Tl
A

OTHER TITLES BY THE SAME AUTHOR

Novels under his own name of FREDERICK E. SMITH
OF MASKS AND MINDS
LAWS BE THEIR ENEMY
LYDIA TRENDENNIS
THE SIN AND THE SINNERS
THE GROTTO OF TIBERIUS
THE DEVIL BEHIND ME
THE STORM KNIGHT
WATERLOO (In conjunction with the Dino de Laurentiis film)
THE WIDER SEA OF LOVE
THE WAR GOD
A KILLING FOR THE HAWKS (Mark Twain Literary Award)
THE TORMENTED
THE OBSESSION
THE MYSTERIOUS AFFAIR

Novels in the same series:
RAGE OF THE INNOCENT
IN PRESENCE OF MY FOES
YEARS OF THE FURY

633 SQUADRON
633 SQUADRON: OPERATION RHINE MAIDEN
633 SQUADRON: OPERATION CRUCIBLE
633 SQUADRON: OPERATION VALKYRIE
633 SQUADRON: OPERATION COBRA
633 SQUADRON: OPERATION TITAN
633 SQUADRON: OPERATION CRISIS
633 SQUADRON: OPERATION THOR
633 SQUADRON: OPERATION DEFIANT
633 SQUADRON: OPERATION SAFEGUARD

SAFFRON'S WAR
SAFFRON'S ARMY
SAFFRON'S TRIALS

A MEETING OF STARS
A CLASH OF STARS

THE PERSUADERS
Books 1, 2 and 3 from the TV series of the same name

Novels under the pseudonym of DAVID FARRELL
TEMPTATION ISLE
STRANGE ENEMY
VALLEY OF CONFLICT
THE OTHER COUSIN
TWO LOVES
MULLION ROCK

Plays
The Glass Prison
A House Divided

Non-fiction
WRITE A SUCCESSFUL NOVEL
(written in conjunction with Moe Sherrard-Smith)

AN AUTOBIOGRAPHY
Volume One: A YOUTHFUL ABSURDITY
Volume Two: AN AUTHOR'S ABSURDITIES

Short Stories
Over 80 short stories published
Short listed for Winston Churchill Fellowship
Short listed for CWA'S Golden Dagger Award

Frederick in his later years

THE FINAL ABSURDITIES

AN AUTOBIOGRAPHY: VOLUME 3

FREDERICK E. SMITH

Emissary Publishing
P.O. Box 33, Bicester, OX26 2BU, UK.
Tel: 01869 323447 www.emissary-publishing.com

First published in Great Britain 2012
by Emissary Publishing, P.O. Box 33, Bicester, OX26 2BU, UK.
www.emissary-publishing.com
www.frederick-e-smith.com

British Library Cataloguing-in-Publication Data.
A catalogue record for this book is available from the British Library.

ISBN: 978-1-874490-82-1

©Frederick E. Smith

SOURCES OF INFORMATION
My mother's autobiography
My father's notes
My own diaries, letter files, and memories

All rights reserved. This book may not be reproduced, in whole or in part, in any form (except by reviewers for the public press), without written permission from the publisher.

Printed and bound by MWL Print Group Ltd., South Wales.

A Tribute To My Late Wife, SHELAGH

Shelagh during the war

I had my first glimpse of her during the dense fog and unbelievable chaos of World War 2. Her perfection and clear untainted eyes told me she had known little of the stress and hard labour of my early days. Stealing a few pecious hours together during that next few weeks, we fell in love, but fate (or was it the Records Office) learned that I had fallen in love with a foreigner and so must be posted.

Posted I was, for over two years in the dangerous Far East. Her last, tear-stained farewell promised me that whatever the cost to her she would be in England with my parents if I survived the next two years.

I did survive, but with little hope because I had received no mail from her for over three months. To see her on my repatriation day standing at the garden gate with Mum and Dad was almost too much to bear. Indeed, I could hardly be blamed for calling it a miracle.

I will not detail our next few years together, they are far better recorded in my second autobiography entitled *An Author's Absurdities* and published by Emissary Publishing in April, 2012.

This third volume, *The Final Absurdities*, deserves another adjective than those I have already given to Shelagh. It is gratitude. My thanks go to those who give us so much and receive so little in return. It is, of course, to the holy saints of our forebears, and to them I want to give my gratitude for giving a lonely man the ideal companion he needed for the task ahead.

Thank you my saints. Thank you for the great gift you gave me.

Frederick E. Smith
April, 2012

ONE

With this final fling of the summer over, it was time to settle down to work and by Christmas I had *The Devil Behind Me* edited and ready for my agent. I had never before written a novel so quickly, but then the story had been given me almost incident by incident. Because it was my first genre thriller, I felt some nervousness while waiting for Reggie's opinion and yet deep inside I felt happy with it.

Not that I had written the Bulldog Drummond or James Bond type of thriller. Having experienced a war, I could not write about bullet-proof men impervious to fear because I had never known any. Perhaps only those who have never seen the impact of a .45 bullet on human flesh can create supermen who throw off such injuries like gnat bites. Perhaps only those who have never experienced real fear can create fearless characters. My characters had to be real, to have doubts and apprehensions, and their attainments had to be possible.

My argument (or was it my consolation?) was that an intelligent reader would find such a character more satisfying because they were true to life. Rightly or wrongly, that was the concept on which the book was based.

The first reaction was favorable. Although Reggie thought I might have included more Swedish characters — an opinion he later retracted — he thought all the characters, particularly the girl, were excellent, the story gripping, and the background superb.

So Round One was mine. My confidence grew. If Reggie liked it so much, surely he would have no problem marketing it. Which would mean we need not worry any longer about our buying a large house.

How wrong I was. The first blow came when Jarrolds turned the novel down. Their reason was much the same as the one given to me after *633 Squadron*. I had led them to believe my intention was to be a serious writer and not a genre one. If I were to write another Sin, they would be glad to see it. But a thriller did not interest them.

The news did nothing to improve my opinion of publishers. I was yet to learn the majority of them wanted genre writers who could capture a segment of the market and extend it with their further books. My problem was, as I realized later, I had too many interests to be so curtailed. But financially it was proving a huge handicap, particularly as I now had a huge house to keep and furnish.

At the time my disappointment about *The Devil BehInd Me* was eased when I heard that Emmet Dalton had sold the film rights of *633 Squadron* to the Mirisch Film Corporation for an undisclosed sum. Initially it was gratifying because at the time Mirisch were regarded as the largest film company in Hollywood and although I knew I was probably getting a pittance to what Dalton received from the sale, it was satisfying that such a prestigious company liked the story enough to buy its rights.

At the same time I knew a film was not certain — film companies were known to buy rights often to prevent others from obtaining them — but at least the chances of a production were better than before, particularly when Hutchinson informed me that Mirisch were also interested in *Laws be their Enemy* and were buying an option on it.

This latter news gave me a real thrill. Because of its anti-apartheid theme, *Laws* was a book very close to Shelagh's heart as well as mine, and the thought of a film exposing apartheid excited us both. When Mirisch took up a second option that year and I was told they were contemplating a major film, I almost flew over the moon. Such prospects were the stuff of dreams.

But what happens to dreams? Ours burst like a bubble only a week before Christmas. To my absolute horror I heard that in spite of their assurances, Hutchinson had failed to copyright the first three of my published novels in the USA. Which meant all three were in the American public domain!

For us it was a huge disaster because it meant Mirisch dropped its interest in *Laws* like a hot brick. I have no words to express how both Shelagh and I felt at this news because we had not only banked on the much needed film sale but had also hoped the film would expose to the world the evils of apartheid.

But it did not stop even there. Not by any means. Because Mirisch had bought in good faith the *633 Squadron* rights from Emmet Dalton — and he himself must have believed American copyright had been obtained — there was now the possibility that not only Dalton might take legal action but Mirish might do the same because of the expenses and the options they had paid. And in such cases it is often the author who is considered responsible.

So for a while it looked as if I might end up in court for an appalling publishing dereliction that had not only cost a film sale but a major one at that. I cannot deny that Shelagh and I were shattered at the news. I was also deeply worried that *633 Squadron* might suffer the same fate.

As if things were not bad enough already, Hutchinson then informed me that some action had to be taken about the American book rights in *633 Squadron* to protect the Mirish company. To ensure copyright for them, the novel had to be published quickly in the States. A publisher had already been found but he, no doubt aware of his importance in the affair, was demanding draconian terms. He would publish the book but only if he were allowed to change its text as he pleased. As Mirisch were only concerned in establishing copyright, he, the publisher, wanted confirmation that I, the author, would accept these terms. I could have my name on the book spine and would be paid normal royalties but only on the condition that I had no say whatever in any alterations to the text.

Such were the terms Hutchinson expected me to accept, telling me the deal must go through to appease Mirisch. Moreover, I was to have no veto on any changes made. In fact — I would not even be allowed to see them before publication.

I found it hard to believe that any publisher could ask any author to accept such terms. It meant no matter what errors or falsehoods appeared in the text, to the critics and general public I would seem responsible for them.

There was only one reply I could give. If no other course was open, then I would have to relinquish the right to have my name on the book spine and my name would only appear in the flyleaves where it would be stated very clearly that the book was only based on my original novel and was not my own work.

Hutchinson had no option but to agree to this and the deal went through. But because principles always have to be paid for, the advance I would have received was greatly reduced and I would receive no royalties whatever. The final irony was an irritable letter from Hutchinson's Rights Manager who, no doubt displeased that his dealings had not resulted in a higher commission, made the comment that 'sometimes young authors need to put their pockets before their pride'.

So Hutchinson's negligence not only cost me a possible second major film but also a lucrative American book tie-in when *633 Squadron* was eventually filmed. I made my complaints in the strongest possible terms to the editorial office but instead of receiving an apology I was told 'these things happen'. When I sent a further letter to Robert Lusty, he replied: 'Members of the staff who should have had the responsibility at that time are no longer with us, so the blame cannot really be apportioned now'.

This was patent nonsense because a company is a legal entity and is responsible for the actions of its staff both past and present. Friends suggested I should sue the company but the law is only for those who can afford to pay its costs, and after these blows there was not the slightest chance we could afford them.

In other words there was nothing I could do but forget my dreams and start again. Life had already taught me there is nothing to gain by lying on the canvas and asking for sympathy. But because it had all brought back my earlier misgivings of publishers, I made one solemn promise to myself. From now on I would learn everything there was to learn about the potential of books and I would check and re-check every word and promise made to me by publishers. It was going to be difficult, if not impossible, for me to trust in their competence again. To remind myself of this I have kept these Hutchinson letters to this day.

So the year that had offered such promise ended in disaster. Numbed by the blow, I was some time in realizing its full implications. Back in Hull it would have been bad enough but there our expenses had been much lower and there had been only one family to support. Since then I had made my parents dependent on me for their shelter. If I failed in the months ahead to pay the mortgage and the bills, two old people as well as Shelagh and the boys might be homeless. From that moment on, no matter how I tried, anxiety was at my elbow day and night.

TWO

If a man can believe in cosmic justice, he might also have to believe in Sod's Law. In my case, after my short stories had gained a market while we were in South Africa, their sales had ceased totally once we came to Britain and needed money for survival. This dearth of sales had lasted for two long years.

Now exactly the same situation arose in 1959. We had bought a house and left ourselves with only enough money in the bank for six months. The auspices had seemed far more favourable than in 1952 and yet they promised only to deceive. I couldn't sell my new novel *The Devil Behind Me* in 1958 and as the first few months of the New Year slipped past, it seemed I couldn't sell it in 1959 either.

I couldn't blame my agent for this. Reggie was trying it everywhere but with no success. As he thought the story one of the best thrillers he had ever read, he confessed to me he was baffled. For my part I began to suspect my concepts were false. Perhaps the average man in the street preferred his heroes fearless and bullet proof. Perhaps in associating himself with such implausible supermen he buttressed up his own ego. I didn't want to think my fellow men were so poorly endowed but the success of such unreal characters was now making me wonder.

In turn my gloom deepened. If it needed comic strip characters to sell thrillers, then where did I, with my wartime background, stand? Did it mean my mental make-up was going to be a handicap in writing thrillers? If it would only allow me to write serious or straight novels, then our financial future looked bleak indeed.

These were my thoughts and they became more feverish as the months passed by. Deciding there was no time to write another novel before our money ran out, I thought of Woman again, and worked out a story of a young Englishman having a romantic affair on a Mediterranean island. Writing a synopsis I sent it to Woman via Reggie.

Woman's first impression was favourable, so taking heart I wrote the first instalment. But once again it seemed I was giving a story too much meat and not enough soufflé. The exercise ended with two months of wasted work and without an extra penny in the bank.

By this time I was getting desperate. All that saved us were *Lydia*'s foreign sales. The French, the Italians, the Norwegians, and the

Philippinoes had bought the serial rights in 1958 and the Norwegians had also bought the book rights. Now the Danes and Swedes also bought serial rights. The income from these sales was only small but nevertheless it made the difference between paying and not paying bills, and once again gave me cause to bless *Lydia*. (For that matter *Lydia* and *633 Squadron* were to go on selling for the next thirty years but in 1959 I had no way of knowing this).

At this time, because of my visits to Woman, whose London offices were in Farringdon Street, I was introduced to the editor of a number of children's magazines. By name, Ken Mennell, he was a balding stocky man with a resemblance to Ernest Hemingway. He had been in tanks during the Second World War when his legs had been badly burned by fire.

This meeting was about my only piece of good fortune during that year. Because of Mennell's history, he liked books on military matters and it turned out he had asked to meet me because of being impressed by *633 Squadron*. In our subsequent conversation he asked if he could have the comic strip rights of the novel for one of his monthly publications. His usual payment was £50 but in the case of *633 Squadron* he was allowed to go up to £60! His magazines were big spenders in those days!

Nevertheless it was money and I accepted it without hesitation. Afterwards he asked if Shelagh and I would care to spend a weekend at his place. I accepted and the two of us drove up to Essex one weekend and met his wife Joan and their two sons, Ian and Danny. It was the beginning of a friendship that lasted until Ken's premature death in 1976.

Ken proved my lifeline in 1959. On my request he allowed me to adapt *633 Squadron* into comic strip format, and the result pleased him because when I asked if he could give me any more work, he let me try my hand at a flying series in one of his papers.

So soon I was writing the prose, the captions, and the exclamations that artists would later transform into pictures and 'balloons' containing such expressions as UGH and WOW and WHAM. It was a come-down for an ambitious young novelist but with the financial screws tightening by the day, I was glad of the work.

The payment at that time was £16 per instalment. The knack was the ability to think up new stories. Ken was a master of this. Writers would come to his office with their latest contributions and before they left twenty minutes later he would provide them with two or three ideas per man. These ideas he would think up while walking up and down behind his desk, with his hands locked behind his back like Felix the cat in the old movies.

Of course the ideas had little if any depth but I challenge anyone to think up ten or more in a day while still carrying out one's administrative work. What came as a surprise to me was his writers' need to be given story lines. I had always created my own and thought all writers, even comic strip writers, did the same. To see an editor giving them out like sweets was a totally new experience for me. Although not impressed by writers who needed such assistance, I could not help admiring Ken's fertility of mind. In this particular field he was quite brilliant.

Although, like us all, he had some irritating habits, I found myself liking the man. One reason was his generosity with his time. If one ever needed to talk about a book or a new idea, he would sit up all night if necessary, and for me who until then had never encountered a fellow writer or one so gifted with fertile ideas, this was no small experience, particularly as he was aware and sympathetic to the problems writers faced.

But such a relationship was to come in the future. In 1959 I was simply grateful for the work he gave me. Although I could not get enough of it to stem the drain on the bank, it helped to slow it down.

Nevertheless by the summer our situation was becoming desperate. Kevan was at school now and two growing boys and the large house with its equally large bills were almost doubling our expenses. With Woman showing no further interest in my island idea, I was at my wit's end. Shelagh, bless her, was more than willing to go out to work but we both felt Kevan was still too young to be left without her attention. In another year it might be possible but by then our fate would be settled one way or the other.

I have never known weeks as long as those that followed. The town was full of holiday makers but I felt a creature apart. I would go for walks in the evenings and think of nothing else but the bills that I soon wouldn't be able to pay. I would rack my brains for new ideas but because of my state of mind, none would come.

Knowing how my parents would worry if they knew the situation, I tried to keep it from them. But to suppress a worry is only to encourage its emergence elsewhere. I became touchy and impatient with everyone around me. Although they never said as much, my parents must have been hurt by my behavior and perhaps wondered if I was regretting having them with us. This in turn only added to my frustration. I had wanted to improve their lives and instead was making it worse for them. I knew some of these morbid thoughts might be imaginary but that in itself only made me feel that an imaginative mind was a curse rather than a blessing.

In fairness to myself I did try to keep the worst of my problems confined to my office which, since Pop had returned to South Africa, was now the front attic. Outside the office the world was moving on in its inexorable way. Peter passed his eleven-plus examination that summer and won a scholarship to the Bournemouth Grammar School, which pleased us all. Kevan appeared to have settled down in his first year at school and my parents, going down to the beach whenever the weather was fine, seemed to be enjoying their new life in spite of my fears.

L. to R. Frederick, Peter, Kevan, Shelagh (Approx. 1958)

More than once I thought about David Doig's interest in my work but because I knew his magazine stories were even lighter in content than those in Woman, the idea seemed pointless. But as my desperation grew, I knew I had to try everything and so I wrote David asking if he were still interested in using me.

His reply came back by return post. He was delighted I had remembered his offer and he and a colleague would come down to Bournemouth the following week to discuss various ideas. This was something Woman did not do and so, although David's magazines paid less, I felt this kind of consultation might improve my chances of getting a story I could handle.

David proved as good as his word. He and his colleague stayed in Bournemouth for three days discussing ideas until we settled on a story that we both liked. Not that I approached the task with any confidence. After my experiences with Woman, my confidence in handling this kind of literature was non-existent. But at least I had the good sense to hide my apprehension until they took the train back to Dundee.

Like *Lydia* the story we had chosen was a thriller with a girl as its main character. From memory, there was no final price agreed. I was expected to turn out one instalment a week until the serial reached its natural ending, and for each one I would receive £25 which would be paid immediately the instalment was accepted. Thus, providing I came up with the goods, I would receive a weekly wage as if I were in regular employment. David told me his writers liked this method of payment and somewhat ruefully I saw his point.

In my heart it was the last thing I wanted to do but equally I couldn't afford to fail. So I motivated myself by deciding to look upon the work as a challenge. I would work and work on the technique until I conquered it, just as I would work on the confounded comic strips until I was one of the best in the business.

It all sounds very pretentious but I had to motivate myself somehow and in the past I had always found that I responded well to challenges. So I studied the magazines David sent me while at the same time I worked on the story we had decided on.

As I still retained Reggie as an agent, I notified him of my decision and told him I would be sending him the commission as if he had made the deal. He didn't want to accept it but as he had been more than fair to me in the past, I insisted he took it. It was, after all, going to be little enough.

Acutely aware how important it was, I spent nearly a month writing the first instalment and my heart was in my mouth when I awaited David's reaction. His letter arrived within a week, saying he was pleased with the instalment and was enclosing his first cheque.

I don't remember feeling any sense of relief. Emotion needs energy and by that time I think I was traumatized. But I know I kissed the cheque before putting it into the bank.

After that the cheques kept coming in weekly and my confidence as a serial writer began to grow. At the same time I knew I had much more to learn so I kept studying the market as I wrote. In the meantime I had a success in the comic strip world. The magazine in which my stories appeared had only one colour feature which appeared on its cover page. With my urgent need to bolster up our income, I had almost doubled my production of these stories but as yet they had only appeared in anonymous monochrome between the covers. However, by midsummer Ken Mennell told me they had become so popular he had decided to give me the colour slot for a flying series. I was surprised at my own pleasure. If I could be successful in one field, I could be successful in another. With this resolution I applied myself even harder to the magazine serial.

I finished the serial, which I called *White Sands* by the beginning of August and David scheduled it for the Sunday Post in 1960. In the meantime I sent copies of the instalment to Reggie and then trimmed up the ending of each instalment so that they ran together like a novel. This manuscript I also sent to Reggie. I don't think I really expected him to sell the book volume rights (although this did happen later) but I was hoping he would try a few foreign countries with the serial rights. This he agreed to do, for somewhat to my surprise he liked the story.

With survival ensured for the rest of the year, there was the next novel to consider. Throughout this time, in between writing the comic strips and instalments, I had been working on the Mediterranean Island idea because it seemed to have book promise even if it was unwanted as a serial, and I wished above all things to remain a novelist. As I knew very little about Mediterranean islands and had now reached the point where I needed detailed information, it was decided I should drive down there and conduct my research. Shelagh felt I needed the break after the strain of the last sixteen months and I couldn't deny I felt like one myself. I also felt that everyone in the house would benefit without my irritable self for a few weeks.

So began a trip as bizarre in its way as the one in Sweden. Packing a small tent into the Husky because it was still necessary to keep travel costs down to the minimum, I started down for the south of France.

Somewhere beyond Lyons, I picked up two German girls who were thumbing a lift. Both spoke good English and told me they came from Leipzig in East Germany. They asked me what I was doing, and when I told them, they looked at one another and then suggested I went to the island they were visiting. It was in the Porquelles group and ought to be suitable for my research. When I hesitated, they pointed out that it was the holiday season and most of the camps on the islands were packed with tourists. But because they had been coming to one camp for years, they felt certain they could persuade the proprietor to accept me if I went with them.

As I had no particular island in mind, it seemed a fair offer and so I took them to Le Lavandou from whence the boats to the islands sailed. There we encountered the never-to-be-forgotten owner of the boats, a muscular character who, stripped to the waist, called himself Lou Lou le Corsair. While the girls got the tickets from him, I parked the Husky on the quay. When I returned, Lou Lou le Corsair bundled the three of us and our equipment into one of the boats and we headed out into the blue Mediterranean.

It was not long before I sensed things were not what they seemed. The girls kept looking at one another and laughing, and there was something about our fellow passengers that didn't quite fit their role of mere tourists.

My suspicions came to a head when we approached a large island with people sunbathing among its rocks. Something about them drew my eyes and as we sailed nearer I saw they were all nude. As I gave the girls a puzzled glance, they both burst out laughing again. They had played a trick on me. They weren't going to the Porquelles but to the Isle de Levant, the famous Mediterranean nudist island. They went there every year but it would make no difference to me because the island would still provide me with all the copy I needed.

By this time I had little choice. The boat was already nuzzling at the small quay. And, to be truthful, I was curious. I had never been inside a nudist colony before and having heard so many different stories about them, I thought it would be interesting to find out the facts for oneself.

So along with the girls I climbed into a jeep, which I was told was the only four-wheeled vehicle allowed on the island, and it took us to the tented camp. This was packed with visitors, and there is no doubt I would have been turned away had not the girls spoken to the manager. When he learned I was a writer, he let me have a small plot on the edge of the camp on which to pitch my tent. The two girls, who had reserved accommodation elsewhere, said their goodbyes for the moment and I began to sort myself out and take my bearings.

I discovered I had a bearded American professor as a neighbour. He told me he had been coming to the island for many years and that I would find many foreigners in the camp, for the island was internationally famous and drew tourists from all over the world. This surprised me because I had never heard of it. Although the island was French, I found few Frenchmen there. The majority of the nudists seemed to be German, but I did find a sprinkling of other nationalities in the days ahead. What did astonish and amuse me was to discover that half the island belonged to the French Navy, the two halves being separated only by a wire fence. One immediately thought of hundreds of matelots swarming over the fence at nights, but I never saw a single one during my stay there. I can only assume they had highly efficient military police.

My bearded professor also helped me not to tread on any eggs during my stay. For obvious reasons one had to get permission to use a camera. Regarding apparel, it was right and proper to go totally naked in the camp or on the special beaches reserved for nudists. But when walking on the paths between these sanctuaries, one was expected to wear a minimum because curious tourists often made trips to the island to view the sights. To some the word itself might explain all. To the less sophisticated, it was a tiny pouch or triangular piece of cloth that just covered the genitals. My professor urged me to buy one forthwith.

The evenings called for a different approach. In the small town of Heliopolis there were shops, restaurants and even a cinema. But to visit them at night one must go fully clothed. I was relieved. The thought of sitting at a restaurant table in the nude or watching dancers doing the twist in that state made the mind boggle.

I experienced little embarrassment that first day because I was fully occupied in putting up my tent and cooking myself a meal. My problems started the following morning when the two girls, now as nature intended, paid me a visit. I found I could strip down to my swimming trunks but no more. And yet with everyone nude around me I felt out of place. In fact I felt almost indecent. When I mentioned these sensations to my professor he nodded sagely. Such feelings were normal. In a day or two I would find nudity as natural as breathing.

It took me a day longer than that. I was still wearing my swimming trunks when I came across four buxom girls playing handball on the beach. I admit I paused to watch, wondering who would be the first to receive a black eye, but none seemed concerned or at risk. Wondering how such bodily dexterity was achieved, I went on my way. The next day I took my courage in both hands. Gritting my teeth, I strode forth naked from my tent. To my relief no one took a second glance at me, although whether my ego was equally appeased must be in question.

Of course my professor was quite right about nudity, as was Bernard Shaw. If the human race discarded its clothes, it would say goodbye to its libido. After a few days seeing the human body with all its imperfections exposed, one soon realized that true eroticism is stimulated not by nudity but by its promise. The beaches of Cannes and Nice, only a few miles away, contained more titillation and sexual stimuli in a few square yards than the whole of this naturalist island. After a few days I became convinced this was the solution to the world's population problem. Off with our clothes and away with our fecundity.

Oddly enough the effect was not disappointing. In some strange way it was very relaxing as life always is when temptation is removed. Because everything could be seen, there was no curiosity or voyeurism. This surely explained the large number of families one saw on the camp. All around the tents were young boys and girls growing up with much of their sexual curiosity satisfied. I wondered if it would put a stop to the wearisome smut of school playgrounds. If it did, I would vote for a nudist camp in every town in Britain.

I also found swimming in the nude very relaxing. Until then I had never believed the lack of a brief pair of swimming trunks could make such a difference but it does. It also gives one a sense of space, of liberation. I remember walking along a cliff path one moonlit night, with the sea below shimmering like quicksilver, and the feeling of freedom was almost godlike.

The lack of clothes also altered the pecking order of the campers. Without an expensive suit to proclaim his position in society, the tycoon more often than not had to give way to the muscular navvy or steel worker. I found that very democratic.

It was my intention to remain only two or three days but eight days passed before I tore myself away. I said goodbye to my new friends and then caught the boat back to Le Lavendou. I then drove to Italy and spent a week on the Isle of Elba before returning home.

It was not long after this that the Berlin Wall was completed and sealed off East Germany from Western Europe. It made me think about those two young girls and wonder if they were ever able to return to their favourite island. Sadly, it seemed unlikely.

THREE

Back home again I worked hard on the island story and soon had it finished. I called it *The Grotto of Tiberius*. Because of my experience with *The Devil Behind Me*, and my need to return to Lapland in spite of all the copious notes I had taken, I had learned that the secret of writing about foreign lands is not to visit them before one begins the novel (unless one has the money to afford a trip before and after) but to write first the storyline and then make the visit. In this way a novelist knows exactly what he needs. Returning home, he then blends and merges the background into the story line and much time and expenditure has been saved. Of course sometimes a visit does trigger off new thoughts and ideas, but generally these can be accommodated in the story line without too much disruption.

This was the method I used in *The Grotto* and in most of my subsequent novels. Although it would be stupid to deny that the practice calls for some judgement and manipulation, these are skills that can be learned, and over a lifetime of writing they pay handsome dividends.

So I sent the completed manuscript of *The Grotto* off to Reggie. Then I took the entire family on a holiday to Cornwall where I had booked a caravan off a farm in Sennen Cove. The plan was that Shelagh and I would sleep in the Husky while my parents and the children slept in the caravan. This worked well and as the weather was good we had a happy week. During it we were visited for a day by a Lancastrian family who had moved next door to us in Bournemouth soon after our arrival. Joe Wilkinson, salesman for a firm of printers, had been given the southern area to manage, and brought his wife Margaret and his young family of two girls and a boy with him. We were pleased because until then the immediate neighbourhood had been filled with elderly tenants and we had felt somewhat embarrassed at the noise two young boys inevitably make. With Joe and Margaret's children alongside ours we felt less isolated. No doubt this was a factor that brought our families together, although we liked them for themselves and soon became good friends.

I began to write my eighth novel as soon as we returned home. I had decided on the theme of this one some months ago. From all I had read in the newspapers and seen in life around me, the taboos and bigotry that surrounded sexual activity in the Anglo-Saxon world were showing signs of strain. In addition, the recent court case permitting *Lady Chatterley's Lover* to be published convinced me it was only a matter of time before a full-scale sexual revolution would take place.

As I have always seen it, the stress and strains between the sexes is caused by our Western World's interpretation of the word love. Then, and particularly today, it is used to mean sex and from that huge error comes a host of problems. Love, a mental emotion, means deep affection, companionship, charity, tolerance, forgiveness: a wealth of positive emotions that have no need of physical contact. Sex, on the other hand, is physical and possessive, and although it is enriched if accompanied by love, it can and often does satisfy entirely on its own. If this were not so, how would brothels flourish?

I saw all this stemming from the mistaken belief that one's love is finite, like water in a bucket. A man, so the conviction ran, could not love a second person without leaving less water in the bucket for his partner. A woman could not give love elsewhere without the same diminution of affection. The fact that love, by its very nature, has no boundaries and expands by its own usage seemed a non-thought in a world dominated by materialism and possessive concepts.

Yet if sex is classed as love, then all these negative aspects of sex taint it. Possessiveness and jealousy become its manifestations to the point when even revenge becomes a yardstick of a person's love for the other. For while Nature entangles the two emotions when one is young and virile, it is vital to recognize the manifest difference between them in later life. Otherwise one can believe one's partner's love is diminishing when sex becomes less frequent, when in fact the cause might be only a failing of physical performance. Such a misunderstanding can cause couples to separate and so lose a love they might never find again.

These were a few of the ideas that I wanted to incorporate in the novel. But although today it sounds ridiculous, I was only too aware at the time of the risks I was taking. I remembered how Hutchinson had made me water down a passage in *Laws be their Enemy* that was only the description of a sexual act and not one inserted to make a controversial point. This new book would be unashamedly attacking false concepts and promulgating new ones, and because sex was involved, a publisher might fear it would become a target for traditionalists. For my part I would welcome this but would publishers whom so far I had found painfully conservative be so content?

But by the time all these thoughts had run through my head, my enthusiasm to write the book was red hot and I decided to damn the consequences. It was a theme I could put my teeth into and I could not wait to get to my typewriter and flesh out a synopsis. As it was a story with a universal theme, I chose as its background my new county of Dorset, reflecting that the novel was going to be difficult enough to write without making geographical problems for myself.

My enthusiasm for the novel made me forget our finances were still very shaky. Or I must have hoped *The Grotto* would not suffer the same fate as *The Devil*.

Here I was soon disillusioned. It was not long before Reggie told me that he was having the same problems with it. Nobody seemed to want my two thrillers.

I was only too aware what it meant. Although I had written six or seven chapters of the new novel and felt it was going well, there was no way I could finish it now. That would take at least another full year and by that time our capital would have long gone. I would have to set it aside and write more of those comic strip stories.

Yet even they wouldn't be enough to keep the wolf from the door if the two thrillers, representing over two years' work did not sell. Once again I would have to go back to women's magazines, the only market that seemed to pay writers a living wage.

So I contacted David Doig again and asked if he would like another serial. I also asked Ken Mennell if I might write a few of the comic strip novelettes that Fleetway House published.

Both editors agreed. David seemed particularly pleased and so we worked together on another story line. This one was set around the Berlin Wall and involved a girl in love with a young pilot. Involved with this and the comic strips, I was left once more with only the odd few hours a week to work on my real love, the new novel.

However, rain is often followed by sunshine and although that year ran its dismal way right to the end, the New Year began by promising better things. Firstly David told me he was delighted with the progress of the new serial, which we were calling *It Happened in Berlin.* Then Shelagh decided Kevan was now old enough to go to school himself and proved again what a wonderful wife and companion she was by getting a saleswoman's job in a large Boscombe store. As she was always a highly capable person, the salary she received made an enormous difference to our circumstances. For me in the attic, its immediate effect meant I could cut down on the comic strip stories and put more time into the novel.

It also meant that towards the end of the year we had enough confidence to trade in our hard-worked Husky for a Bedford Dormobile: a thing we would never have dared to do when I was the sole breadwinner. These mobile caravans were cheap at this time because they carried no purchase tax and although we took a risk in laying out £800, we argued it would provide us with cheap family holidays and also be invaluable for me when away on research. On both counts we were proven right.

Nevertheless it was a risky purchase and I for one had my fingers crossed that we wouldn't have to suffer for it. To cover ourselves I kept on writing comic strip stories, using the weekends for the work so they wouldn't interfere with the new novel which I had now decided to call *The Wider Sea of Love.*

But although 1960 was proving a better year, I couldn't get over the failure to sell my two thrillers. After the enthusiasm shown to my first two novels and then the successes of the next two, it had seemed only a matter of time before I would be an established working novelist. Now I seemed to be back to square one again and surviving only by living off Shelagh's wages and by turning myself into a hack. Although I had worked hard on the two serials and given them my best, my heart was in novel writing and I knew I would never be happy until my books were published again.

But when, if ever, would that be? I would have moments of depression but then I would remember *The Wider Sea of Love* and tell myself it would sell because of all the ideas locked within it. Publishers would see I was right about the forthcoming sexual revolution and would jump at the chance of publishing it. Perhaps in spite of my anxieties and frustrations, beneath the skin I was always the perennial optimist.

FOUR

Sometime in the winter of 1960 I had a rush of blood to the head. I noticed somewhere that the editorial director of Hodder & Stoughton had changed and suggested to Reggie that he tried him with the two thrillers. As Reggie had already tried Hodders along with other publishers, he naturally hesitated. An agent hardly endears himself to a publisher by subjecting him to a second refusal.

But I still believed in the two novels and because Hodders specialized in the genre, I couldn't escape the feeling that something untoward had happened to the earlier submissions. Perhaps the editor had been off sick the day they were rejected and some colleague had instigated their refusal. Perhaps the editor had quarrelled with his wife that day and kicked the cat and all his writers in his frustration. Whatever the reason, a brand new editor seemed to offer as good a chance as any to see if a misjudgement had been made.

To make it easier for Reggie and to clear him of any involvement in the affair, I suggested making the submission myself. This I did and a month later, without any reference to their earlier refusal, Hodders made me an offer for both books.

If anything proved to me how subjective the opinions of publishers are, that acceptance was it. Needless to say, I was delighted. After two dismal years that had suggested my days as a novelist were over, I was back in business again. A great load seemed to fall from my shoulders.

Not that the advances would pay the mortgage for long. Hodders' offer was £175 for each novel. But as from their point of view I was starting as a new novelist, this was something I had to accept. The great thing to me was that every novel I had so far written, no matter what its theme, had ultimately found a publisher. This seemed to prove my faith in myself was not misplaced, and encouraged my belief in *The Wider Sea*, which I had worked on throughout that winter.

The Grotto was published in 1961. Although the reviews were reasonable enough, and a few excellent, I was disappointed with the promotion, which seemed very lack-lustrous. Realizing this meant it was unlikely I would receive any royalties in six months time, I approached David again to ask if he were interested in my doing another serial.

He said yes and between us we worked out a likely story line. I had no sooner taken on this commission when Reggie told me that his foreign agent had managed to sell both the Norwegian and Danish serial rights in *White Sands*. Although the monies were welcome, they gave me the uncomfortable reminder that the only real monies I was earning at this time came from serials.

With this news under my belt and with Shelagh secure in her job, we decided we could risk a holiday that year and asked our neighbours, Joe and Margaret, if they would like to go over to the Continent with us. Dying to use our Dormobile, we were considering driving down through France to the Mediterranean. To our delight they agreed, and in the August school holidays our two families were on our way, Joe, his family, and a tent in a tiny A40 Austin and we in the Dormobile.

House in Southbourne with camper van. (Circa 1958)

It proved a highly successful holiday. We reached the Mediterranean in a couple of days and found ourselves a campsite only five minutes walk from the beach. We found Joe and Margaret good company and the five children seemed happy playing together. On our return we voted it had been a great success and we must do it again in the near future.

During the rest of that year I worked on both the serial and *The Wider Sea*. In the early autumn Shelagh's mother came over for a holiday. With our relationship on a firm footing again, we were delighted to see her and did our best to give her a happy time.

She was desperately unlucky that winter, however. It was the coldest since 1947 and although Bournemouth usually escapes the worst of the weather, there was a spell of severe frost and snow that lasted for over six weeks. As we had no central heating and could only provide her room with an electric fire, the contrast between the South African summer she had just left and the Arctic conditions here made life hard on her.

She returned home in the spring but not before she had bought gates for the front garden. Until then we had never been able to afford them, and there had been an unsightly gap in the wall to give my Dormobile access into the garden. Such niceties as gates were beyond our means at this time and we were grateful for her help.

Hodders published *The Devil* in January 1962. It received the same meagre promotion as *The Grotto* yet its reviews delighted me. Books of the Month chose it as their 'Book of the Month'. Vanity Fair said: 'Suspense! From the very first chapter right through to page 220 the chase is on. If you normally find it difficult to put a book down, you'll be burning gallons of midnight oil with this one.' Eric Dehn of the BBC said in a broadcast: 'Terror is communicated to the pit of the reader's stomach as in those nightmares of stumbling pursuit when limbs refuse to respond.' Even the conservative Guardian gave it a good review. I was thrilled by these professional comments because they seemed to prove for once and for all that I could write thrillers when given the chance.

One effect of the publication was a letter from the Crime Writers Association inviting me to join them, at the same time putting *The Devil* up for their yearly crime writers' award (it eventually made their short list). I hesitated a while about joining because I didn't see myself as a crime writer but I did need to meet some fellow writers, so I joined and found some interesting people among its members. Realizing the organization might also be used as a pressure group for Public Lending Rights, I agreed to serve on its committee.

Feeling *The Devil*'s reception must be a good omen for *The Wider Sea*, I sent the first few chapters and a detailed synopsis of the novel's aims to Reggie. His first response delighted me. He said he agreed with all my views — he had shared them secretly for years — and he congratulated me for incorporating them in a novel. But — it seemed there must always be buts in this profession — he was wondering what publisher would stick his neck out by publishing such views. He also wondered if it was the right kind of book to follow two thrillers. Might it not be wiser to put it on ice for a while and in the meantime write another thriller for Hodders?

His letter depressed me because I felt he was right. A sensitive book written through the eyes of a woman would seem a strange novel to follow two thrillers written through the eyes of men. And if Hodders were to turn it down, my image would hardly be improved by my losing yet another publisher.

There was no doubt that my changing the genre and theme of my books was making life difficult for me. I knew by this time that if I had continued to write books about war or about women in peril like *Lydia*, I would soon be firmly established with a publisher and earning substantial royalties.

Although such popular story tellers might not always be invited to the top table at literary functions, this is what publishers want. Authors whose names become synonymous with a certain genre and who corner more of that market with every book they write. The sales they gain and the money they make please publishers and shareholders alike.

My problem was I couldn't do this. My need to write had stemmed from the things I needed to say, and not to say them seemed to make all the sacrifices we had made pointless. Somewhat idealistically, I saw a writer as someone who should be allowed to write on whatever subject he chooses, as many Victorian novelists had done. To me an artist should never be constrained, no matter what market forces demand. His greatest gift is an unruliness of mind that urges him to wander from the broad highway into brush or woodlands where treasure is sometimes hidden. He is not, nor should ever be, tagged in the way a can of beans is tagged with a label. Businessmen can have the tags and may even wear them with pride but not writers. Give them freedom and sooner or later they will come up with a novel that surprises or even amazes their sponsors. Restrict them with the harness of specialization and their work will slowly sink into mediocrity.

I believed it then and I believe it now. 'I have nothing against writers who write only for money. Practically everyone else in the Western world does it so why not writers? But I do feel that publishers ought to respect more the writer whose ideas demand a wider range of novels and not be so influenced by their sales managers and accountants. In the long run it is the rebel who is most likely to bring prestige to an imprint.

So *The Wider Sea* was put on ice and I worked on the new serial. By the spring David had received all the instalments and published the story in his magazine My Weekly. He told me the response from readers was as favourable as for *White Sands*, and that he would always be ready to accept another serial when and if I were ready. After all that had happened since moving to Bournemouth, I found his offer very comforting.

For the moment, however, our shaky finances were topped up by the Toronto Star buying the Canadian serial rights in *The Devil*. A week or two later Reggie told me a film director named Don Chaffey had bought an option on the film rights. The final figure if he took up the option would be £1,500. This excited me not only because of the money that would make us safe for another year but because of the chance of seeing the story filmed. To date nothing had come of my earlier film sales and I was positively thirsting to see one of my novels on the screen.

But as always in this profession, there was the waiting to endure. I have no record of the exact duration but it was certainly some months before Reggie cabled me to say all was well and the deal was going through.

The trouble with this waiting is that it is emotionally draining, so that if good news does eventually come, one's feelings have been so pulverized by the uncertainties that it is impossible to enjoy a success. I feel sure that any author who might read these memoirs will know exactly what I mean.

A few weeks later I received a cutting from the Cape Times, South Africa, with the photograph of a girl and the caption: 'The 22 year old blonde, Mercedes Alonso, is in London to star in the film *The Devil Behind Me*.' From this it looked as if I was to have a film behind me at last.

But this profession does not give its goodies away that easily. For months, even for years, we looked for news of Mercedes Alonso and her star role in *The Devil,* but we never heard of her or of the film again.

Nevertheless, on the whole 1962 was a better year for my work, but I was soon brought up with the reminder that life could hurt in other ways than by rejections. In mid summer my father, who had always helped me out by doing odd jobs in the house or garden, was repairing our garden fence when he suffered a severe pain in his chest. Realizing it might be angina, I wanted to call for the doctor immediately but that wasn't my father's way. Wanting to prove to himself that he wasn't finished yet, he refused my offer of a lift and walked by himself to the surgery. He returned forty minutes later saying he had to take some pills whenever the pain reappeared.

Later I went to see the doctor, who confirmed it had been an attack of angina. When I told him it had long been my father's wish to have a trip round the First World War battlefields, he advised me not to leave it much longer as none of his arteries were in good condition.

Angry with myself for putting it off for so long, I had a word with Shelagh and she agreed I must drop everything and take him. So in the late summer my father and I set out for Belgium and France in the Dormobile.

It proved to be the most moving and rewarding journey of my life. Our first stop was the Yser Canal where the British and the Germans had confronted one another with only the narrow strip of water separating them. The British trenches were still preserved when we walked along the canal bank and as we came to a decayed, moss-grown dugout entrance, my father halted and told me he thought he remembered manning this stretch of trench in 1917.

My first reaction was scepticism. Forty-five years and a second war must surely have disguised all its original features. Seeing my disbelief, my father tried to climb over the pile of rubble outside the entrance. When I drew him back and attempted the climb myself, he told me that if he were right, there would be a large, flat-topped rock three or four paces inside. I moved forward in the semi-darkness and there was the rock my father had remembered.

We went on to Ypres and the Menin Gate and heard the Last Post played at sundown. We then followed the British Army's road of death to Sanctuary Wood, where a quarter of a million men had died, and when there listened for the birds' song. It is said birds never sing there and certainly we never heard any, although this might be because it is a conifer wood. We visited an estaminet at the road corner and gazed at dozens of old sepia photographs of the local countryside littered with British and German corpses. We drove past Hill 60 and my father said it had looked much higher in 1917. Again I suspected his memory until, reading my guide book, I learned that the eight million shells the hill had received had pounded it down to half its original height. After that I fell completely under the spell of that emotional journey.

We visited war cemeteries where we found the graves of men he had shared his rations with. I watched him wandering through the endless rows of graves with their captions and time warped and made no sense. There was my father, seventy-two years old and growing frail and old, and here were his comrades aged eighteen and twenty and twenty-two, all in the bloom of youth. 'Age shall not weary them, nor the years condemn.' My thoughts of my own war as well as his disturbed me. If years did not condemn them, what about we who had survived? How did we match up alongside them? Wasn't it better to die in the full flush of youth with one's ideals intact, then live on into old age with all its humiliating infirmities? To live to see the world as it is, cruel, avaricious, and corrupt? To become as corrupt oneself? Then I looked at my father again and my mood lifted. He had become none of these things. In so many ways he had retained his innocence. I had never loved him more than at that moment.

From there we drove south to the Somme and then on to Verdun, the immortal French citadel that had claimed the lives of a quarter million Frenchmen and as many Germans. We reached the plateau in the evening when all the visitors had gone and the underground passages were locked for the night.

It would have been hard to find a more apt evening. The air was still, a black shroud hung over the fading sky, and the sun, sliding down the western horizon, was staining red the gun cupolas and battered forts.

We visited the huge mausoleum where endless rows of marble caskets reached out as far as the mind could encompass. Caskets not full of single bones but the bones of regimental units. The presence of so much death awed us both and we returned to the Dormobile in silence.

We drove on to some of the ruined forts, Faux, Souville and

Douaumont. Arriving at Douaumont when the light had almost gone, we were about to drive away when I noticed a splash of colour on its front wall. Approaching, I found a tiny basket of newly-cut flowers resting in a niche in the scarred wall. Pinned to the basket was a handwritten note which I was able to translate. It read: 'Since your eyes closed in sleep, mine have never ceased to weep.'

Forty five years had passed. Flesh and bone had long crumbled to dust and yet a woman still remained true to her lover. Nothing has ever brought to me the mysteries of life and death more than that posy. To this day my throat tightens when I remember it.

The trip ended on a more cheerful note. We visited Paris and I took my father round the sights. We took a river boat along the Seine and went to the top of the Eiffel Tower. We sat outside many a cafe sipping beer or wine and watching life pass by. With the capacity to enjoy life that he had always possessed, he loved every moment of it.

As the Dormobile was too clumsy to park in the crowded streets, it did mean he had a great deal of walking to do. Yet he bore up marvellously until one evening around eleven when he dropped on a seat and gave me a wry smile. "I'll have to take a rest. Do you mind?"

Knowing him and what his words might mean, I ran most of the way back to the campsite where the Dormobile was parked and drove it back to him. To my relief he was still sitting there and assured me he was in no distress.

So ended one of the most rewarding trips of my life. In the years left to him, he never stopped talking about it, and the photographs we took were among his prized possessions. For me, although that had not been its intention, it proved to be an invaluable asset to my work in the years ahead.

FIVE

With Shelagh in need of a holiday, and with an invitation from David Doig to visit his family in mind, I drove her and the boys up to Scotland in the school holidays.

It proved an adventurous two weeks. On the way, reaching the Pass of Glencoe, we parked in a bay off the road to allow Shelagh to prepare lunch.

Telling the two boys to keep off the road, although there was little traffic that day, we let them out to work off their energy. Inevitably they began to climb the mountainside alongside us. Not ten minutes passed before we heard Kevan shouting and saw him running towards us. Looking frightened, he told us Peter had fallen on to a car and hurt himself. Wondering what he meant, we ran with him up the mountainside to a small but steep corrie that was invisible from the road.

Peter was climbing out of it as we arrived. He was looking very pale and blood was streaming down a leg. As we reached the corrie I understood what Kevan had meant. An old car had at some time been driven up to the corrie and pitched into it. It must have been the only corrie in that entire vast mountainside that contained a jagged, rusted old car but our sons had inevitably found it, with painful consequences.

The gash was a good inch and a quarter long and clearly needed stitches. Bandaging the wound as best we could, we hurried back to the Dormobile and tried to find a doctor.

L.to R. Shelagh, Kevan, Peter, Frederick

We drove for ten minutes before we came across a stone cottage tucked into the mountainside. Throwing open a gate and hurrying down a path, I heard a fearsome barking and snarling from behind the cottage door as I knocked on it.

The noise would have made the Hound of the Baskervilles jealous and I wondered if I would escape alive when the door was opened. When it was, for no more than a few inches, I could just see an old woman's wizened face. When she croaked something I couldn't understand, I guessed it was Gaelic and tried again. "Will you help me, please? My son's had an accident and I must get him to a doctor. Where can I find one?"

Her wizened face seemed to sharpen. "Are ye a Sassenach?"

"Yes," I said, bewildered. "Yes, I suppose I am. Can you tell me where I can find a doctor, please? It's urgent."

Her reply seemed to be a cross between a curse and a denunciation, although as it was in Gaelic I couldn't determine its gist. But when she turned to White Fang behind her and the snarling rose in crescendo, the message was crystal clear. About to run for my life, I heard a man curse and the dog's snarling cease. A moment later the door was flung wide open and a middle-aged man appeared. Pushing aside the old crone, he addressed me in English. "What di'ye want?"

With my courage back, I explained. He pointed up the pass and gave me instructions. As I thanked him and turned back for the Dormobile, I heard his angry voice as the door swung closed. "Ye stupid auld woman. Do you no ken those days are over? How many times do I have to tell ye?"

We found the doctor twenty minutes later. He sewed up Peter's leg in expert fashion, gave him an anti-tetanus injection, and then mixed up a medicine for him to take if he developed a temperature. In between he chatted to us about our holiday and gave us advice where to go. He was the kind of doctor I had known as a boy, a pharmacist, a surgeon, and a philosopher all in one. A far cry from the doctors who had treated me in my adult life and light years from the doctors who sent one to hospital for an ingrowing toenail. In one day we had seen the worst and the best of Scotland.

Our last stop before going to Broughty Ferry, where David lived, was to pay a call at the famous Soldier's Leap which, for those not versed in Anglo/Scottish history, is the river that an English soldier was supposed to have leapt over when chased by ferocious Scotsmen with claymores. On the way down was an old tree with many of its roots lying like aged veins above ground. I must have had my Scots porridge that morning because, as the four of us walked down the slope towards the leap, I suddenly let out a Tarzan-like yell, ran full pelt down the slope, and threw an arm around the tree.

My purpose was to use my momentum to swing me right round the tree and land back on my feet. But such crazy gymnastics don't always work according to plan. My momentum took me halfway round the tree but the slope, which I hadn't allowed for, meant I was swinging downwards and not sideways.

It was nearly a fatal mistake. What I hadn't known was that one of the roots was severed and was sticking out of the ground like a pointed stake. As I swung down with my body weight behind me, the stake struck me on the sternum.

Everything stopped on the impact: my breath, my heart, my vision. I collapsed as if I had been pole-axed and lay on the path certain I had only seconds to live.

I don't know how long passed before the anxious faces of Shelagh and the boys came back into focus and my heart re-started, but for me it felt like minutes. As other faces appeared I felt the world's biggest fool when finally I was helped to my feet.

I soon discovered how lucky I had been. The pointed root had struck me at the very base of the sternum. Half an inch lower and there is no doubt that it would have gone right through me.

But although it was painful to breathe for a while and I remember coughing up a little blood, I didn't feel it was necessary to see a doctor and so we continued on our way. In later years it was to prove a wrong decision but I had no way of knowing it at the time.

In fanciful moments during the rest of the holiday, I couldn't help wondering if my old crone was psychic and had anticipated the coming of an idiot Englishman. One could just see her cackling away while she chopped at the root with an axe while White Fang howled at the moon. After all, what better place to put paid to a Sassenach than at Soldier's Leap?

After a very pleasant holiday with David, when we met his charming

Irish wife Kay and his three young children, we returned home to continue the battle with publishers. With no royalties arriving from either *The Grotto* or *The Devil* I knew I must continue writing for the only market that was paying the bills, the women's magazines. As My Home were interested in a serial, I discussed the theme of my play *The Glass Prison* with their fiction editor and was told she would be interested in a serial adaptation.

So I made this my work that winter and My Home published the serial in the New Year. It seemed to go well and indeed some years later the Robert Hale company published it in hardcover.

But with *The Wider Sea* still in cold storage, I had to produce another novel for Hodders if I were not to lose them, and this time I decided to obey the rules and to write another thriller. I thought for some time about a background and finally decided I'd use Scandinavia again. It had done well for me in *633 Squadron* and *The Devil* and perhaps because I am an East Yorkshireman, the Nordic countries seemed to strike some atavistic chord in me.

So in the spring of 1963 I set out in the Dormobile, sailing from Harwich and driving through Denmark, Sweden, and finally over the Hardangavidda to Bergen. With the Dormobile providing nightly accommodation, I was able to do the trip without recourse to hostels and long hikes for buses and trains. This proved a bonus because it was a poor summer that year and I went through heavy snowstorms on the high Hardangavidda. I spent about two weeks in Norway doing research, then began the long journey back. I missed the fraternity of the hostels in the evenings but with nothing else to do, I was able to work on the plot and by the time I arrived home I was able to plunge into the novel itself.

It was set some years after the Second World War and concerned a rich Norwegian family who had kept their fortune intact by collaborating with the Germans. When they discovered a touring Canadian skin diver has been persuaded by a local ex-partisan to locate a sunken ferryboat which might expose their guilt, they took steps to stop them both.

Aware that mystery stories of this kind can easily become run-of-the-mill, I needed a theme to give the novel depth and after writing a few chapters I believed I had found it. The theme would be friendship and loyalty. The ex-partisan, a man of strength and passion, wants the wreck found because he believes a wartime friend's besmirched name would be cleared by the discovery. For this purpose he is prepared to risk his life. He is also in love with his dead friend's daughter who is also encouraging the Canadian to make the search. If I worked the plot so that the Canadian also falls in love with the girl in circumstances that make it feasible, I felt I had enough mystery and conflict to produce a substantial thriller.

There was one problem before I could finish the novel: I had to learn all I could about skin diving. So I made enquiries from local sources and did some diving myself to get the feel of it.

But before I could finish the novel, there were the family's holidays to think about and we decided to visit the Continent again with Joe and Margaret. Once again we went camping in Spain and once again we enjoyed ourselves.

It was, however, our return home that made that holiday memorable. We had barely entered the house before my father hurried excitedly down the stairs and handed me his newspaper. There on the second page was a large picture of a crashed Mosquito and beneath it a caption stating it was a scene from a film the Mirisch Company were making at Borehamwood. The film was entitled *633 Squadron.*

Having had no warning the film was being shot, I made a phone call that same day to Borehamwood. I was put in touch with the film's executive producer, an American named Lewis Rachmil, and he invited Shelagh and I to visit the studios the following week. My agent, Reggie, was also invited.

None of us had been on a film set before and we found it fascinating. Although many of the flying scenes had already been shot in Scotland, using real Mosquitoes diving through steep valleys, the final scene had to be simulated and so a massive artificial fjord had been constructed with papier-maché, mountains and a huge lake laid down between them. Here near-perfect scale models would fly between them and be destroyed by controlled explosives.

This action was not yet ready to be filmed but we were invited to see one or two current studio shots. Here I received a lesson on trade union practices. A short scene of an aircraft cockpit being hit by bullets was delayed because of some minor technical hitch. As the actors waited in the cockpit and the crews crouched behind their cameras, a loud voice was suddenly heard counting off the seconds. Forty, thirty-nine, thirty-eight...the voice echoed on while the technical crews feverishly worked to correct the fault.

Puzzled, I turned to Rachmil alongside me. "Who's counting and why?"

He grimaced at me. "It's the union foreman. Here in England the union breaks off for the day at six pm promptly unless the cameras have started rolling. Then we're allowed to finish the shot."

"You mean if you're not ready by the time he reaches zero it all stops until tomorrow?"

"Yeah. It'll all have to be done again. Fresh make up for the actors, fresh lighting, fresh everything. All for a shot that takes less than ten seconds."

"Is it the same in the States?"

At that moment a relieved cry from a technician telling the fault was cleared interrupted us but not before Rachmil's expression gave his negative answer. While I have never been a 'union basher', this did seem to carry industrial practices to the heights of absurdity.

We spent the rest of the day meeting the stars of the film, when press photographs were taken. Afterwards Rachmil drove us into London to Michael Wilding's ex-home where he and his wife were staying. Here we met Bradford Dillman and Peter Graves, two more film actors who were in London at that time. We returned home with my believing that my earlier exclusion from all news of the film had been due to some innocent mistake and that from now on I would be kept in touch with all its progress.

I could hardly have been more mistaken. While Rachmil and his producer had been courteous enough, I was soon to discover that such rapport was not commonplace between film companies and authors. From that one visit to Borehamwood I heard nothing more about the film and its progress until it was completed.

Nevertheless, with a film on the stocks, this was the time to market the book again. When Hutchinson had let it go out of print some years earlier, Reggie had obtained the British Empire Rights back for me, which meant they could be sold again. To date this had not been feasible, but with a major film in the offing, with stars as famous as George Chakaris and Cliff Robertson involved, the situation had vastly changed. A publisher could tie-in with the film's publicity machine and the outcome could be extremely beneficial to both parties.

Thus we had every reason to hope for a large advance when Reggie offered the novel to Corgi Books, the English branch of Bantam Books in America. Even in those days tens and even hundreds of thousands of pounds were paid for paperback rights with film tie-ins, and so my hopes were high. Even if we received only a half or even a quarter of the likely advance — my previous experiences had made my expectations modest — our financial problems should be solved at last.

But even our modest expectations were put to rout by Corgi's offer. When I received it from Reggie, I thought his typist must have missed at least one nought from the offer and more likely two.

No, it was correct. Just as Hutchinson had believed in 1955, Corgi believed a war film would have little impact on the market in the Swinging Sixties and a £300 advance was all they were prepared to make. Worse, because there were few paperback publishers in business at that time, Reggie advised me to accept it.

Although I tried not to indulge in self-pity, I began to wonder if it was my fate to suffer from publishers' lack of foresight. Reggie tried to console me by pointing out that if the film did well, I ought to get royalties from the book in the months and years ahead but with creditors disinclined to await such prospects, my feelings were that a bird in hand was worth a dozen in the bush.

Nevertheless £300 advance it was, on a book of a film that was later to break box office records. I can only hope that by chronicling it I don't depress those starry-eyed would-be writers who believe to publish a book in itself is a passport to the Cote d'Azur and to have a film made of it means a Beverly Hills swimming pool and the fields of Elysium.

My next contact with the film people came when the Royal Air Force Association and the RAF Benevolent Fund threw a joint publicity dinner. They were involved because United Artists, who were to distribute the film, were offering to donate the proceeds of the film premiere to the RAF Benevolent Fund. To add glamour and newsworthy copy for the Press, five RAF VCs were to attend.

I was invited to the dinner by Group Captain Hamish Mahaddie. Mahaddie, with a distinguished military record, had been chosen by Don Bennett during the war to recruit crews for his elite Pathfinder squadrons, and the film unit had made him their technical advisor. Known by squadron commanders as The Horse Thief for his ability to woo skilful crews away from them, he retained this charm in peacetime and in 1964 he was an aviation consultant with offices in London. I don't remember how I first met him, but when the dinner was mooted, he sent me an invitation.

So one evening that winter I found myself sitting at a long table laden with food and drink in one of London's finest hotels. It was an affair typical of its kind, with somewhat extravagant speeches, blinding flashlights, and reporters paying more attention to their whisky glasses than their notebooks. I was sitting beside Bill Reid VC, a big Scottish ex-pilot who, after receiving a serious wound over Germany, had courageously brought his Lancaster and crew back to base.

It proved one of the most embarrassing evenings of my life. From the speeches it was soon evident that my novel had long been forgotten as the mainspring of the film. Praise was liberally bestowed on actors, producers, directors, Uncle Tom Cobley and all, but the book itself might never have been written. I began to feel I was a charlatan sitting there, particularly when photographers, ordered to take pictures of the guests, passed me over as if I were a member of the servicing staff who had sneaked in for a free meal.

It was all too much for Bill Reid. Like the other VCs, having been told nothing about the novel, he had assumed it was the child of the screenwriters. On discovering there was a book from which it had all stemmed and that a fellow airman had written it, he had been growing more and more irritated by my isolation, and whenever some name was mentioned and cameras clicked, he would growl under his breath that it was bloody time the author was acknowledged.

By this time it was the last thing I wanted and I kept nudging him to keep quiet. But the wine was flowing and Bill wasn't the kind to back out of a situation if he believed his cause was just. After a further fifteen minutes in which everyone from the executive director to the studio sweeper had been photographed, he suddenly smashed both his big fists on the table and shouted that if I wasn't given some credit for the bloody film and my photograph wasn't taken, he would walk out and take his fellow VCs with him.

In the sudden silence that followed I wanted to die or slip through the floorboards. No doubt the organizers had the same wish. But

Bill's threat was a mortal one. Whispers were heard and less than a minute later I was hauled to my feet while photographers snapped me from every angle. No doubt all the prints were over-exposed in the dark room afterwards, but at least Bill was appeased and the dinner was allowed to continue.

My next encounter with the film people came when I and Madge Lake, who was Corgi's film tie-in manager, went to see Charles Berman of United Artists. Berman was everything one expects of an American film publicity manager, big, brash, confident, and smoking a cigar only a little smaller than a World War One Zeppelin. I have forgotten most of the conversation but the part that mattered I could never forget. Berman removed his cigar and fixed Madge Lake with a challenging stare. "Book sales help us too, Miss Lake. So if your people will put up 25,000 dollars, we'll match it dollar for dollar and that'll mean streamers about the book in just about every street in the land. What d'you say?"

It was a moment when my entire fate as a writer rested on Madge Lake's reply and I knew it. As I watched her with bated breath I saw her eyes falter and knew my moment had come and gone. "I'll talk to my directors," she told him. "But I'm fairly certain they won't put up that kind of money."

Berman shrugged and put the Zeppelin back into his mouth. "If they don't have that confidence in the goods, why should we? Talk to 'em and get back to me. Only do it quick. I gotta know by next week."

I don't think I was ever more depressed than when I left his office that day. I had already learned that publicity can sell anything from chalk to iron filings but without it one gets nowhere, and to be so close to a massive campaign and lose it was worse than anything I had yet experienced. I was left thinking that if a publisher wouldn't give me promotion when a major film was behind my book and when a film company were offering to share publicity costs, then when could I ever expect any in the future?

But a true writer is nothing if not resilient and I pushed my disappointments aside by working hard on the Norwegian thriller. Also I had a piece of good news from Reggie. The Paperback Library of New York liked my 'Gothic' novels *Lydia* and *The Other Cousin* (the new name for *White Sands)*, and were making an offer for both. The advances were only modest and the royalty percentages low, but the offer could not have come at a more bracing time for me. So I signed the contracts gladly, although they reminded me once again it was women's serials coming to my rescue.

As I expected, Corgi turned down Berman's offer. Indeed, I was soon to learn they were more than lukewarm about the book's prospects. In May a preview of the film was shown in the London Corner Cinema for their directors and for their wholesale buyers. Along with my agent, I was also invited.

Until then I hadn't even seen rushes of the film, much less a completed version. I met my Corgi editor and we went to the preview together. Not knowing what to expect I felt nervous as the credits began to roll. Although the advance on the book had been agreed, there was still the print run to be determined, and although publishers often denied it, the size of their promotion campaign is usually determined by the number of first edition copies they print. So I sat in the darkness wondering what fate had in store for me this time.

My first viewing of the film left me with mixed feelings. The script writers had kept to the main story line and it was well handled and the flying scenes were superb. Indeed they were the best I had ever seen. It was the omission of some of the sub plots that I found disturbing. To me they were important because their intention was to show that war is a filthy, obscene business. By leaving them out but retaining the main plot and the highly exciting flying sequences, the film seemed to me to glamorize war rather than condemn it.

At the same time I wasn't so naive not to realize the result was a highly commercial film. Moreover the flying scenes — possibly the best ever photographed — would appeal to flying buffs all over the world.

Thus when the curtain fell my feelings were ambivalent. The film would do nothing for my artistic image but as a box office success, which I felt certain it would be, it should do a great deal for our bank balance. Which in our current financial state was a great deal better than nothing.

So when I turned to my Corgi editor I felt confident he would endorse my opinion of the film's chances. Instead he shook his head. "I'm not impressed. It's just another run-of-the-mill war film."

I couldn't believe what I was hearing. "But the action scenes and flying sequences are marvellous. I've never seen anything like them. And the music is sensational."

He shrugged. "They won't make a successful film in themselves. See if I'm not right." Knowing now what was coming, I braced myself as he went on: "Sadly, poor films don't sell books. I don't think our print run can be more than 40,000. Sorry but there it is."

And there it was. 40,000 copies was barely more than an average printing for a paperback without a supporting film. That was Corgi's decision on the book of a film that was destined to break records everywhere, to be shown on television dozens if not hundreds of times, and had music so compelling it is played on State occasions.

Not that I was so stupid not to realize that a downbeat opinion could well be a business ploy to excuse a modest promotion campaign. But genuine or not, it did nothing to liven my faith in publishers. Indeed I began to wonder if they lived in the same world as the rest of us.

SIX

My frustrations with publishers did not end there, not by any means. From the money or lack of it the film was producing for me, there was no way I could ease up on my work, and so between my infrequent journeys to London, I continued working on my new novel, which I called *The Storm Knight,* and before the film was premiered I felt I had produced a thriller at least on par with *The Devil* I posted the manuscript off to Reggie to forward on to Hodders and awaited their reply.

Although well acquainted with the foibles of publishers by this time, I felt as confident about that book as about anything I had written. I felt its characters were lifelike and the plot contained the right percentage of sentiment, conflict, and excitement. I also felt that the spectacular Norwegian scenery added an extra dramatic quality.

I was more than surprised, therefore, when Hodders turned it down. I've forgotten the exact wording of their letter but by this time I was well acquainted with the multitudinous excuses editors use on these occasions. It seldom if ever gives their true reason. If it did, the wording would be something as follows: 'We are sorry but the poor sales figures of your previous books doesn't justify our publishing another. Yours with regret....'

The author, of course, has a different interpretation. He blames his books' failure on the poor promotion given to them and so feels he is being punished for the publisher's sins.

This most certainly was my interpretation and Reggie agreed with it. At the same time there was nothing we could do but try the book on other publishers. Presuming one eventually took the novel, it would be my fourth publisher for eight novels and I had the rueful thought that I was perhaps breaking a record in this field for a young author.

However, my bruised feelings were eased when Reggie let me know that a film producer named James Whittaker wanted a year's option on it. As the story hadn't yet sold to a publisher, this seemed to us both a huge vote of confidence and reinforced our belief that Hodders' decision had not been based on the novel's quality.

In the meantime things were moving fast on the film front. I had now learned that the premiere was fixed for early June but Corgi were not publishing the book until late July. After Corgi's refusal to accept United Artist's promotion offer, this delay of seven weeks upset me because of the publicity that would be lost, and I made a complaint. In reply I was told the fault lay with United Artists. In October 1963, when Corgi had signed up the book, they had been told the film was unlikely to be ready before August 1964. Accordingly Corgi had scheduled their edition to appear in July.

I had another reason for concern. Between the 10th and 20th of June, London was holding its World Book Fair and with the film premiere only a week before, I had naturally hoped my book would be ready and given a prominent display. Now it seemed this opportunity would be lost too, although once the facts came out I could hardly blame Corgi. Instead I felt that once again my career would be harmed by errors over which I had no control.

Realising there was conflict between Corgi and United Artists — perhaps because of Corgi's refusal to match the film distributors' publicity offer? — I took matters into my own hands and managed to obtain a 16mm film from Mirisch on the making of the film. It was the best I could do but I felt it might give the book some publicity when the Fair began.

The date of the world premiere of the film was the 4th June at the

Leicester Square Theatre. Because the proceeds of the evening were donated to the RAF Benevolent Fund and the Queen Mother was a patron of many RAF associations, she had been invited to grace the occasion. In the event she declined but in the days that followed I couldn't help wondering if she might have changed her mind had she known the author was the airman she had encouraged to continue writing in the dark days of WW2. Probably not but it was a pleasant thought to consider.

Shelagh and I took the train up to London where we met Hamish Mahaddie. In turn he introduced us to Don Bennett and we were driven to the theatre in some style in Bennett's Rolls Royce.

All the ballyhoo of opening nights was in full swing when we arrived but Shelagh and I had no problem in slipping unnoticed through the crowds. I did, however, pause to look at one of the outside posters advertising the film. Credits were given to the director, the screenplay writers, the executive producer and the English producer but my name was conspicuously absent. 'I discovered later that my Rights Manager at Hutchinson had never insisted on a credit clause in the contract. At the same time, seeing that I had received less than a studio sweeper for the film rights, one might have thought the film people capable of a grand gesture. But perhaps such thinking meant I was still naive.

We met none of the film unit people on our entry and were shown to our seats in the upper stalls by a cinema attendant. This anonymity worried neither of us because neither Shelagh nor I felt comfortable in the limelight. We bought a programme and then, not without some trepidation, settled back to watch the film.

As is usual on such highly charged occasions, when one wants to take in every nuance and reaction of the audience, the opposite happens. The mind seems to go blank and is left afterwards with only fragmented impressions. I seem to remember a military band playing stirring music (although to this day I can't be certain if it was a band or only taped music), I remember how huge the auditorium looked with its tiers of seats, and I remember thinking how formal and well-dressed people looked around us against the usual cinema audiences. Those were the sum total of my impressions until the curtains closed and the lights came on. I had absolutely no idea how the film had been received and had to ask it of Shelagh. She laughed. "Didn't you hear them applauding?"

I hadn't heard a thing. "No," I said. "Did they?"

"Of course they did. They clapped time and time again. Some even cheered. They loved it."

"Are you serious?"

"Of course I am. It's been a big success."

My next memory was standing with Shelagh downstairs and talking to Leonard Cheshire. We were at one side of the foyer, half-hidden by a pillar. In the center of the foyer, standing in a pool of brilliant light, celebrities connected with the film were being given beautiful models of Mosquito aircraft. I can't remember if Leonard Cheshire was given one or not but halfway through the presentation, he turned to me. "Aren't you getting one too?"

To be truthful, my mouth was watering because the models were exquisite. "I shouldn't think so," I said.

"But why not? You're the author of the book, aren't you?"

I thought it was a subject better not broached further, particularly as I wasn't offered a model, and we talked instead about other things, in particular his homes for cancer victims. Somewhat to my surprise, he asked if I would care to write a book on them if he provided me with the necessary material. I said I would be delighted to and gave him my address. (Regrettably I heard no more about the project in the following weeks). Then the presentation ended, the celebrities drove off in their huge limousines, and the crowds dispersed. My big day was over and although Shelagh told me it had been a big success I can't say it left me with lasting memories. But perhaps that is a common experience. Perhaps anticipation is always better than reality.

The rest is history. The Kinematograph Weekly reported that the film not only topped the West End cinema business during its week's showing but also made more money for the Leicester Square Theatre than any other film in the theatre's history except for the film *Charade*. Since then, after its sale in 1968 to American and British television, it has been shown time and again in the States and over here. It also soon appeared in video under different guises, (all lacking an author's credit, of course) and, from the letters I still receive, its popularity seems undiminished. So much for Corgi's opinion it would not do well, and so much for the £1125.00 film sale of 1955, the only payment I ever received out of the entire financial harvest.

A situation, in complete harmony with all that had gone on before, happened immediately after the premiere. Cecil Ford, the English producer of the film, phoned me the following day. Unlike the film corporations' general cavalier behaviour towards writers, Cecil Ford and Lewis Rachmil, the Executive Producer, had shown some interest in my contribution: indeed Rachmil had gone so far to ask what work I had in the stocks and if I would show any of it to him.

Ford's purpose in phoning me was more immediate, however. "F.E., am I right in thinking you are going on holiday soon?"

"We were planning to, yes. As soon as the Book Fair is over. Why?"

"Take my advice and don't go."

"Why? What for?"

"Because of the film. It's making money hand over fist and I know it's going to do just as well when it goes on general release. Don't you realize what that's going to mean?"

"You mean it's going to help the book sales?"

"It'll do that, of course, but I'm not thinking about the book. I'm thinking about your next one. When film companies see a film making money like this they want a fat slice of the author. As soon as the word gets around, your phone'll never stop ringing."

I burst out laughing. "Cecil, nobody gives a damn about authors. That's one thing I have learned."

"In general terms I agree. But not when a film makes money like this. They'll be after you in a day or two like wolves after a big fat stag. See if I'm not right."

I knew he meant it. I also remembered another writer I had met who had received a quarter of a million dollar offer for his next book after a film not half as successful as *633 Squadron* had been screened. I had a talk with Shelagh and we both decided it would be madness to miss offers that could permanently cement my career, for a mere holiday. We could take one later in the summer.

So, with apologies to the children who took it very well, we cancelled the holiday and while the film continued to break records, we waited for those frenetic offers Cecil had prophesied. In all we waited for two months and not a single call was made. As it made no professional sense, I began to wonder if my old RAF officer was right and my stars were hopelessly and irretrievably crossed.

My next foray to London was during the Book Fair. Although their official publishing date for the book was the 24th July, Corgi had met my complaints to some extent by producing a few dozen early copies and these were displayed on a stand at the end of Earl's Court. To augment interest in them, I had personally asked two VCs to attend, Bill Reid and Norman Jackson, and, along with Hamish Mahaddie, the four of us were busy all day autographing copies. I don't expect it did much to promote the book on a national scale but at least my personal involvement made me feel better because I couldn't stifle my worry that the long gap between the film and book publication would do great harm to sales.

It was this concern that brought me into conflict with Corgi a week or two later. The RAF Association offered space in their magazine Air Mail for an advertisement of the forthcoming book but when Corgi made their approach, the Association's secretary made it clear the magazine expected some payment in return. Corgi bridled at this, pointing out that as the film premiere had devoted its takings to the Benevolent Fund, which I was told later was £76,000, it was more or less incumbent on the Association to give us free mention. In turn the Association pointed out that it had been United Artists, not Corgi, who had made the donation, so why should the publisher expect special treatment.

It was a petty quarrel over nothing, because the cost of the advertisement was less than ten pounds. At the same time the Air Mail, being the organ of ex-RAF servicemen and women, had a circulation of around half a million at that time. As these were the very people likely to read a novel of this nature, I believed it was extremely important we informed them about it.

The stupid argument continued, making me feel like a small nut suffering extinction between a sledge hammer and an anvil. After all, if the half million would-be readers were not informed, I would be the only one harmed. A company the size of Corgi would hardly notice the loss of sales and the Association would lose only ten pounds. Finally, to shame them both, I offered to pay for the advertisement myself. From memory someone gave way and my offer wasn't accepted, although which one made the supreme sacrifice I can't remember.

For those who know little about the ways of publishers, this reluctance to advertise might seem surprising but it is endemic. Years later, when having a novel published, I believed an advertisement in a certain newspaper would pay excellent dividends to both the publisher and myself. The editor had repeatedly refused to pay the required forty pounds but when I insisted on seeing him about it, he humoured me and offered to take me out to lunch.

Like most publishers, he favoured expensive restaurants but this day I had other intentions. "Mike," I said. "I don't feel like a three course lunch today. Why don't we go round the corner and have sandwiches and a pint of beer."

He gazed at me, then shrugged. Perhaps he thought I'd grown so used to bread and jam that my stomach could no longer cope with expensive food. At any rate he humoured me and we had a roll each and two half pints of beer. I waited until he had downed his second glass before playing my ace. "Mike," I said. "We were going to the

Mirabelle, weren't we?"

He nodded. "It's where I usually go, yes. Why?"

"What would the meal there have cost you? We'd have shared a bottle of wine, wouldn't we?"

He frowned, no doubt at the bad taste of my question. "Of course we would. Oh, I don't know.... Forty-five or fifty pounds, I suppose. What's your point?"

"Then I've saved you at least forty pounds today, haven't I?"

He stared at me. "Yes, I suppose you have. But so what?"

It was then I struck. "I want you to spend that forty pounds on my ad. That's all it'll cost."

His eyes opened wide at my duplicity. "You cunning bastard," he said.

Cunning or not, I got my advertisement and felt pleased with myself. At the same time the point deserves amplification. That editor would have spent fifty pounds or more on our lunch without batting an eyelash; in all likelihood he did it two or three times a week. Yet the same man had been quibbling for weeks about spending forty pounds on an advertisement that might substantially increase his firm's profits, never mind my own. No doubt the answer is bound up with some accountancy ploy of setting off expenses against tax liabilities, but to authors it is time this crazy business sorted itself out and learned what its priorities are.

The film was put on general release later that year and appeared in Bournemouth in the late summer. Being resident in the town I somewhat naturally expected that the publishers would lay on some extra promotion

I could not have been more wrong. In my letter of complaint, which I have before me as I write, I note that I found four *633* books in the largest of Bournemouth's bookshops and six in one other. That was all. No posters, no show cards, no anything. A bookshop sited almost alongside the cinema displaying the film didn't have a single copy. I tell this with my hand on my heart, because I can understand that anyone who lacks first hand knowledge of my profession must think I am exaggerating or telling a falsehood.

SEVEN

It was my parents' golden wedding in 1964. Wanting to give them a celebration, we made our plans and then wrote my brother reminding him of the date.

He wrote back to Shelagh, not to me, saying he wouldn't be coming. I couldn't believe it at first until I remembered a quarrel we'd had the previous year when I had been staying in his flat. To be truthful it had been as much my fault as his. He had been complaining about the number of black people who were entering the country at the time and I, having lived under the crime of apartheid, had taken him to task about his views. When the quarrel had become heated I had remarked it was an odd way to feel about one's fellow human beings when one claimed to be a committed Christian.

It had been a stupid and unkind remark because I knew well enough that he was basically a kind person and would help any man whatever his colour if the occasion arose. But he had taken it to heart and walked out of the flat, leaving me regretting my comment.

Aware now that he hadn't forgiven me, I wrote to him and apologized. When he did not reply I realized the real cause of our dissention lay in the past and wrote him again, saying that if he came I wouldn't consider he was giving any ground on our quarrel but coming solely for the sake of our parents.

It was no use. He still wouldn't come. My mother sobbed bitterly when she heard and although my father said nothing, I knew he was equally distressed. In turn I felt responsible and although we had our little party, the undertone of sadness spoilt it for us all. I felt quite dreadful that my parents should receive this reward for all those years of life together, and for a while felt bitter towards Ray. Then, as the bitterness turned into regret, I found myself wondering if the long shadows cast by my grandmother would ever lift from our lives.

Reggie was still trying to sell *The Storm Knight* and receiving the most extraordinary reasons for its rejection. He sent me one of these rejection letters while enclosing excruciatingly funny comments of his own. It seems Jarrold's reader had turned down the book on the grounds that its heroine was too old for the romantic role I had given her. The decision had made Reggie conclude that in the Swinging Sixties publishers were now using school children to vet their submissions. Checking my manuscript again, I decided he could well be right. My heroine for whom romance was a thing of the past was 28 years old!

Reggie suggested I should join the London Savage Club that year. It was a club that catered for writers, musicians, and actors and Reggie felt I would benefit from the people I would meet, for it was a prestigious club of long standing with some illustrious members.

I hesitated for some time, not solely because basically I am not a club man but because I felt I wouldn't be able to attend often enough to make my membership worthwhile. But Reggie took me to one of the concerts the club gave every fortnight and I was won over. I remained a member until Reggie's health broke down and then I resigned. My infrequent visits hadn't enabled me to get to know many members, and without Reggie to meet there, I found the incentive had gone.

In spite of its disappointments 1964 couldn't be called a boring year and it did bring me in touch with people who were to influence both my professional and personal life in the years ahead. One such person was Lewis Rachmil whom I have already mentioned. After the film of *633*, he went off to Malta to make another film, but kept in touch and informed me he would like to see any ideas I had on his return to England.

With *The Storm Knight* still searching for a publisher and *The Wider Sea* still on ice, I needed new material and began considering writing about the First World War. It had always fascinated me — I had always thought of it as the worse catastrophe this turbulent world has ever known — but that was not the only reason for my interest. As I recorded in *A Youthful Absurdity,* I had suffered nightmares of trench combat when only a small child, which had puzzled both my parents and doctors alike. Whether this meant I had inherited such memories by some mysterious transmigration is something perhaps only a reincarnationst will believe. For myself I have no explanation. I simply testify that the nightmare plagued my young life and inevitably left its effect on me. To this day I have only to hear the songs of that war or see pictures of khaki clad soldiers marching to the trenches for my eyes to moisten and an inexplicable melancholy to sweep over me.

Without any doubt this is why the expedition my father and I had made had affected me so much. Now, as I toyed with the idea of writing a novel about the war, I realized those impressions were urging me to set them down on paper. So I wasted no more time and began working on a synopsis.

I had no problem over a theme. The book would be a violent attack on war lovers everywhere. In doing this it would explore the relationship between courage and morality. Having been through a war myself, I had been left with an ambivalent attitude to both. I had known brave men whose private lives would not bear scrutiny. Equally I had known brave men whom I greatly respected.

Thus I had long decided there was no kinship between the two elements. Yet for centuries societies everywhere had allowed physical courage to take priority over other virtues. Padres on the eve of battle had promised soldiers direct entry into heaven if they died on the morrow. Courage and sacrifice would purge a man of all his sins. Such redemption I found absurd.

At the same time I knew the dangers of attacking these credos because I would be twisting many social and religious nerve ends. But a belief that such things should be said had nagged at me ever since I left the Services. It did not mean I had no respect for physical courage. On the contrary I knew only too well the will power it demands. My case was that it should not be given priority over more beneficent virtues, and that for society to claim it should earn absolution from sin was a dangerous nonsense.

So, with the decision made, my next task was to create characters whose behaviour would present my case. At first I made them soldiers but then I paused. I knew a fair amount about ground forces in World War One but I knew a great deal more about the old Royal Flying Corps because of my interest in flying as a child. Why not make my unit an RFC squadron in 1917? In this way I would be getting the best of all worlds while still tapping the wellhead of emotion I felt for that terrible war.

With this decision made, I found my synopsis went well and it was completed in two weeks. This was fortunate in that its completion coincided with Lewis Rachmil's return to England. I showed it to him and he said he would like to take out a film option on the completed novel.

His offer was £500 for a six months' option. My agent tried to secure more and for the option to extend until the book was ready but this Lewis wouldn't do. He said he needed to consult certain people in the States before he went any further but he did suggest there was every chance he would renew the option in six months time.

Although we knew the offer was small, Reggie felt it could do no harm to take it. And the possibility of another major film being made from my work was too tempting for me to pass over.

So we accepted. There was, however, one large snag. Lewis said the book must be finished by August 1965 and Christmas was only weeks away. Until then I had seldom completed a novel under a year and I was anticipating this one would be at least forty thousand words longer than anything I had written since *Laws*. Conscious that every day might count, I began work immediately and only allowed myself one free day at Christmas. My hope was that Shelagh would not hold it against me, which, bless her, she did not.

It was my first experience of working to a deadline and I found it stressful. Although on the whole the novel was going well, any book poses its particular problems and by May I had only half of the first edition written. When I began working in the evenings too, Shelagh broke her silence and told me I was being stupid. The novel wasn't a matter of life or death. The Paperback Library in America were doing very well with my serials and Lewis Rachmil had just sent a cheque for another six months option. Even Corgi were contemplating a reprint after swiftly selling out their first edition of *633 Squadron*.

It all meant, as Shelagh pointed out, that for the first time in years we were not draining our bank balance. And if I broke down through overwork, the new book wouldn't get finished anyway. I must at least keep my evenings free and get more exercise to ease the stress.

It was all sane and sensible advice and I took it. But neither of us had taken into account my personal gremlin. He clearly didn't like my living normal hours because one evening he made the point in his usual unambiguous way.

We were having an early season tennis tournament at the club and I was perched up on an umpire's chair refereeing one of the matches. Behind me was a shoulder-high wooden fence. It was a typical early spring evening and a chilly wind was clearing the fence and catching me on the back and neck. As I was wearing a coat I can't say I felt particularly cold throughout the hour long match. But when I climbed down from the stand I noticed players staring at me and Shelagh showing alarm when she ran up to me. "What on earth's happened? Are you feeling all right?"

I stared at her. "Of course I am. Why shouldn't I be?"

"Go and look at your face in the mirror. It looks frozen."

I went inside the clubhouse and couldn't believe what I was seeing. The right half of my face was normal enough but the left half had lost every feature. My left eye stared at me unblinkingly and the left side of my mouth drooped down mournfully. In short I looked like a freakish version of Janus. My cheek had also lost all feeling and I could taste nothing on that side of my mouth.

Shelagh, who had followed me inside, tugged at my arm. "Can you move your face?"

I could not. The right side obeyed me, the left side wouldn't even twitch. I couldn't even blink its staring eye. My God, I thought. I've had a stroke.

We drove home and I phoned my doctor. "Can you use your arms and legs?" he asked.

I told him I could, that everything else worked but the left side of my face.

"Then you've probably got Bell's Palsy," he told me. "Don't worry. It won't kill you. Come and see me in the morning."

I did and he confirmed his diagnosis. "It was probably the draught coming over the fence and catching you beneath your ear," he told me. "That is where the nerves meet. Motorists who drive in cold weather with their window open often catch it."

I was thinking about that open eye, already becoming inflamed by being unable to blink, and my still unfinished novel. "Will it come right?"

"It will eventually. But if you don't want to be permanently disfigured you'll have to wear this," and he handed me a short chain with a hook at either end. "If the mouth is allowed to droop for long it hardly ever recovers. So you have to counter that by connecting it with this chain to your ear. It won't be too comfortable but it's the best we can do."

"How long?" I asked, thinking in terms of weeks.

"Not too long, although nerves do heal very slowly. If you're lucky, perhaps in six months."

I yelped. "Six months? With my eye open all that time? How am I going to work?"

I suspect that my doctor had little sympathy with my profession, thinking no doubt like so many others that its practitioners are all rich dilettanti. "Keep bathing the eye with Optrex. If it still bothers you, then give up work because you could do it harm. I shouldn't worry. The rest will do you good."

There was a tennis club dance that night and prior to Bell's Palsy we had promised friends we would go with them. Deciding I must finish the novel no matter what, I felt the best way to handle the situation was to defy my gremlin and to behave as if nothing had happened. So I went home, fixed my mouth and ear together, and then took Shelagh to the dance.

The effect was hysterical. People stared at me as if I were Banquo's ghost. And, to be fair, with my mouth chain in place and my bloodshot unblinking eye staring back at them, I can't have been every woman's idea of a dreamboat. But although I felt as if someone was beating a bass drum inside my head, I survived the evening and on returning home felt the first round had been won.

But there was still a long way to go to win the second. My first problem was sleeping. As my Cyclops' eye wouldn't close, it became a prey to any sheet or blanket within range and I found the only way to prevent its being scratched was to wear an eye patch. This I could cope with during the night but when I tried to work at my typewriter with the patch in place the other eye, unused to carrying the full load, began to ache and blur after a couple of hours. As I had to put in at least eight hours work a day if I had any hope of finishing the book in time, this forced me to tear off the patch. In turn the bad eye, receiving no natural moisture, took its revenge by developing conjunctivitis.

There is no point in dwelling on the complications of the next four months except to say no book has caused me more problems. It was not as if only physical discomfort was involved. When the idea had come to me I had not considered that when writing about the carnage of World War One I would be conjuring up my old ghosts for eight hours of every day, seven days a week. Normally I pride myself in having the mental control to switch off at the end of each working day and return to my family my normal self. With this book I couldn't. I would go downstairs to dinner with my mind still in waterlogged trenches or in bloody aerial combat, and it would be half an hour or longer before the present world came back to me. Taking all things into account, I must have been an impossible man to live with that summer.

Nevertheless I learned something during that time. Some novelists believe hardships diminish their creativity and if allowed a better life they would produce better work. They are quite wrong. Fiction is emotion and emotion is never as powerful as when the mind and the body are under stress. If the writer allows that emotion to feed through muscle and bone to his pages, he can turn dross into gold. Moreover, if his subject is about suffering and pain as mine was, then he is being handed a gift not a handicap. I truly believe that my novel would not have been the book it became if I had not suffered that setback in April.

Mind you, I had great difficulty in giving it a title. I tried *The Eagles of Arast* but felt it too melodramatic. Finally I wrote myself a piece of poetry which summed up the theme of the book. It ran: 'For some men do cherish life and some men life destroy and all the breadth of heaven lies between them. Curb then thy barren contentions lest again the hawks have a killing.' Then I extracted the last five words, re-arranged them, and entitled the novel *A Killing for the Hawks*.

I actually finished the book three weeks before its deadline. I confess I was exhausted and as Shelagh had suffered almost as much as I during the last few months, we decided to be rash and pay a typist to type out a final copy rather than have Shelagh do it herself.

I remember as if it were yesterday the two of us lying out in the sunshine in the garden. The long struggle was over: the huge novel was finished after all, and I felt it was my best yet. The sensation was almost ecstatic. While someone typed that final copy which we could pass over to Rachmil on his arrival, we could relax and enjoy life again.

We really should have known better. On the second morning we had a phone call. Our typist had been offered an immediate holiday in Majorca and had decided to take it. Would we please collect the manuscript? She was very sorry but had only managed to type one chapter!

So it was all hands to the pumps again and we had to work almost to the day Rachmil arrived. It really did seem that my gremlin's sense of humour was insatiable.

EIGHT

It was autumn before Reggie succeeded in selling the book rights in *The Storm Knight* to Harrap. As I was a new author to them, I started at the bottom of the ladder once more and received only £150 advance. Nevertheless, it meant all my novels except *The Wider Sea* had been accepted for publication and I had every confidence it would be taken soon. As novels were my real love, the sale heartened me and I soon shook off the effects of the last year and began thinking about my next work.

I was concerned about my face and eye, however. I knew the strain I had put on both eyes had had some small effect on them and was becoming worried that if I continued working I might do them serious damage. At this time my face was still frozen and my mouth badly ulcerated from the chain.

Not that I hadn't fought the affliction. Every morning and night during the previous four months I'd stood before a mirror and attempted a smile in order to make my mouth move again. The effect was grotesque. The right side would respond, the left side wouldn't even twitch.

The result was demoralizing. Until the affliction I think I had harboured the secret but common belief that if I ever had a stroke I would defeat it by pure will power. By massive concentration I would make the stricken limb work again

I soon learned the falsity of that belief. I would concentrate on the left side of my mouth with every atom of my being and will it to lift in a smile. I would order my left eyelid to move and blink until the sweat burst out all over me but nothing made the slightest difference. The ugly misshapen face staring back from the mirror seemed only to mock me.

But the really frightening thing came after a month or two of trying. Until then my mind had remembered the right signals to give to the paralysed muscles. Then one morning I found myself trying to remember them. I succeeded but only after a few panic-stricken seconds. The danger became alarmingly clear. If the paralysis lasted many weeks or months, the mind would lose all contact with the afflicted muscles and with it would go one's ability to fight back. Although I kept on trying throughout the four months, this in fact is what happened.

But by August there had been a few hopeful signs. I imagined I could taste certain foods on the left side of my mouth again and I occasionally felt a nervous twitch down my lower cheek. When my doctor told me these were signs the severed nerves had grown and were in the process of knitting together, I began hoping my eye might have recovered by the time I began my next novel.

This better news cannot have pleased my gremlin because, less than a week after I saw the doctor, a film company whose name I have forgotten made me an offer for the rights in *The Storm Knight*. Not an option offer but an outright sale which most likely meant they intended to make the film.

At any other time it would have been an occasion for rejoicing but with our option to James Whittaker still with months to run, it could hardly have been more frustrating, particularly because by now it looked as if Whittaker's company weren't going to make the film. Reggie asked them if they would release us from the option but somewhat understandably they declined. Reggie then asked the other film company if they would wait for the option to run out but they told us it was now or never. So it was never, and as Reggie phoned to give me the news, I thought I could hear my gremlin roaring with laughter.

It was during this period that I met Jerry Cassidy. Jerry was the manager of a film theatre in Mayfair that specialized in film takes and previews. The owners were the makers of the James Bond films. As rushes (unedited prints of movie picture scenes for quick viewing) were shown in the theatre, everybody who was anybody in the film world was likely to pass through it at some time or other, and Jerry knew them all.

In fact, Jerry seemed to know everybody in London. If he said to you "I had lunch with the Duke of Edinburgh yesterday", it was probably true. At first I thought him the world's greatest line-shooter but soon discovered I was wrong.

How he got to know so many people outside the film industry I never found out because Jerry kept some cards very close to his chest. But to me he was a good friend and when I went up to London I would usually call round at the theatre to have a drink and a chat. He was a small Irishman who had never learned to pronounce the English th but his popularity was unquestioned among the producers, directors, and film stars who used his theatre.

It was through him that I met the Beatles. At that time they were at the height of their fame and whenever they wanted to see rushes of their films, it was usually Jerry's theatre they used. Jerry was something of a fan of theirs and suggested I met them sometime when they were making an evening visit.

To be honest, I had never been entranced by their music and was baffled by the hysterical praise it was receiving. Such comments as 'On a par with Beethoven' had sometimes made me wonder if the entire artistic establishment had gone raving mad. But as they were undoubtedly a phenomenon, I was curious to find out what they were like as individuals and so was happy enough to accept Jerry's invitation.

My first meeting with them was not at the theatre but at the Hammersmith Odeon where they were currently performing. I had been up in London for the day to see my new editor, Ian Harrap, and when I called round to see Jerry he told me one of the Beatles (I think it was Paul McCartney but can't be certain) had expressed interest in *633 Squadron* and would like to meet me. He, Jerry, was going to the theatre that evening to see the manager so would I care to go with him and meet the Fabulous Four?

It sounded like an interesting evening and so I agreed. We went in Jerry's car but had to park hundreds of yards from the theatre because of the immense crowd of fans surrounding it. Unable to pack into the theatre, they were venting their frustration in hysterical screams that could be heard halfway across London.

To get through them we needed the help of a police escort. Even then it was an astonishing experience. The possibility we might in some way be connected to the Beatles caused the screaming crowd to surge around us and clamour for autographs. Some wanted to touch or grab us as if the act might put them in mystical contact with their idols.

Aided by the police, we forced our way into a side door of the theatre. At that time the Beatles were on the stage, so Jerry suggested that I waited in the wings to watch them while he conducted his business with the theatre manager. Afterwards we would visit the Holy of Holies, the Beatles dressing room.

My memory of the next half hour is pure surrealism. Someone gave me a stool and I sat down in the shadow of the wings. Ahead was the brilliantly illuminated stage with the four Beatles playing one of their numbers. What that number was I had no idea. Although their amplifiers were at full blast, they could not compete with the screams of the audience. Its decibel count was horrendous: a massive wave of sound that swept forward and drowned everything in its path. Although I was less than twenty feet from the nearest Beatle, he could have been playing Handel's Messiah for all I knew.

From my vantage point I could see the storm troops of this teenage army. Clearly intending to tear their idols limb from limb if released, they were being held back by a row of sweating policemen who filled the entire front row of the stalls. Now and then a girl would break through the cordon and hurl herself on the stage. A desperate policeman would leap after her and bring her down in a rugby tackle before she could reach her first victim. Each time the screams would reach a new crescendo that had seemed impossible a few seconds earlier.

Yet the Beatles played on. If their music was not to my taste, their courage won my deepest respect. A team of wild horses could not have dragged me in front of that fearsome teenage army.

The lights blazed down, the enormous din raged on, and from the darkness of the wings a midget ran forward and did a cartwheel alongside me. He was followed by an enormous man nearly seven feet tall whose facial expression suggested he was laughing as he bent down and said something in my ear. Although I couldn't hear a word, I decided to nod. This seemed to amuse the midget who did another cartwheel beside me. Who the grotesque couple were and what their purpose was I had no idea, but when they disappeared behind me into the darkness again, I felt certain the din was turning me delirious and I had imagined both of them. It was a huge relief when the Beatles left the stage to despairing screams from their fans and Jerry appeared to take me to their dressing room.

Even then the nightmare wasn't over. From my bemused memory the dressing room had one or two glass windows and as I was talking to Paul McCartney there was a crash of glass and a girl's bare arm reached through the window to touch him. We both turned sharply and saw the white arm slashed by glass almost from wrist to elbow. Although the girl had fainted when we reached her, I haven't the slightest doubt that on her recovery she would beg the hospital to make sure a scar remained after the stitches were removed. After all, it was an arm that had touched a god!

I met the Beatles twice more in Jerry's theatre. On both occasions they arrived around seven thirty, each in a different taxi. All had to be disguised so that a frenzied mob wouldn't follow them and tear the theatre down. I can't remember which ones were wearing false moustaches, but once inside the theatre, with the outer doors securely locked, they became the Beatles again and spent the next half hour watching their rushes. Afterwards we all had drinks and a chat.

My interest was in their conversation. For months and even years the popular press had suggested that in them we had not only four fabulous musicians but four great sages too. The range of their intellect was profound: their every comment full of wit and wisdom. The British Cabinet was mad not to use their intellect but their puissance did not end there. Weren't a million fans demanding that God recognized His limitations and should stand down for Lennon?

So my expectations were high in the interviews I had. In truth I found myself talking to four young lads from Liverpool who were likeable, who were bright, and who were professional, but who were extremely unlikely to unseat the Government or put God in fear of His golden throne.

I say this not to be spiteful because I liked the four of them and they could hardly be blamed for the garbage the newspapers and journals were serving up. But did not Beatlemania illustrate on an international level the frightening power of the media to delineate some particular person or group and then enlarge and distort beyond recognition their image and value?

If my earlier comments of the cavalier treatment of film companies on authors sounded like self pity or sour grapes, I feel they can be cleared of suspicion by what happened later that year. One evening after his returning from school my elder son Peter ran up to me in some excitement. "Dad, didn't you once write a short story called *The Devil Doll*?"

"That's right," I said. "I wrote it in South Africa."

"Didn't you sell the film rights of it?"

"In a way, yes. A magazine editor made me give him the rights before he bought the story. Why?"

"Well, there's a film called *The Devil Doll* on at the Carlton Cinema. A boy at school told me. Do you think it could be your story?"

I picked up the evening paper to look. Sure enough a film of that name was being shown at both the Westover and Carlton cinemas. With Shelagh seeing a friend that night, I took both boys to the Westover. And there was my story on film, starring Bryant Holliday, Yvonne Romain, and Sandra Dorne. I had not been told a word about its production or its release. If Peter had not heard about it by pure chance I might never have known that the film had been made. It made me wonder, as it does today, if any of my other stories have been filmed without my knowledge.

I wrote to the film company and in return received a few stills from the film. But there was not the slightest suggestion in the correspondence that they might have acted discourteously. The inference was clear. Why should film producers tell writers when their work is being filmed? The rights have been bought, haven't they? What more do they want? Such is the warm and cosy relationship between authors and the film world.

Lewis Rachmil purchased a third option on *A Killing for the Hawks* after his second option expired. He was very impressed by the completed novel but he couldn't give Reggie any idea when he could set up a production because he still needed to awaken Mirisch's interest. After our frustration over *The Storm Knight* this worried us, but as *Hawks* hadn't yet been published, we allowed him this third option.

At this time things in the book world had changed for the better for me. Not only were my serials going well in America but *633 Squadron* had recovered from the publicity mistakes of 1964 and its sales were on an upward curve. For a time it even appeared in the W.H. Smith's best-seller cabinet in Waterloo Station, which gave me a pleasant thrill when I made a day trip to London. By this time Corgi were in their sixth printing and even went as far to admit they had underestimated the book's potential. Their excuse was that the book was a 'sleeper'; a designation for a title that begins slowly but speeds up its sales as the years roll on (*633 Squadron* eventually went to twenty-six editions). I, of course, had my own explanation for its slow beginning!

All this meant that for the first time we were able to buy some furniture for the house, although we still felt the decorating of the large back room was beyond our means.

Our reasoning was based on the disappointments that had gone before. We had found the profession of writing defied all logic. It was based so much on subjective taste, on publicity, on luck, and on the strange whims and behavior of publishers, that to live up to one's current income was pure folly. The quality of a book seemed to have little bearing on the final formula. If this sounds unduly cautious for two people still in their early forties, it should be remembered that we had two elderly parents as well as two growing children to consider. We also had a deep distrust of my gremlin!

It was around this time that I was invited with other writers to a party at John Masters' house. Peter George, the author of *Dr. Strangelove* was there, and during the evening he drew me aside and asked if I was getting any big offers from America after the success of *633 Squadron*. When I told him I hadn't received any, he was shocked. He had received a huge offer via his American agent for the rights in his next book and he openly confessed that *Dr Strangelove* had not done as well financially as *633 Squadron*, which was all that mattered to American publishers.

"It's quite ridiculous," he told me. "You need a high-powered American agent to put your case over there. If you had one, I'd guarantee you'd get offers that would take your breath away."

I gave a wry shrug. "It sounds good but how do I get an agent like that."

Peter was nothing if not generous. "Leave it to me. I'll write my agent tomorrow and recommend you. Don't worry. We're good friends and in any case with *633 Squadron* behind you, you've got all the credentials you need. He'll take you on and it'll make the world of difference to you."

My thanks were heartfelt. I had known for a long time that I needed a good American agent because to date the one linked to my English agent had done nothing whatever for me. I had tried to find one but failed because the good ones have no need to advertise their wares. They are selective and usually only accept a writer by recommendation. I went away that night glad I had gone to John Masters' party.

I wasn't so glad a few days later when I picked up my morning paper. On discovering he had cancer, Peter had committed suicide. Horrified, I almost felt the fault was mine.

I had another of Reggie's comical letters at this time. It seemed a news programme on television had featured a man who for some reason better known to himself had spent 130 days alone down in the Cheddar Gorge, and Reggie wanted to know if I had seen the feature.

I hadn't and regretted it when Reggie went on to explain its relevance. According to this odd character, he had taken over a hundred books into the Gorge to help him pass away the time and had read them all twice. Amused, his interviewer had asked him which one of the novels he had enjoyed most and the man had said it was *633 Squadron*.

Although Reggie wasn't partial to cranks, he chuckled over this one, pointing out what splendid free publicity it was. But, as Reggie had to confess at the end of his letter, there was one small snag. When asked who the author of the book was, our cave dweller could not remember his name!

I heard a disturbing story about book publishing that year. One day when I was in London Ken Mennell introduced me to a man who had been a sales director in a large publishing house but had been forced into early retirement by ill health. Knowing that my views on publishers left something to be desired, Ken felt I'd be interested in something he had to tell me.

I was. He told me that sometimes a book was earmarked as a 'tax-loss' book before it was published. There could be two reasons for this. One might be the book's contents, which the publisher believed unlikely to appeal to the general public. He would publish it but then use the poor sales to offset against other profits.

The other reason was much more disturbing. The publisher might receive a manuscript from a new author whose style and quality matched or even surpassed the quality of one of his best-selling authors. Rather than risk this new author taking his book to another publisher, who might recognize its promise and so produce a rival in the market place, the first publisher would sometimes take on the new writer with the intention of destroying him. He would give the book just enough advertising to prevent the writer or his agent complaining, but subsequently give it little if any promotion in libraries, shops, or in the media. In other words the book would be quietly allowed to die, and in dying diminish the threat of a rival to his best-selling author and the profits he brought to the house.

Although I realized the ploy could not be proven, and that similar ploys are often practiced in the business world, I found it difficult to believe such a thing could be done to literature and by the very people involved in it. Feeling I must know one way or the other I sought out a book editor I knew very well and invited him out to lunch. I waited until he had drunk a couple of glasses of wine before putting the question to him.

I expected indignation but he remained silent. When I pressed him again he gave a rueful sigh. Sadly, he said, it did just occasionally happen. It was usually arranged that the book just covered expenses but it wasn't difficult for a good accountant to make it appear to have lost money on the company's balance sheet.

I remember feeling quite sickened at this discovery and I wrote my agent to tell him about it. I have this letter before me as I write but although I did mention the name of the whistle-blowing editor who confirmed the story, I had better not give it here as his confession might not endear his name in the publishing world. It is one reason, however, why I advise young writers to always don their flak jacket and tin helmet when they complete their work and send it out into the bold, bad world of business.

NINE

To my relief Harrap liked *A Killing for the Hawks* and bought the volume rights before they published *The Storm Knight*. I knew this signified a great deal of confidence in *Hawks* and my meetings with my editor, Ian Harrap, confirmed this. He even told me it was the firm's intention to have a launching party for it — something I hadn't been given before — and he asked me if I had any suggestions for the venue.

My choice was The Pathfinder Club, of which I am a member, a club founded for the survivors of the air crews chosen for wartime pathfinder missions. At that time the rooms were in Mount Street and although relatively small they were rich with wartime memorabilia. The Queen Mother was the patron.

Harrap agreed and the club was ear-marked to be used. At the appropriate time I was to ask various Air Force personages of my acquaintance if they would attend.

In the meantime Harrap succeeding in selling the paperback rights in both *The Storm Knight* and *Hawks* to Pan Books. Apart from the welcome fifty per cent I received, it was an entry into Pan Books which I was to find rewarding later on a number of counts.

Storm Knight duly came out in the spring. It received excellent reviews in the nationals, which pleased Harrap. The Daily Mirror said it was 'a very exciting yarn about skin diving and skulduggery in Norway' and The Sun said 'it was a splendidly atmospheric novel with excellent underwater scenes': reviews that ought to have guaranteed good sales for the thriller it was. But I can't claim the book broke any records although Harrap seemed satisfied enough. It made me wonder what authors had to do to get good sales. After all, unless he seeks other sources for publicity, he can do little more than please the critics. Perhaps I should try another way, I thought, such as throwing eggs at the Prime Minister or taking off my trousers and streaking one night around Trafalgar Square. After all don't most celebrities gain their publicity in similar anti-social ways?

But Shelagh put paid to that. She pointed out that if I were ever so stupid to leave off my trousers, didn't I realize there would be a lunar eclipse that night and all London's lights would blow a fuse and go out. So all I would get for my gesture would be frostbite in my extremities. Knowing she was right I abandoned the idea.

Nevertheless I managed to remain optimistic and there were other things that summer than writing. England won the World Cup after two exciting weeks, during which I hardly worked at all, and directly afterwards we took the children in our motor caravan to Spain for a couple of weeks. In all it was the longest period I had taken off writing since our return to England.

The months flew past and once again Lewis Rachmil's option was due for renewal. He wrote from America requesting a fourth but this time Reggie advised caution. He pointed out that *Hawks* was due to be published in a few weeks and if we agreed to a fourth option we might have exactly the same situation we had landed with *Storm Knight*. A film company might make an offer for the full rights and once again we would find ourselves tied up and unable to accept. Moreover, as Reggie felt *Hawks* was the best book I had written, that made the chances of a large film company picking it up more likely.

I saw his point and so we asked Lewis what was moving at his end. He said he loved the story but at the moment could not obtain the finance for a film. Nevertheless, the novel deserved screening and he felt sure it was only a matter of time before he persuaded a backer to put up the money.

It put us in a difficult position because I liked Lewis and would have been happy working with him. At the same time I knew there was no sentiment in these deals. The key factor was always money and profit. Reggie and I met in London and talked for an entire afternoon before coming to a painful decision. We would tell Lewis that we had been patient for eighteen months but if he wanted the rights, he would now have to buy them outright. We couldn't risk the same thing happening as had happened with *Storm Knight*.

Lewis's reply came back a couple of weeks later. Our decision had greatly disappointed him because he had been in the middle of promising negotiations. These plans were now terminated and he could only hope I didn't live to regret the advice I had been given. I remember reflecting how difficult decisions were to make when one had become acquainted with the wheelings and dealings of the business world. Liking Lewis as I did, I couldn't help wondering why it was only now that he had mentioned these promising negotiations.

At this time neither the novel rights in *Storm Knight* nor *Hawks* had sold in America. Some of the reasons for rejection were ludicrous. One publisher rejected them because their sex content was too graphic! When one took into account the stuff that was being published in America even in those days, I found that to be the joke of the year.

Summer, however, brought better news from America. David McKay bought the USA volume rights in *Hawks*. It was my first hardcover sale in the States and neither Reggie nor I were too happy that a clause in the contract committed me to give the publisher 10% of any subsequent film sales. English contracts made no claim on such rights. Nevertheless, the sale did seem to confirm Reggie's belief that it was my best novel to date.

The book was launched by Harrap in the autumn at The Pathfinder Club. I managed to get Bill Reid and Norman Jackson there, as well as Hamish Mahaddie. Another interesting guest was the father of Peter West (a then current BBC personality) who had appropriately won his VC in the RFC in the First World War. Although because of budget restraints the number of guests were limited to thirty, I also managed to get my old RAF friend Des Matthews invited.

So, with plenty of copy for the invited journalists, the evening went with a swing. Afterwards Shelagh and I stayed the night in London with my brother.

As I had hoped, the theme of the book was picked up by critics and in the subsequent controversy I was invited to appear on four television programmes. One stands out in my mind above the others. It was a station on which I had appeared a couple of times before. This time I was given half-an-hour and artfully set up by the producer. Without telling me beforehand, he produced a dear old vicar well over seventy years of age who had won a VC in the First World War. Frail in appearance, gentle of voice and manner, he nevertheless totally disagreed with my belief that physical courage bore no relationship to a man's moral character.

He was scheduled to share the entire programme and I wasn't so stupid not to see the trap set for me. He was frail, elderly, and a vicar to boot, while I was in the prime of my life. If I were to argue forcefully with him, I might seem intolerant and perhaps lose the case I was defending.

So I had to soft pedal and not interrupt while he repeated the hoary old chestnuts that my book had challenged. Allowed by the producer to take an interminable time in making his points and with myself unable to cut in for fear of appearing a bully, I felt my case didn't get the best of hearings.

I had one more memorable experience while helping Harrap to promote *Hawks*. Hearing about an old man in a nursing home in Lyme Regis who had won a VC in World War One, Harrap asked if I would visit him. If a date were arranged, the appropriate Press coverage would be there. From the snippets I had been given, the old man sounded a fascinating character. So I took my father with me to Lyme Regis, and while he was taking a look round the town, I paid my visit to the nursing home.

The old man's name was Alan Jarvis. He was sitting in an armchair when I was introduced to him but looked very frail. Earlier a staff nurse had told me he had a brain tumour and had not long to live. But there was nothing wrong with his mind and at first he gave me the impression he hadn't much time for writers and their stupid novels.

But as we talked I think he began to realize my interest in flying was genuine and not just a subject I was plundering to make a living. He asked me if I had been in the RAF and when I told him I had served for over six years, he invited me to sit down beside him.

I found the next half hour fascinating as he re-lived his past. I believe he enjoyed it too because as we talked his eyes began to shine. He spoke about dawn patrols and artillery spotting and aerial fighting but made no mention of the extraordinary feat that had won him the VC until I asked him the question outright. "Is it true that you once shot down five Fokker DVIIs in one day?"

He looked almost sheepish as he nodded. "Yes. But I think I was a bit lucky."

I looked at him sitting in that armchair, a dew drop on his nose, a sick old man no doubt treated like a child by the young nurses, and thought of the hell raiser and warrior he must have been in his youth. Before I left I asked him to sign a copy of my book while waiting reporters took photographs. Then I went off to meet my father. Reminded he too was growing old, I took him to a pub. I needed a drink. I had never disliked the humiliations of old age more.

I had an even deeper reason for disliking old age a couple of weeks later. A brother-in-law of my father paid us a visit and as he hadn't seen Dorset before, I offered one afternoon to take him and my father out for a drive. To that date, having no car, my father hadn't driven since his days in Hull, but this day I sensed he was longing to have a wheel between his hands again and so when we reached the quieter country roads I suggested he took over.

He clearly appreciated the gesture and for my part I had no qualms. He had held a clean driving licence since the First World War, something of which he was secretly proud. But as we neared an approaching van and I felt our near side wheels bump against the grass verge, I realized he had allowed more clearance than was necessary.

Feeling it was due only to lack of practice I didn't concern myself too much until we approached a stationary lorry and he swung too far across the road, causing an oncoming car to swerve away. Seeing my uncle glance at me, I began to break into a cold sweat. I was beginning to realize my father's reflexes had gone and with them his sense of spatial awareness.

I sweated it out until a juggernaut lorry swung round a bend towards us. This time my father kept too far over the crown of the road, making the lorry swerve violently. As its angry driver gave a loud blast on his horn, I saw my uncle's face and knew he was about to protest. To save my father from humiliation I knew I had no option but to take back the wheel myself.

But there was no way of saving his feelings, no matter how diplomatically I tried to make the suggestion. He knew the reason as well as I. He showed no resentment: he just quietly moved seats with me. But I knew his last possession, his pride in his competence as a driver, had been taken from him and there is no way I can express my feelings. I felt quite dreadful and later wondered if that disastrous day had begun the decline in his health.

I was in contact with the comedian Norman Wisdom at this time. He had read a short story of mine called *The Last Lie* and wanted me to adapt it into a vehicle for himself. As it was a story about a mousy little Parisienne who is tricked by a letter into believing a handsome young lodger is in love with her, it was asking a lot of me. Before receiving a penny for my work, I wrote at least four variations and went up to Norman's flat at least as many times, but still without satisfying him. It really was a clown wishing to play Hamlet situation and as such was doomed to failure. In the end he bought the story as it was for £500 and we parted on good terms. It was the last I heard of the story.

Christmas approached with Corgi suggesting that I wrote a sequel to *633 Squadron*. With the film having made money all over the country and overseas and the book having yet another reprint, they were now convinced there would be a future in another book about my squadron.

I'm not certain why I didn't take up the offer at that time. Perhaps it was because I had thought of the novel as a testament to my friends and for this reason had never contemplated another. Or perhaps it was because I was already making plans for my next novel or that I couldn't see any way of writing a sequel. The cardinal rule of sequels is to keep one's characters alive and nearly all of mine had been killed in the Svartfjord. To produce a valid sequel seemed an almost impossible task.

So I thanked Corgi for their offer but declined it, no doubt making some comment that I might consider the idea at a later date. In view of what was to happen, it was one of the worst decisions of my writing life: a misfortune that for once I couldn't blame on my gremlin.

So 1966 came to an end. It had provided its ups and downs but on the whole it had been my best year since our arrival back in England. Publishers were now asking for my work instead of my peddling it to them and when we made our toasts that Christmas, it did seem a new era had dawned. None of us had the slightest suspicion that a storm was developing just below the horizon and soon would be heading straight towards us.

TEN

Peter, my elder son, went to university in 1967. He had obtained eleven 'O' levels and four 'A' levels at the Bournemouth Grammar School and gained entry into Manchester University. His first choice was engineering but after a few weeks he changed to psychology. It was a popular subject in the Sixties and although I had my doubts about its efficacy and the people who practised it, I raised no objection to his making the change.

It was about this time that I learned my father was having pain in his right leg. It seems he had been suffering cramp in it for some time when out walking but feeling I had enough to worry about, he and my mother had kept it from me. But now the twinges of pain were too severe to be hidden.

It was not the first time in my life, nor would it be the last, that my ambivalence towards my work became evident. I was absurdly dedicated to it and my ambitions had no limits, but at the same time I was always conscious that in pursuing it so single-mindedly, I was not giving sufficient attention to the people I loved. Shelagh had made countless sacrifices for me and I had never given as much time to the children as other fathers seemed to give. Now this dedication had led to my father keeping his illness a secret and I felt shame and resentment that my work should make me so blind I had not noticed it. As guilt or worry tend to make me irritable when I can do nothing to mitigate them, I made things worse by practically quarrelling with him for not telling me before.

I made him see a doctor and to my dismay learned that a main artery in his leg was almost blocked. I was also told by the doctor that he had general arteriosclerosis and we must be prepared for a rapid worsening of his condition in the days ahead.

It was a discovery that shadowed everything that happened that year for us. The thought of losing that reliable, lovable man was like a stab in the heart, and my ambivalence towards my work grew when I thought of the times he had gently hinted it would be pleasant to go out for a drink and a chat together and I had prevaricated in order to write a few more paragraphs. Now it was too late as it was too painful for him to walk more than a few yards from his sitting room and I reviled myself for my neglect.

I had to go into hospital for medical checks myself that year. For a long time I had suffered from indigestion but recently I had experienced sharp pains under my right ribs. I had them only occasionally and they lasted only a minute or two, but during the attacks I would not be able to move for the pain.

I was prodded and poked and given X-rays and finally told there was a dark shadow beneath my ribs whose cause was a mystery to my doctors. Not liking the sound of it I was reassured it was not a growth but a long sharp object shaped like a needle. Indeed, they believed it was made of metal.

As everyone was baffled by this, I was questioned about my activities and finally asked about my war history. It was only when I mentioned my German bomb experience that their ears pricked up and a doctor suggested that the explosion had not only caused the fracture of my neck but a sliver of steel must also have penetrated my body. Because of its dart-like shape it would have left the merest puncture on my skin which would have gone unnoticed by the medics who had attended me.

If they were correct it seemed my German bomb had had it in for me in more ways than one. For myself I couldn't believe it but they seemed satisfied by the explanation and gave me liver and other tests to ensure my vital organs weren't affected. As they were not I was discharged. I asked if the thing shouldn't be removed and they advised against it. Removal could be dangerous whereas, apart from the occasional stabs of pain, which only seemed to occur when I was sitting down, it presented no health threat. Taking their word for it, I went on with my life.

As *A Killing for the Hawks* had now been on the bookshelves for over three months, Reggie and I felt there had been ample time for readers to scan it and notify their film companies about its screen possibilities. So, as one week followed another, our anxiety grew. Was it possible we had made the wrong decision again?

By March it seemed certain we had. Because of the *Storm Knight* fiasco we had turned down Lewis Rachmil's ongoing interest, and now we seemed to have no one interested in its screen possibilities. Yet had we let Lewis have another option, Sod's Law would have made certain we received a huge film offer. At such times one felt there was no way one could win.

However, I rallied on remembering the novel was being published in the USA in 1967. Surely it would be seen and recognized there? I think I had to believe that to avoid jumping off the pier and drowning myself.

Hawks was duly published by David McKay and, anxious to hear the views of the critics, I paid an American Press Cutting Agency to send me reviews. They were as startling as my British ones had been. I quote some from both countries without shame because of what happened then and later:

'A graphic and horrifying account of the air war over France during World War One as seen by a Canadian pilot in the Royal Flying Corps.' (Library Journal, New York)

'All in all, this novel should in time rank with the classics of fiction dealing with the 1914-1918 war in the air.' (St. Louis, MO Post Dispatch)

'Delightfully and accurately told by a veteran of World War Two, Mr. Smith handles his material with great skill.' (Louisville KY Courier-Journal)

'A KILLING FOR THE HAWKS by Frederick E. Smith is perhaps one of the finest novels ever written about air combat over the Western Front in World War One.' (Blackfoot, Idaho News)

'One of the best tales of human emotions and human conflicts that I've read for a long time.' (Wolverhampton Chronicle)

'Smith's research has been meticulous and he has some superb flying sequences.' (Books and Bookmen, Britain).

'The descriptions of dog-fighting over the Western Front are as good as any of their kind.' (Daily Telegraph, Britain).

'This gripping novel with its remarkable authenticity of the air struggle in World War One is obviously destined to gain a wide audience.' (Southern Evening Echo, Britain).

'Brilliantly told, with vivid and detailed descriptions of the squadron's sorties and tactics against the manoeuvrable Albatross. The novel undoubtedly portrays accurately front-line squadron life in 1917. It will be thoroughly enjoyed by all who read it.' (Aeroplane, England).

There were many more of similar vein but the one that made my eyes widen in astonishment was the letter I received from Cyril Clessens of the Mark Twain Journal. It read: *'In view of your outstanding contribution to American fiction by your A KILLING FOR THE HAWKS, you have been unanimously elected Knight of Mark Twain.'* I read the commendation twice before passing it over to Shelagh. It seemed I was no longer plain Frederick E. Smith. The ceremonial sword had fallen on my shoulder. Thanks to *Hawks* I was now Sir Frederick!

From dozens of such reviews plus a literary award I think I was entitled to believe the book would be a reasonable if not a best seller in the States, there would be film interest, and its paperback rights would be in instant demand. Not so. Not one little bit so. The hardcover didn't go to a second edition, no film offers came, and McKay couldn't sell the paperback rights to any of the leading firms. They were eventually bought for a small fee by a third-rate company who sold a few thousand copies and that was all. None of it made any sense to me. It almost seemed as if sales were in adverse ratio to a book's success with the critics, bringing rueful thoughts that perhaps the critics would be kinder to me if in future they adjudged my work to be banal and untellable.

But life has to go on and there is little to be gained from lying down and feeling sorry for oneself. When it was finally clear *Hawks'* sales was not matching its reviews, I felt it only fair to Shelagh to relieve her of my disgruntled self for a while. So I took myself and my motor caravan to Cornwall. There I walked the cliffs for a week and badly blistered my feet in an effort to burn out my disappointment. When the week was over, I was myself again and discovered I had thought of another novel. So I hurried back to commence it.

It was nothing like *Hawks*, being about a young woman in danger from jealous forces. I suspected Harrap would not be keen on it after the pungency of *Hawks* but perhaps my disappointment accounted for the change of theme or perhaps I needed to write a lighter novel after spending so long in war-torn skies. Whatever the reason and whatever the outcome, I worked on the novel through the winter. I called it *Mullion Rock* after a cove of a similar name in Cornwall.

As I expected, Harrap didn't exactly turn cartwheels at my presenting them with a Gothic type novel but to do them credit they took the book on the understanding they could publish it under the pseudonym I had used for my earlier serials, David Farrell. Knowing it was hardly the type of novel to follow *Hawks*, I agreed, although once again it meant bottom-of-the-ladder payment. However, this time I had no one to blame but myself.

Harrap did something equally commendable that year, although I knew it was to keep me on their list in the hope I wrote another *Hawks*. They took *The Wider Sea of Love* and agreed under protest to publish it under my name. By this time Reggie had been negotiating it for over a year but to date had found publishers still nervous of the ideas expressed within it. This had worried and irritated me because with my son bringing home friends from university I was in a position to know that the sexual revolution I had prophesied was well under way by this time. When young girls of eighteen, looking as if butter wouldn't melt in their mouths, could sit in a family drawing room and talk without the slightest embarrassment about the affairs and abortions they'd had, one knew that in the sub culture of the young the revolution had not only occurred but reached its Robespierre days. The Swinging Sixties hadn't won their epithet for nothing, and my fear was that by the time publishers and the general public took notice of the changing scene, with its credits and its debits, my book would be out of date.

However, worries of this nature were nothing beside the anxiety my father's health was causing us. By the autumn he could no longer walk and was in great pain with his leg. He bore it like the man he was but although his cheerfulness tended to hide the brutal facts from the rest of the family, I knew in my heart he hadn't long to live and that knowledge shadowed everything else for the rest of the year.

It was during this time that I met Charles (Jerry) Juroe. Juroe was the assistant to Arthur Jacobs, a film producer who had made the highly successful film *The Planet of the Apes* and was regarded as the current Golden Boy of Hollywood. Juroe was a fanatic about the aircraft and air battles of the First World War and was said to have one of the world's finest collection of memorabilia. He had read *Hawks* and wanted to know if the film rights had sold. When I told him they had not, he asked me to hold on to the rights while he contacted Arthur Jacobs.

Within a week or two I was dining with both of them in London. By this time Jacobs himself had read the book and was as enthusiastic as Juroe. He mentioned a huge figure for the full film rights and then offered me a cheque for a six months' option. Knowing Reggie would be delighted and offer no objection, I accepted the deal.

In normal times I would have been on Cloud Nine, for an Arthur Jacobs production would not only ensure the finest actors of the day but would receive world wide publicity. It would make up for all past disappointments, but as I travelled back to Bournemouth in the train that night, I couldn't work up any real excitement. The shadows of my father's illness reached out too far.

It was a depressing Christmas. With father unable to climb the stairs to his bedroom, we set up a bed for him in my parents' sitting room. Needing attention day and night now, we all took it in turns in nursing him but as his pain worsened it became obvious he needed the attention only a hospital could give, and not long after Christmas our doctor insisted he went in for treatment. Within days we were told he must have a mid thigh amputation if he were to survive.

The night before the amputation was an experience I would never want again. Knowing my father's sensitivity, I lay wondering what his thoughts were as he waited to be mutilated the next day. I prayed he was heavily sedated but my imagination gave me no sleep. Nor did I find much comfort in the ward sister's words over the telephone after the operation: "Your father is as well as can be expected, Mr. Smith."

"Can we see him today?"

"No. Phone again this evening and we'll let you know how he is progressing."

We were allowed to see him the following evening. At first it was an agreeable surprise. Pink-cheeked, he looked in better health than he had looked for a year. But as we talked, my eyes were drawn to the depression in his bedclothes. He must have noticed it because he gave my hand a little squeeze. "Stop worrying, lad. I'm all right. Really I am."

While Shelagh and my mother chatted to him, I had a talk to the ward sister whom previously I had ear-marked as a dragon. But when I mentioned my father's name she melted. "Oh, yes. You are Mr. Smith's son, are you?"

"What does the doctor say about him?" I asked.

"He's very pleased with his condition."

"He's a better colour than I expected."

"That's due to the blood transfusions he's been given. Even so, he's doing very well."

I felt let down at that. I think she understood because she gave me an encouraging smile. "Has he told you what he did this afternoon?"

"No. What was that?"

"He got a crutch from one of the other patients, then climbed out of bed and hopped along the ward. Isn't that wonderful? Only one day after a mid-thigh amputation? And he's the oldest man in the ward."

I didn't understand. "Why did he do that?"

"Don't you understand? There are other men in the ward awaiting the same operation and he wanted to show them they've nothing to fear. Your father's a remarkable man, Mr. Smith. A remarkable man."

"How long is he going to be here?" I asked.

"Our doctors say the next fourteen days are the critical ones. If he survives them he should be all right and you can take him home."

I don't think any of us had any real sleep during that fortnight. Every time the phone rang our hearts would leap and thump painfully. Shelagh and I took my mother to see him every night and we all thought he looked better at every visit. And yet those fourteen days dragged as none has ever dragged before.

At last they were over. The old man had made it! I couldn't remember Shelagh looking happier and my mother's relief was a joy to see. After we visited him in hospital, we spent the rest of the night making plans to ensure his life at home would be as comfortable as possible.

The phone rang the very next day just after 5 a.m. It was a grey winter morning. I heard it before Shelagh did, but it took me all my will power to answer it. It was the ward night sister, her voice sympathetic. "I'm very sorry to tell you this, Mr. Smith, but your father passed away an hour ago."

All emotion seemed to die in me. It was now a stranger talking on the phone. "Do you know the reason?"

"Not yet. We would like your permission to carry out an autopsy. But we think it was his heart. We're very sorry, Mr. Smith. Your father was greatly liked and respected here."

I had to fetch his possessions that same winter afternoon. They were in a paper bag which I took upstairs to my mother's room. I poured them out on her table: a cheap wrist watch, a lighter, a half-filled tin of Three Nuns tobacco, a blackened pipe, a pair of spectacles, and a handful of silver and copper coins.

Those were his possessions, his rewards for a lifetime of service and unfailing kindness. A few cheap baubles. As I stared down at them, the long-held vat of acid from my childhood suddenly fumed and exploded. Afraid of myself, afraid of what I wanted to do or destroy, I walked out of the house and down to the sea front. Spray was breaking over the promenade but I felt nothing of it. I walked into the greying night and cursed the entire universe for its broken dreams and its lying promises.

ELEVEN

After my father's death I was lost. My mind could settle on nothing and as the days and weeks passed by I began to wonder if I would ever write again. Then one day I understood myself. I had to put down on paper all that had happened.

I sat down at my typewriter and the words poured out as if a dam were bursting. I don't remember how long it took me, a day or a week, but when it was over I could think clearly again. I made no effort to publish the pages. I put them into a drawer and closed it. Then I settled down to life again.

My next novel had already been planned during 1968. It was based on the idea that had come to me in 1959 and which I had not felt experienced enough to write. But the idea had simmered in my mind all those years and, not surprisingly, both a theme and a plot had developed during that time.

Yet although I believed it was a marvellous idea (one can boast about ideas because they seem to be given to one rather than be created) I had still found excuses not to write the novel. Perhaps I knew that I would never get a better idea and if I ruined it by inexperience I would never forgive myself.

But I was now nearing fifty and there was an epidemic of men dying of heart disease in their fifties. With this in mind, I had decided somewhat neurotically that it would be as frustrating to die before writing the novel as to ruin it through lack of skill.

I had one great regret. To date I had always visited countries I had written about but South America was one continent I had never visited and at this time it was beyond my means. Yet I needed a great deal of information to give the book a factual background.

To circumvent this problem, the previous year I had taken a step I had never taken before and applied for a grant. As it was the year when literary grants were available, I'd applied for a Winston Churchill Fellowship. In return I was asked for details and for my case history. These I provided and to my surprise I was put on the Foundation's short list. When the list was whittled down further, it looked as if the Fellowship might be mine. Instead the award was eventually given to a member of the BBC. It was a decision that disappointed me because I felt a man with 'Auntie' behind him could afford to travel without requiring a grant.

With no help there, I'd had to try elsewhere. Reading that Cuba was giving some writers hospitality to see the improvements Fidel Castro was bringing to the country, and convincing myself that the interior of Cuba would be near enough to my novel's background for me to fill in the rest, I had approached the Embassy to see if they would grant me free travel. The reply from the Embassy took over a week to reach me and had clearly been intercepted and opened en route. With the Cold War still chilly, I found it highly amusing that anyone could suspect I might be a member of some off-beat political party.

The letter had granted me a brief interview with the Ambassador. On arrival at the Embassy, I was told I had ten minutes to state my business. When ushered in, I was expecting to meet some grey-bearded elderly man or a ranting political fanatic. Instead there was a beautiful, raven-haired girl in her early thirties sitting at a desk. Puzzled, I told her I was hoping to see the Ambassador. At that she laughed and waved me forward. She was the Ambassador and what was the purpose behind my request?

I did my best to explain. She questioned me about my work and when she heard I had lived in South Africa and had written a book attacking apartheid, her interest quickened and she began asking me questions about the country.

As one question led to another, I began to worry about my allotted ten minutes but it proved unnecessary. As the door opened and an aide reminded her of the time, she told him to make excuses and cancel her appointments for the next hour. Her interest in South Africa was such that I could only think it was a case of one extreme finding the other extreme fascinating. Whatever her reason, her questions were intelligent, perceptive, and good humoured. During the conversation I learned that she was an aristocrat in her country who had been converted to communism by the deeds and aspirations of Fidel Castro.

In all my initial ten minutes was stretched to one and a half hours before she smiled at me and rose. I hesitated and then took the plunge and kissed her hand. After all, I thought, it wasn't every writer who could claim he had kissed an ambassador's hand. Before I left she informed me I would be made a guest of her government for fourteen days and my flight would leave for Cuba in two weeks time.

I returned home delighted with my invitation. But although my father had had a remission prior to my visit, his health deteriorated so quickly during the following week that it became clear I couldn't possibly be away at such a time, particularly as Shelagh was still going out to work. So there was no option but to contact my gracious host, apologize for wasting her time, and withdraw myself from the trip.

Thus, now I had decided to write the novel, research became a major problem. In a novel of the scope I was contemplating, topography, climate, and even flora and fauna might have a bearing on the story line, and so had to be defined even before a synopsis could be written.

Initially it had been my intention to use an actual country for my novel. Now my only option seemed to be a fictional country: one that contained the features my story needed. By doing intense research I hoped it would have the flavour of South America but would also be insured against any terrestrial criticism.

Aware how factual errors can damage a novel's credibility, I spent over two months creating my fictitious country which I called Montaguay. Only then did I work on my synopsis. But by this time my father's health had deteriorated so much that it had pushed the project aside and after his death I had wondered if I would ever find the enthusiasm to return to it.

But after setting my emotions down on paper, my earlier urgency had returned and today I believe I know why. My father's death had been a catalyst and given me the need to bury myself in a challenge that would take my mind off my loss.

The initial idea behind the novel had been the question that all pacifists must surely ask themselves. Although a man has the individual right to turn the other cheek, has he the moral right to stand aside when others are being violated?

From that question my synopsis developed. As the war had taught me that violence begets violence, supposing I made Montaguay a corrupt dictatorship and my main character an expatriate Englishman, named Mason, who, ashamed of his combatant role in World War Two, has become a doctor, swanning with high society but also running a clinic for the poor. While Mason knows that violence is self-corrupting, what will his thoughts be if one of his dearest friends is imprisoned and tortured for political resistance? What will Mason do if he has the means to aid his friend's escape and yet knows the price he will have to pay if he surrenders to the temptation?

This initial supposition took some time to develop but once it came I found it the entrance to a gold mine with its possibilities. Will not Mason soon discover that to remove a pernicious system one's ideals might become corrupted by the evils one is fighting against, that in destroying corruption the visionary might become corrupted himself, sacrificing every dearly-held belief in the name of expediency.

Many questions can arise from this discovery. Can violence ever attain the idealist's objectives? How far can a man go in the fight for his beliefs without corrupting himself? It is considered a truism that a man's life is the greatest sacrifice he can make for his fellows. Might not a greater one be the sacrifice of his principles — what some would call the loss of his soul?

The political aspect could also be stressed. Political fanaticism, which blinds the mind to self-criticism, can turn men against their brothers, lover against lover, nation against nation. How true is it that 'nothing makes a greater fool of Man than his reason'? Can the dreams of a visionary sometimes be of surer coin than the plans of the realist?

As those possibilities would not only lead to an intriguing novel, they would also be timeless in their message. From this I knew my earlier instincts had been right. This could be the most important novel I had yet attempted. What I didn't know at the time were the difficulties I would have to face before it was completed.

I had never worked harder than I worked that year. I found the theme immensely rewarding but I had only written a third of it when Clarence Paget of Pan Books made me an offer.

It seemed Pan had obtained the book rights on a film Dino de Laurentiis of Italy was making. It was of the Hundred Days before Waterloo and the battle itself. The film, which was to feature units of the Russian Red Army and have Rod Steiger as Napoleon and Christopher Plummer as Wellington, was to be the most expensive film ever made. It was to be released in 1970 and Pan's book had to be ready at the same date for a tie-in. Did I want to take it on? My advance would be £1000 but I would have to share royalties with the film makers.

It was a difficult decision to make. My heart wanted to continue with my South American novel but my head told me I should accept the offer. It was clear by this time that my novel was going to take me at least two more years to write and that the only money coming in that year would be royalties on *633 Squadron* and dwindling royalties from my serials in America.

I had another reason for my hesitation. I knew Pan wanted me to write the book on the strength of *Hawks*, which had sold over 150,000 paperback copies, and as I liked Pan as publishers, my reasoning went that if I did a good job for them they would be that much more likely to take on my South American novel. Another, although lesser reason, was the subject itself. I knew very little about the Napoleonic wars, having taken the Elizabethan period at school, but to write a novel about the titanic clash between two of the world's greatest military leaders seemed a fascinating challenge.

So, not without some pain, I put aside my South American novel and began reading about the Hundred Days. I read at high speed and read over twenty-four books in a fortnight.

I did not need to make many notes. My memory was still almost photographic and although I couldn't claim to remember all the information stored in the books, I knew I could remember which book and which page to scan for any facts I might need when writing the novel.

Although the film script was at my disposal to use and the book was later, regrettably, billed as being based on the script, the truth was I didn't use very much of it. I approached the work as my own novel and although here and there I used a turn of phrase from the script that I thought apt or vivid, by and large I wrote my own version of those tremendous times.

I had reasons for this. One was probably egotistical: my belief I could do better literary work than film writers. Another was the occasional historical discrepancy I found in the script. Undoubtedly these had been introduced to heighten the drama but I have always held the belief that a writer can and should be able to make satisfactory drama out of the true facts and should never warp history to suit his plot.

Not that the script lacked talent. In its genre it was very good but the book would have my name on its spine and so personal pride demanded I kept to the facts. The only discrepancy I allowed myself was Marshall Ney's meeting with Napoleon after the latter's escape from Elba. The script had the site in an Alpine valley. As the real meeting took place in a dismal and undramatic office in Lyons, I felt artistic licence could be allowed this one change, particularly as there is a painting of an Alpine meeting in the Louvre.

I made one important addition to the script. I felt that many readers would know little about the history of the two men and the circumstances that led up to the Hundred Days, and so I wrote an historical foreword. To condense so much within a few pages and yet keep it clear and readable was not easy and I kept asking myself if such a history lesson was appropriate to a fast-moving story. In fact it proved to be what the novel needed and Pan congratulated me for including it.

One interesting sidelight of my research was the discrepancies in the history books I read. To this point I think I had believed historians kept to basic facts. In other words although their interpretations of historical characters' motives might differ, their actions and venues were based on universal accord.

I soon found my mistake. The Duchess of Richmond's Ball on the eve of Waterloo must surely be one of the best documented events of the 19th Century and yet I discovered three different addresses for its locale in the books I read, and all were by well known historians. I mention this as a gentle admonishment to all those who put their noses in the air at historical fiction. Perhaps there is an element of fiction in all history books.

While I was spending my days (and often my nights) with Wellington and Napoleon and riding with them to their destiny at Mont St Jean, Arthur Jacobs took out his second option on *Hawks*. He also told me that he had commissioned Terence Rattigan to write the screenplay. Although disappointed he hadn't asked me, I nevertheless knew that producers needed big names to sell their film packages to financiers, and few were bigger in the screen writing world at that time than Rattigan. It also indicated that Jacobs was fully committed to making the film.

So I sold him another option and accepted Rattigan's role with good grace. I had no inkling at this time what a disaster Rattigan's participation would mean to me.

I finished Waterloo by its deadline and sent it off to Clarence Paget. As its subject had been a new departure for me, I awaited his reaction somewhat anxiously, only to be delighted when he wrote to say he thought it was a 'superb' novel and he expected to do very well with it. Greatly relieved, and receiving the £1000 advance to subsidize my South American novel, I pulled my manuscript out of my desk drawer and began work on it again. My hope now was that there would be no further interruptions before it was finished.

In November Arthur Jacobs bought his third option on *Hawks*. This time I learned he was assembling an all star cast with Sophia Loren and Gregory Peck in leading roles. With Rattigan soon to finish his screenplay, the entire package seemed certain to interest any large film financier. My excitement grew by the day.

Harrap's publication date for *The Wider Sea of Love* was the 11th November that year. Two weeks beforehand they sent me a courtesy copy for my approval. To date I had found Harrap one of the most equitable publishers I had encountered but the jacket of *The Wider Sea* upset me. Some artist had given it the kind of cover that would make a Mills and Boon author wince. I needed only one look at it to know it had doomed the novel from its onset.

The design of jackets is often a cause of discontent to authors It is hard to express one's feelings when a year of thought and hard work is put at risk or even ruined by a totally inappropriate one. An author wonders why on earth publishers don't consult him beforehand. While one accepts that their sales manager might have more knowledge of which jackets appeal to the public, it would surely be possible for a compromise to be reached between two reasonable people.

In my case, apart from my alarm over the jacket and the sales it might deny, I was wondering about the ultimate fate of my South American novel. Harrap had published two novels after *Hawks* and neither had done that well. Being human, I believed the fault was inadequate promotion but what publisher would ever make that admission? Poor sales are almost always blamed on the author, and it was quite possible Harrap might already be doubting my worth to them. If *The Wider Sea*'s jacket affected sales badly, what would they decide when they received a novel so entirely different as my new one would be? Could I risk a further two years of work on it or should I hedge my bets and write something more certain to be accepted and to sell?

I wanted above all else to write this novel because of its subject and its scope but felt it was only right to discuss these problems with Shelagh. Knowing her courage and her faith in my work, I should have known her answer before she gave it. We must do what we had always done, she said. Believe in ourselves and let the future take care of itself.

TWELVE

During the spring of 1970 I received irritating news from the States. Rattigan had introduced homosexuality into the screenplay of *Hawks* — homosexuality was becoming the 'in thing' to write about at that time — but Arthur Jacobs had rightly felt it totally inappropriate in my novel. Accordingly his plans were delayed while another script writer was employed to write a second screen play. Dying to have the film made, I could have kicked Rattigan for tinkering with the story, but I tried to console myself it would only entail a short delay.

My novel *Waterloo* was published by Pan Books on the 7th August, 1970, three months before the premiere of the film. Pan's reason for this early publication was given in the September edition of Books and Bookmen. They considered the book, along with a publication by Paul Davies called *The Field of Waterloo*, (which was a double-format pictorial appraisal of the battle) would have 'two lives' — one in their own right as books and the other a tie-in publication when the film was released in the autumn.

I had no complaint about publicity this time. The book was featured prominently both in photograph and purple prose in Smiths Trade News, the Bookseller, and other trade journals; was listed for Star Treatment in the Retail Newsagent; and review copies were sent out to most newspapers and journals in the land. Huge colour posters were produced, combining stills from the film with captions of the novel. From the early press releases I learned that Pan would be printing 125,000 copies for its first edition and 70,000 copies of Paul Davies's book, which was an excellent companion volume.

If anything proves that advertising and promotion sells books, it was proven here. Sales soared as reviews poured in from all quarters, including Eire who, in spite of Wellington's protests, had always laid a claim on his birth. Although the novel was being marketed as a 'book of the film', I was pleased and relieved to find that most reviewers accepted it as a book in its own right. I was also delighted to discover that nearly all the reviewers shared Clarence Paget's high opinion of it. It was listed among the 'top tales of the month' in the National Newsagent and listed as a non-fiction best-seller in 'This Week in Ireland'. It seemed my six months of work had paid off handsomely.

Mr. Dino De Laurentiis and the
Directors of Columbia Pictures Corporation Ltd.
cordially invite you to the
PRESS SHOW of

DINO DE LAURENTIIS presents ROD STEIGER · CHRISTOPHER PLUMMER
'WATERLOO' u
ORSON WELLES as LOUIS XVIII
co-starring JACK HAWKINS · VIRGINIA McKENNA · DAN O'HERLIHY
Screenplay by H.A.L.CRAIG Produced by DINO DE LAURENTIIS Directed by SERGEI BONDARCHUK
FROM COLUMBIA PICTURES Ⓒ
TECHNICOLOR / PANAVISION

at the **ODEON MARBLE ARCH**
on Monday, October 26th 1970 at 10.30 a.m.

ADMIT ONE — CIRCLE

"WATERLOO" HAS ITS ROYAL WORLD PREMIERE AT THE ODEON LEICESTER SQUARE ON
OCTOBER 26th 1970 AND OPENS TO THE PUBLIC AT THAT THEATRE ON OCTOBER 27th

    Not long after the book was published, Shelagh and I were invited to London for a preview of the film. The media were there in great attendance because some of the film stars, including Rod Steiger, were present. I was asked to meet him and give him a copy of the book, which I did, but for me the most pleasant part of the afternoon was meeting Tom Carlile again, who was the publicity manager of Dino de Laurentiis. I had been in correspondence with Tom for some months because of the film tie-in and had sent him a manuscript copy as soon as it was ready. It seemed to have impressed him because from then on he had done everything in his power to make sure there were none of the obstacles that so often occur between film companies and authors. He had arranged to see me during a quick trip to England and we had struck up a friendship right away. He was a rangy Texan six foot eight inches in height who towered over the press men he interviewed, but busy though he was on that preview day, he made sure Shelagh and I were comfortable and sat with us when the film credits began to roll.

    The publicity handouts claimed the film had cost $45,000,000, which made it the most expensive film to date. Although money is no guarantee of quality, I did find it an impressive production. Christopher Plummer could hardly have been bettered as the cold, disdainful Wellington and Rod Steiger was excellent as the emotional, tempestuous Napoleon. Actors like Virginia McKenna, Orson Welles, Jack Hawkins, and Michael Wilding also lived up to their billing and the thousands of Red Army soldiers, fighting as if they meant it, gave the scenes great virility and colour.

My only real criticism lay in the battle scenes. With regiments of the time wearing different uniforms, it was often difficult to identify which were Napoleon's soldiers and which Wellington's when cameras were engaged on horizontal takes. A few aerial shots from a helicopter, locating the regiments' positions on the ridge, would have solved this problem.

In a way I had faced the same problem in the book and had made the point that a few maps interspersed throughout the text would make the battle manoeuvres easier to follow. No doubt because of the extra cost, Pan had only allowed me one map of the battlefield which I drew myself and placed just before the prologue. However, perhaps because it is much easier to explain manoeuvres in text than in vision, I don't remember receiving any complaints about this.

Apart from these occasional pleasant forays to London, I spent the rest of 1970 working on the South American novel. It was going extremely well and its subject was giving me scope to express long-held beliefs and ideas. To include them in the average novel might have slowed it down and irritated the reader. In this novel, because of the rebellious and disparate characters I was using, I could actually present my tenets in a way that strengthened both the story line and the characters themselves. In other words, the main theme was like the trunk of a tree, throwing out branches that added weight to the story and yet aided its symmetry at the same time. It made the book immensely satisfying to write, and at last I had a title, *The Tormented*.

Because of the time spent on the novel, our financial situation became a worry again, and when Pan Books approached me to write more tie-in books, I had little choice but to accept.

This time it was a twenty-six part television series called *The Persuaders* and featured the popular actors Roger Moore and Tony Curtis. As most of the action was outdoors, which meant using film in those days, it was going to be a very expensive project and so would receive a high promotional budget.

As the series was only comedy/adventure with no real substance, I didn't really want to take it on but again it was a case of beggars couldn't be choosers. Accordingly I signed my contract and was given the twenty-six scripts to choose from. I put aside what I felt were the best seven and then asked to visit the film studios.

The Independent Television Authority, who were funding the series, were co-operative enough. My problems began when I visited the studios. Although I pointed out that if I were to write worthwhile books I must get the feel of the series and its main characters, the directors tried to keep me out of their studios and also told me that neither Moore nor Curtis would agree to an interview. Indeed I was even told that Curtis had been known to strike out at would-be interviewers.

By this time I had lost all patience with the way the entertainment industry treats writers, and my reply was short and to the point. If I wasn't allowed to see Moore and Curtis, I would walk out and they could find another writer.

My belligerence seemed to work because soon afterwards I was introduced to both stars over lunch. The outcome was exactly as I expected. Both were charming and helpful, cracked a bottle of wine with me, and asked for copies of the books when they were finished. I made certain to keep my promise and in return I have today a copy in my bookcase with a signature and a humorous little comment from Roger Moore. 'Thank you, Frederick, for making me seem so strong!'

In all I was to write three of these *Persuader* books, using the seven scripts I had chosen. As I seemed to have a knack for adaptations of this kind (and in any case the plots were ready made for me) none of them took me more than two months apiece to write. I didn't expect, nor particularly want, any reviews because I was worried they might affect my name as a serious writer. But they came in nevertheless and were surprisingly good.

The books themselves sold like hot cakes, although no doubt the popularity of the two stars had everything to do with that. Indeed they sold so fast that a Persuader Fan Club made the ridiculous threat to sue Pan Books for allowing the first edition to sell out before their 30,000 members could obtain copies. On the strength of this success I was even made guest of honour at one of the publisher's Pantime occasions and couldn't help thinking ruefully of the novels I had written over the years for which I never received as much as a free lunch. Such is the world of writing and publishing.

Sometime in the middle of the year Reggie phoned me to say Arthur Jacobs had not applied for a fourth option. Had I received any word from him?

I had not and suddenly became alarmed. Surely after all this time and all those plans, he hadn't turned against the film. I found the thought intolerable and made anxious enquiries. The answer when it came was shattering. Arthur Jacobs had suddenly collapsed with a massive heart attack! He was dead and my film was dead with him.

By this time I was used to disappointments but this was one of my worst. *Hawks* meant so much to me and I had been counting the days to see the film. What hurt and rankled the most, however, was the full story when I heard it in detail. It had been Rattigan's distortion of my story that had brought about the disaster. Had he done what was expected of him, Jacobs would have been alive to start the cameras rolling and in all probability both he and I might have seen the film completed. Instead, he had been forced to wait while another writer worked on the script and during that time his health had deteriorated and caused his sad and untimely death.

If ever a book was unlucky it was *Hawks*. Some time later an American named Lynn Garrison flew over to see if he could buy the film rights. He told me he would have approached me years ago but until then had heard the rights had passed to 20th Century Fox. His reason for approaching me now was because he had news that Fox had suffered some crisis that had compelled them to axe and return all recent contracts, which included *Hawks*. At this point Garrison had jumped in and flown over to buy an option.

I was only too glad to sell him one, particularly as at that time he claimed he owned the aircraft used in the film *The Blue Max*, but not long afterwards his source of finance dried up and he couldn't take up his option. Soon after that another film producer whose name I have forgotten bought one but he fell foul of his studio and was sacked. And so it went on. Even Tom Carlile bought an option but couldn't raise the money for a production. *Hawks* seems to possess all the right ingredients for a film but along with it ill fortune beyond belief. I can only hope that one day its luck will change because nothing would please me more than to see it filmed.

I had to change my literary agency at this time because Reggie was forced into retirement through ill health. In many ways he had been like a father figure to me and I missed him greatly. His partner, Ian Thompson, had already retired which left me no choice but to look elsewhere.

It was during this period while I was without an agent that I made contact with Howard Baker. Baker had been originally one of Ken Mennell's colleagues at Fleetway House but had left to begin his own publishing business. He appeared to be prospering and when he offered to re-publish some of my earlier out-of-print novels, there seemed no reason to refuse the offer.

Accordingly I signed a contract that gave him five year volume rights in *Masks, Laws, 633 Squadron, Lydia* and *The Devil*. He also obtained permission to bring out a hardcover copy of *Waterloo*. Although my advances were very small, I accepted them in the hope there would be royalties later that would help to subsidize *The Tormented*.

In the event there were little or no royalties. I had not known it at the time but when Baker had taken my books, his business had been close to bankruptcy. Before this happened he had sold my books in considerable numbers to the public libraries. This meant they could be read freely by the public because there were no public lending rights in those days, and so my chances of obtaining any income from them became nil. One way and another my gremlin had excelled himself that disastrous year.

THIRTEEN

Choosing an agent is a little like choosing a bride: one is never quite certain how the relationship will develop. I paged through the Writers' and Artists' Year Book and finally wrote to John Farquharson to see if they would take me on. They did and I found myself working with Innes Rose, a director of the firm and a middle-aged man of the old school, which meant he was courteous at all times, although I found him not quite as approachable as Reggie.

Although *The Tormented* was still not completed and I had nothing new to give Innes, his Foreign Rights assistant, Vanessa Holt, impressed me by asking for the case histories of my earlier novels. When I gave them to her, she wrote to the foreign publishers to see if the books were still in print. Where they were not, she asked for the rights back and began marketing them again. In this way this highly efficient foreign agent sold some books twice to the same countries. Two of these were *Lydia* and *White Sands* (now entitled *The Dark Cliffs*) making me reflect again how well those novels had done for me.

In spite of still having some way to go on *The Tormented*, I had a talk with Innes about my next project. I had a need to write something light-hearted and mentioned the adventures I had shared with Ken Addey during the war. Innes liked the idea and so I drew up a synopsis of two disparate RAF characters, their chequered relationship, and their adventures. It then went into my drawer as my next project when *The Tormented* was completed.

Our tennis club in Queens Park closed at the end of the season. The Council were building a new road that would run right through it and so the sale was enforced under the Compulsory Purchase Act.

Shelagh and I were sorry to see it go. It had been our sole recreation in recent years and held many happy memories. We had fought many a stern tussle on its courts, won a title or two as doubles partners, and Shelagh had been the singles champion for the last seven years. Indeed at the time, although now fifty, we were both still playing in its teams. In addition, with our friends Joe and Margaret, we had attended ballroom dances in its delightful old clubhouse and I have nostalgic memories of my mother asking to see Shelagh's dresses before we left for these dances. The poor old dear had never had the chance to attend dances in her youth and she found a vicarious pleasure in witnessing Shelagh's attire. I remember how very sad I found those requests of hers.

After the club's closure we could have joined the prestigious West Hants Club, but it was quite a long drive away. Perhaps we might have joined had we been younger or our circumstances different, but, rightly or wrongly, we decided to hang up our rackets. This we did but I know we both missed the sport in the years ahead.

During this time we allowed ourselves no thought of holidays. But then a freak respite lightened the load for a few weeks and I suggested to Shelagh we should use it while the opportunity existed. At first she resisted but then realized we both badly needed a break and so we booked a two week holiday in Majorca.

The first week was a farce as far as a holiday went. We were so tired that we spent almost the first seven days sleeping in our room. For the first time I realized how deeply our well of reserves had been drained and that we had taken the rest only just in time.

Although we left our room the second week, we did little else than lie on the beach, go for walks, or play a little tennis. Then it was the plane back home to resume the battles again.

I did one other short trip that year. I needed some general South American information and some colloquial expressions, and a writer named Stephan Frances, who lived in Spain, had a South American living with him. I had met Frances through Ken Mennell, and we had visited him during one of our trips to Spain in the Sixties. He was a writer who published under the name of Hank Jansen. I had seen these Hank Jansen books before and during the war. Invariably they had yellow jackets and were about the adventures of a 'private eye'. Although today they would be considered innocuous, in their day they were the kind of book a boy felt deliciously wicked to read and hide beneath his mattress.

Stephan, married to a Spanish nurse, lived in a flat above Rosas Bay. Although a complicated character, he could not have been more helpful during my brief visit. He introduced me to his South American guest, who thankfully could speak English, and also brought in his wife to help. I returned home after a couple of days grateful and pleased with my research.

An amusing thing happened at this time. Reggie's daughter, Gillie, was a talented sculptor and had asked to make a bust of me. From the glimpses I had seen of it when I popped into her studio during my trips to London, it was quite a flattering affair, and I was looking forward to surprising Shelagh with it when it was finished.

But then Gillie had to move flats which also meant moving all her work. Two days after the move she phoned me. Her removal had gone well and everything had arrived safely except one item.

I didn't need telling what it was. "My head's been broken, hasn't it?" I said.

She sounded surprised. "How did you know that?"

How do you tell people, even friends, that you have a gremlin who never misses a trick? I didn't even try. "I just guessed it from your phone call," I said. "Don't worry about it. It was sure to happen."

My younger son, Kevan, left college that year. Although through no fault of his own he hadn't attended the local grammar school prior to college, he had obtained eight 'O' levels and three 'A' levels. He soon found work in the Bournemouth Treasurer's Department and it was not many years before he became a director in the local Transport Company. By some genetic miracle it seemed we had produced two very intelligent sons and, much more importantly, two very likeable ones.

I was now working on the last stages of *The Tormented* and had never felt happier with a novel, for it had allowed so many personal beliefs to be integrated into its story line without cloying or holding up its progress.

One element of the book dealt with the massive gap in the world between the rich and the poor. It was the reason I had set the novel in South America. It was the injustice of this situation that enabled John Mason, my major character, to overcome his scruples about the use of violence.

Another element of the novel dealt with the United States' one time habit of funding and arming South American dictators to keep their rebellious peasants in thrall. With America almost paranoiac about Communism at this time and seeing a Red under every bed, I was aware how, to prejudiced eyes, my criticism could make me seem like one, which in turn would not aid the book's chances in America. But I had the view and still hold it that a man's novels should portray his beliefs and dislikes, and the writer who disguises them for success and profit is not worthy of the title.

So the work neared its end. Conscious of the years I had spent on it and not wanting to spoil the ship for a ha'p'orth of tar, I spent a long time touching up the final draft but when I finally laid it down, I felt fulfilled and contented.

This was unusual for me because in one sense a completed novel is always a disappointment due to the loss incurred between the golden dream in the mind and its arrival on paper. Because of one's imperfections a loss is inevitable and with earlier novels I had always felt some disappointment no matter how many times I had edited the work. For some reason, although it might have been due to relief felt now the long task was over, I did not have these feelings about *The Tormented*.

Moreover, the final chapters pleased me. They came about through the thematic progression of the novel — in other words they were not planned beforehand but came naturally — and with their Samson and Delilah imagery I felt they gave the book an entirely satisfying ending.

The only work left now was the huge task of typing a hundred and ninety thousand words. Here I was lucky. A friend Shelagh had known since her school days, Dorothy Nolan, was having a holiday in the UK and staying with us. As she worked for Hansard in South Africa, she was an excellent typist. Another good and close friend, Monique Register, whom I had met during my visits to Ken Mennell in Newport, also offered to help. So with the two of them sharing the work with Shelagh, the novel was typed and checked in less than two months, which only left me to send it to Innes Rose and cross my fingers.

To be honest, I felt reasonably confident about its acceptance. Any writer worth his salt knows when he has done a good job just as he knows when he has done a poor one, and I was more than satisfied with this one. So when Harrap turned it down and it was then rejected by publisher after publisher, it made no sense to me.

It made no sense because of the reason publishers gave. It was not the story they rejected, it was its South American setting. Indeed from the tone of their letters it seemed the moment they had realized the book was set on that continent, they hadn't even bothered to have it read.

It was my first experience of the common prejudices that seemed to infect publishers at that time and perhaps also does today. Quite suddenly they would turn against a novel of one genre or one background. Thus historical fiction or WW2 novels would suddenly become unwanted. No matter what gems of that genre arrived, they would be rejected. At another time it would be detective or spy fiction. It is as if all publishers were under the influence of the same research organization and when that organization put a veto on one type of book, publishers followed its dictates like a flock of sheep.

In my case it was the South American background of the novel that was its bête noire. If that background had been an essential element in the novel, it might have made some kind of weird sense. But that was not the case. Mason's problem and the social inequalities and messages the story line raised could pertain to any country in the world, and I had chosen South America only because of its social inequalities. I could have chosen Africa or Asia or even Eastern Europe with equal effect.

But no matter. South America was the cross the book had to carry. After Innes, who liked the book, had tried six or more hardcover publishers, in desperation I asked him to try for original paperback rights. He sent the book to Corgi, who would not take it without hardcover backing, but did promise an offer of £750 if any hardcover publisher would publish it first.

This offer, small though it was, held out the slight hope that a hardcover publisher might risk an offer knowing he would get his advance back from Corgi when paperback rights were offered them. On this possibility, Innes told me he would try two or three more hardcover publishers before the book was finally put to rest.

Months passed while all this was going on and my frustration grew by the day. I had put nearly three years work into the book, only for it to be condemned by a ridiculous prejudice. My feelings about publishers at this time are better left unrecorded.

But life must go on and like the pilot who must fly again immediately after a bad crash, I had to write another novel quickly. So I pulled out my synopsis based on the war and Ken Addey and began to develop it.

I found it a great relief to write a humorous book at such a time. I think it was good for Shelagh too because I often heard her laughing when she was typing the manuscript. After everything that wonderful companion had been through in recent years, I found great comfort in her laughter. With all the facts at my fingertips I wrote the novel in four to five months and called it *Saffron's War*. I followed it immediately with a sequel, *Saffron's Army*. Both were dispatched to Innes, who, being an ex-serviceman himself, said he loved them. Yet even so, he found neither Pan nor Corgi would take them as paperbacks. It seemed the darkness that surrounded us at that time did not possess a single glimmer of light. So when Corgi asked me once again if I would write a sequel to *633 Squadron,* I had little choice but to agree.

I had another reason for accepting their offer. Shelagh's father, now an old man, had been very ill recently and although Shelagh never once put the slightest pressure on me, it was obvious she would like to see him in case the chance did not come again.

So the contract with Corgi was signed and I was committed. I use that expression because at the time I had no idea how I was going to write a sequel with all the major characters killed off in the first novel.

With the disappointment over *The Tormented* still with me, I struggled for weeks to solve the problem and got nowhere. I must have been an impossible character to live with during that time because nothing frustrates and drains a writer more than to rack his brains all day and end it with a blank sheet of paper. Finally I was driven to desperate measures. Telling Shelagh I would be away for two or three days, I drove off in my motor caravan to my old wartime airfield in East Anglia.

I arrived in the early evening, to discover the field had long been ploughed over and returned to agriculture. But a few of the old Nissen huts remained, the water tower was still standing, and there was a long low building at its far side that I recognized as the Administration Block. A few dozen yards of the perimeter track could also be seen at my side of the field, although grass now sprouted through its cracked cement.

Seeing nobody about, I walked round the field for a few minutes, then returned to the motor caravan. There was a low bank on the northern side of the field with a disused road running along its ridge and I drove along it until I could see the entire field below me. I parked there, sat on a deckchair I had brought, and surrendered my mind to memory.

I could hardly have chosen a better evening. There was a pennant of cloud on the horizon and shafts of light were radiating across the sky. I sat there while the sun dipped down below the horizon and almost imperceptibly time became a cloud in which I drifted back over the years.

I sat outside all night absorbing that old airfield's atmosphere, and when the summer dawn came I had an entire novel in my mind. Elated, I drove straight back home and got my synopsis down on paper. A week later I began writing the novel itself.

No idea, except perhaps *The Devil,* had ever come to me so quickly and yet until that night I had believed the novel would defeat me. I had learned a lesson in the evocative power of nostalgia.

Shelagh went over to South Africa to see her father while I worked on the novel. My main problem, what characters to use, had come to me during my vigil by the airfield. In the original story, a number of aircrews had been wounded on a mission and hospitalized on their return. This had meant they had been unavailable for the final, fatal mission, and I could use them as my main characters in the sequel. The rest of the squadron could be made up by new men. Because conflict is important in drama, this merging of old 'sweats' and 'sprogs' would provide plenty of scope for internal strife in addition to the squadron's external conflict with the enemy.

This proved to be true and once the novel was started, it went very well, although my concern for *The Tormented* remained as acute as ever. I knew I couldn't expect Innes to go on trying it for ever and Corgi's offer was its last hope.

I had written around three chapters of the *633* sequel when the nightmare spell broke at last. The hardcover publisher Cassell decided to take on *The Tormented.* Their advance was small — little more than a thousand pounds, and of that Cassell would keep half of the £750 Corgi would pay for paperback rights.

Nevertheless, I was elated and so was Shelagh, now back from South Africa. The book would be published after all and a paperback edition was certain. Moreover, I could now afford to visit Bavaria to research the *633 Squadron* sequel.

I did the trip in the motor caravan before *The Tormented* was published. It only took a few days and I returned home to finish the novel and to discuss *The Tormented* with Cassell. It was scheduled for a summer publication. Looking forward to its appearance as no other book I had written (except perhaps my first novel) I was encouraged by my Cassell editor. His name was Edwin Harper and he was one of the few novel editors I have respected. In his sixties, loving books, and with a lifetime's experience, he understood authors' problems as no editor I had met before, and moreover was prepared to listen to them. I felt a confidence in him I had seldom felt in others.

Because he was my editor I saw him a number of times before the book was published, and as we got to know one another better, I gained the impression he did not have a high respect for his fellow directors. But because he was loyal enough not to make the confession, I never knew whether my impression was correct or not.

But there was no doubt he thought highly of *The Tormented* The things he said about it made me wonder about his sincerity until I saw a pull-off of the jacket he had designed and written for it. It said things about the book that almost made me blush, but when I spoke about them, he assured me he meant every word.

So all seemed set fair for its publication. The one thing I couldn't establish was the size of its first print run. Publishers are always loath to give this to authors and I couldn't find mine out even from Edwin, although it was possible he was kept in the dark himself. Politics are as endemic in publishing houses as in anywhere else.

I wanted to discover mine because I knew by this time that a publisher's promotion and advertising are commensurate with his initial outlay, and I wanted to be certain *The Tormented* was going to have a fair showing. However, when Edwin had a handsome brochure printed about the book, I felt I had no reason to worry.

The novel was eventually published and the first results were startling. Not only did it get excellent reviews but it very quickly topped the best seller chart in Australia, New Zealand and South Africa. It seemed all my hopes had been realized and I had a best seller on my hands at last.

Excited, I asked Cassell how the first edition was going and to my dismay was told that only 6,000 copies had been printed. It seemed Edwin Harper's confidence in the book had not extended to his Board.

Nevertheless, now that the book had taken off, I naturally believed a new edition was already rolling off the press.

I couldn't believe the truth when I heard it. Cassell did not think a second edition was worthwhile! Aghast, my agent and I made strenuous protests but the company remained unmoved.

The consequences were inevitable. With no more books available in shops here or abroad, there could be no more sales and so *The Tormented* vanished from the best-seller list as fast as it had appeared. My feelings were impossible to describe.

There is a sequel to this story. Five years later I visited South Africa and while there visited a large bookshop in West Street, Durban. The manager was a man called Rabjohn and he met me at the door of his shop with a bottle of wine in his hand. As I wasn't accustomed to such bookshop greetings, I was puzzled until he told me about *The Tormented.*.

He said he had sold nearly two hundred copies of the book while it was available. Astonished that a book on modern revolution should sell that way in South Africa of all countries, he had tried to obtain more copies but without a second printing stocks had been exhausted and he had been told no more were forthcoming. The decision had astonished him. He had never known a book so successful to be abandoned in such a way.

Such was the outcome of nearly three years dedicated work. I can say in all truth that I had never worked so hard on a book and never been more satisfied with one. To see it reach best-seller status and then have that success tossed away because Cassell lacked Edwin's faith in the book was astonishing as well as heartbreaking. I admit it did take me longer than usual to recover from this blow and I suspect its mental scars have remained to this day.

It was about this time that I was beginning to discover from fellow writers and such investigative publications as Private Eye and The Guardian, that our profession suffered manipulation by a literary clique whose effects could not be discounted. Indeed a Welsh novelist friend of mine was so affected and disgusted by it that he called it The Literary Mafia.

Their home base is London. More often than not it begins in one of our public schools or universities. Ian, whose ambition is to be an agent, becomes friendly with Dominic whose ambition is to be a writer. Both become friendly with Maurice who intends to enter his father's publishing business.

From then on the game is in progress. They gain their degrees and because of their favourable backgrounds they achieve their ambitions. Dominic writes his first novel, Ian handles it, and Maurice makes certain it is published.

So far so good, one thinks. Is that not what friends are for? But regretably the game does not end there. Other books are being published by other authors and many do not wear the old school tie or share our heroes' views. So what is to be done?

What is to be done is far less praiseworthy. Neither Ian, Dominic nor Maurice can allow authors of lesser station to gain prominence of writers of their own statue. And so the game of back-scratching changes its tactics. By articles, reviews, and the old boys' network of nudges. winks and glasses of port, the lesser men are put in their place and authors like Dominic are pushed into the centre of the stage.

For those who do not want to believe me, watch the newspapers at Christmas, the peak time for book sales. Gaze at the authors' photographs and then check their agents and publishers' backgrounds.

I am fully aware such shenanigans of this nature are evident in all professions but I love mine and would like nothing more than to believe it free of such shabby practices. But after a lifetime within it, I know it exists and find it sad that literature, which ought to enrich and broaden our minds, should be influenced and sometimes impoverished by a narrow clique whose ideas and values are so often at odds with the real world in which the rest of us mortals live.

FOURTEEN

In spite of my state of mind, I managed to finish the *633 Squadron* sequel that winter. By some miracle it turned out far better than I had expected and as the original novel was now in its tenth or eleventh edition and selling more copies than ever, its chances ought to be good. 'Ought' was the only hope I allowed myself those days, for my optimism had taken a bad battering after the disaster of *The Tormented*. If it were to do well, I knew the public must recognize it as the son of *633 Squadron* and that meant giving it a title that provided a direct link. This wasn't easy, particularly as Corgi had hinted they might like more books about the squadron if this sequel did well. Because of this I sent them a few titles but they showed no great enthusiasm for any of them.

Three weeks must have passed before I hit on the idea of using *633 Squadron* as a prefix and following it with the book title. That would surely give me the better of two worlds. But what title could I use?

I must have scribbled down thirty or forty titles before I thought about Bavaria. I toyed about with the name and its associations and Wagner came to mind. Something mythological and with German connotations would be ideal. Then I had it. *Rhine Maiden*. It had the right ring and was appropriate to the main story line. Moreover if I pre-fixed it with Operation, the format could be used for any subsequent novels if written. So I ended up with *633 Squadron: Operation Rhine Maiden*. I sent it and the book to Corgi and they said they were delighted with both. They asked me how I felt about them sub-licensing the hardcover rights to Cassell now that Cassell had published me. Their idea was that Cassell could come out first with a hardcover version, which would provide useful advance publicity, and they would follow six months or a year later with their paperback.

It was an idea I liked because it meant I wouldn't have to share half my paperback royalties with my hardcover publisher. Using Cassell was another matter, however, and I asked Innes Rose for his opinion. He felt I should stay with them because now they had learned their lesson they might do better for me. I wasn't fully convinced but I told Corgi to go ahead. Cassell accepted their suggestion and the hardcover version of *633 Rhine Maiden* was scheduled for publication in 1975. Before it appeared, Cassell invited me to suggest an appropriate jacket design. As this was something I had always believed publishers should do, I was perhaps ungracious in thinking it was done to appease me.

Whatever the reason, I told them I favoured a royal blue background with a squadron crest imposed upon it and a Mosquito aircraft bursting through the crest. As other books in the series were being considered, I pointed out that the only changes they would need for them were different coloured backgrounds and different titles. In this way a series would be instantly recognizable.

Cassell accepted the idea and allowed me to design the jacket. With the help of my friend Hamish Mahaddie, I sketched out a crest and Mosquito and the publisher's artist did the rest. Although I say it myself, the result was effective. Like a woman's simple but stylishly cut dress, I believed it would stand out among the many fussy and garish creations around it.

Certainly Cassell seemed to like it and suggested that I gave a talk to their sales representatives a few weeks before the book's publication. Facing a bunch of hard-bitten sales reps was not a welcoming prospect, yet at the same time, being an author who had constantly argued publishers did not work hard enough to sell books, I would be stupid not to take my opportunity to say it.

As it was summer, the event took place outdoors. I gave them the history of the original *633 Squadron*, how it was conceived and developed, and then went on to describe my problem in writing a sequel when most of the original characters were dead or prisoners. When I discovered they were both amused and interested by my solution, I became bolder and began talking about my past experiences with publishers. Warming to my subject as painful reminders of *The Tormented* and other lost sales came back to me, I forgot all my inhibitions and said that there had been many times when I had suspected that the last thing publishers wanted to do was sell books. Books, surely, were only the cloak of the profession, the deceptive facade to deceive the law and the police. Publishers' real occupation was the selling of hard drugs and prostitution and books were only a bothersome but necessary facade to hide the real lucrative trade.

The loud gasp that followed brought me back to earth with a jolt. Had I gone too far and antagonized the very people who were going to handle my book?

I need not have worried. The gale of laughter that followed sent pigeons clattering up from rooftops. Perhaps there is in all men a healthy need to have the mickey taken out of their occupation every now and then. Or perhaps I had run into a crowd of men and women with a corporate sense of humour. Whatever the reason, both the management and the reps took it well and afterwards I was assured the reps would try that little bit harder to push my book. As events were to show, this was true.

A few weeks later Cassell and Corgi united to launch the book in some style at the RAF Club in Piccadilly. Shelagh went with me, along with a few close friends I had been allowed to invite. I was introduced to this and that buyer and wholesaler, none of whom I knew, and soon the event became a blur of faces and chatter. My one firm memory of it is the numbers of hangers-on we met. I heard later this usually happens. A high number are well known names in the arts and literary circles which in turn gave me unworthy thoughts. In spite of their names, do their egos still need to be seen and draw attention? Or are their motives even less worthy and it is the free drinks that draws them in?

We returned home to find the Bournemouth shops packed with copies of *Rhine Maiden*. The local rep, a young man named Brown, had broken normal rules and given them to the shops on sale or return. As a result managers had taken in dozens of copies and built up impressive window displays, which in turn awakened the public's interest. In less than two weeks the young rep told me he had sold nearly two thousand copies in the local catchment area alone.

If other reps had been allowed the same procedure, the book might have broken selling records. Although they were not given this permission, the book sold well enough for a second edition to be put into print right away. When reviews began pouring in, nearly all full of praise, I began wishing I had taken Corgi's offer and written the book shortly after the film's premiere.

Nevertheless, the omens were good and made some recompense for the stupidity shown over *The Tormented*. We celebrated by deciding to adopt a retriever puppy. Hearing good reports about a breeder named Harley in Potterne, Devizes, we drove out there to see what puppies were available.

We were lucky. A bitch had dropped a litter only seven weeks earlier and we were taken to see them.

They were gorgeous. Six golden, furry, cuddly creatures with black noses lying around their beautiful mother. They showed curiosity as we approached but only one took the courage to toddle up to me, sniff at my shoes, and then wag his tail.

Bold and friendly. I knew at once he was for me. We inquired about him and learned that his Kennel Club name was Butterscotch Gallant and he had an ancestry of show champions a mile long. But none of this mattered a scrap to me. Butterscotch Gallant had won my heart and I wanted him badly.

But it wasn't that easy. Over tea and scones Mrs Harley chatted to us while she made up her mind whether or not we deserved our beautiful puppy. When we passed the test an hour and a half later, she paraded Butterscotch's grandparents before us to ensure we were satisfied with our choice before signing any papers. It was an impressive display of a breeder's duties to both dog and owner and we both respected her for it.

We drove away with the tiny creature curled up into a furry ball on Shelagh's lap. We felt some guilt at taking him away from his mother and his siblings, so it was a comfort when he fell into a peaceful sleep.

On the way we discussed what we should call him and I came up with the name Saffron, derived from my two comedies. Shelagh liked it and so Saffron it was.

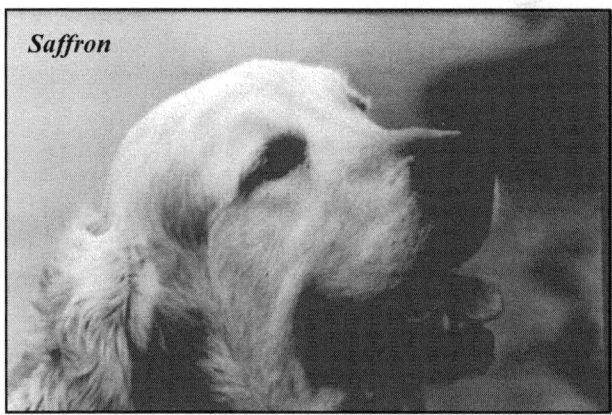

Saffron

We arrived home in the late afternoon and put him out in the garden for a tiddle. But there was the night to follow and expecting the worst, we laid papers all over the carpets and erected defences against vulnerable pieces of furniture. As a further safeguard, I slept downstairs on the settee.

What followed astonished us both. I woke up halfway through the night hearing a whimpering. Expecting to find the puppy sitting miserably in a pool of water, instead I found him at the front door. When I opened it, he rushed out as fast as his little legs would take him and cocked a leg against the garden gate. Looking immensely relieved, he toddled back and flopped thankfully back into the box we had made for him. The same thing happened three hours later. His little bladder could not yet last throughout the night but some instinct prevented his fouling his bed or the papers around him.

It was the same with the carpets and the furniture. He never tore or scratched at them nor did the slightest damage to anything in the house. All this sounds like a case of fond memory embellishing the facts, but every word is true. We appeared to have adopted a puppy without a blemish and it was almost a relief to discover his desire to dive into water sometimes overrode our efforts to keep him dry.

As he was a young pedigree dog, our instructions were to keep him clear of places other dogs frequented until he was six months old, a precaution against disease. As his breed was also prone to hip trouble, we were not allowed to take him for long walks for the same length of time. Neither instruction was easy to obey, as anyone who has owned a young active dog will know. I overcame the first problem by taking him down to the beach at low tide as soon as he was old enough, and keeping him below the high water mark, arguing that the salt tide would have kept that area of the beach sterile.

His energy was more difficult to contain. I kept him on a long leash and limited his walks to three or four breakwaters. Even so he would scamper about and cover three times as much beach in his joy of living.

He was so beautiful in appearance that he brought me aesthetic pleasure as well as the pleasure one gets from seeing a young creature so full of life. People would stop to look at him and I remember one elderly lady, after watching him playing about with a ball, approaching me and saying: "I've kept dogs all my life but I have never seen anything as beautiful as that puppy. Where on earth did you get him?"

Saffron was beautiful. He made me realize what I'd missed in my life since I lost Pride when a child. He brought laughter into a house that had not known much joy during recent years but, even so, I don't think either Shelagh or I guessed the pleasure he was to bring us in the years ahead.

My illness came on quite suddenly. The first warning was an unusual thirst that began while I was making a business trip to London. By this time my brother and I had made up our quarrel and my plans were to stay for a couple of days in his new flat near Waterloo Station. But my thirst became worse and during the night I passed an excessive amount of urine. Compelled to return home, I was sent to see a specialist who diagnosed diabetes.

It came as a total surprise because until then I'd had no reason to suspect that I was anything but a very fit man. Fortunately, unlike my brother Raymond who had suffered the illness for years and needed insulin, I only needed a diet low in carbohydrates. As far as sweetmeats were concerned, this was no hardship because, somewhat ironically, I had never liked cakes or sweets. However, the diet I was given in 1975 consisted almost entirely of fats and protein and within a month I barely had the strength to walk.

Realizing the cure was more harmful than the disease, I modified it myself by taking in more carbohydrates in the form of slow-absorption foods until I believed I had got the balance right. Today this is the diet the experts advise. Somewhere here is the message that although the experts do their best, no one knows his body better than the man who lives inside it.

Although to this date diabetes is incurable, I can't say that it slowed me down in any way. I worked as hard as ever, I exercised as hard as ever, and if just now and then I felt a little shaky, a biscuit or a glucose tablet quickly put me right. Indeed thirty-five years later I think many of my friends will be surprised to hear I carry this illness. Chronic disorders can all too easily become an obsession with their victims, and I am convinced that to pander to them is to make them worse. Like children, they behave better when they know their place and aren't allowed to dominate one's thoughts and behaviour.

Saffron's War was published by Futura in 1975. If nothing else, its cover design was striking, being a nude girl with a champagne bottle in one hand and a red, white, and blue RAF roundel draped round her bottom. As the subject was principally comedy, I couldn't complain too stridently about the design but I had the uneasy feeling it might be too risqué for at least one section of the public.

The book received little advertising but by this time I was resigned to books not being brought to the attention of the general public. Instead, I was sent on a publicity tour with a member of Futura's staff. We visited Scampton airfield where, in the hope of obtaining space in local newspapers, photographs were taken of me standing beside the resident Lancaster bomber; we met a few press reporters; I did one or two radio broadcasts; and we were finally driven by the local rep to Yorkshire Television where we had been promised an interview on a regional program.

It proved a minor disaster. To begin with we were running late, which meant a mad car dash over the Pennines to reach the Leeds studios in time. There my publicity man and his rep were consigned to an anteroom with a TV monitor while I, with *Safron's War* and its nubile girl held under my arm, was marched into the studio. I was introduced as the author of *633 Squadron* and then the interview began.

It had an appalling start. After introducing me, my interviewer turned to the camera and asked the viewers that if any of them had served in *633 Squadron* they should phone the studios. Their names and phone numbers would then be taken so that the author could talk to them afterwards.

I was horrified. It was true that many people believed *633 Squadron* had existed and it was also true that some ex-RAF veterans had claimed they had served in it. Standing at the bar in the Pathfinder Club one evening, I had almost choked in my beer when a distinguished ex-pilot had come alongside me and made the claim. My sons and my wife had also run into men who boasted they had flown with the squadron and such claims are made even to this day.

But these can be handled by a cough and a change of subject. In the television studio we were being overheard by heaven knows how many people and if men made the claim over the air, what was I going to say to them? Men could be humiliated before their friends or lose the trust of hero-worshipping sons forever. Unless the interviewer himself believed *633 Squadron* had existed, I thought it a dreadful trick to play and for the rest of the interview was worried more about what was to follow than about the questions I was being asked.

Not that these questions had any relevance to my new book. My interviewer talked of nothing but *633 Squadron*, how it had begun, how long it had taken me to write, how it had become filmed, etc, etc. Conscious I had only ten to fifteen minutes and aware that my two colleagues in the ante-room would be wondering when we were going to talk about their book, I began to sweat. But each time I tried to change the conversation, the interviewer switched back to *633 Squadron..*

Finally I was driven into desperate action. Clearing my throat, I said I would like to talk about my new book and held it up, nude girl and all, to the camera. Almost immediately the camera swung away to my interviewer who thanked me for my presence and then asked the switchboard for the names of any *633 Squadron* members who had phoned in.

To my immense relief no one had. I've forgotten exactly what I said to the interviewer but I made it clear what I thought of his ploy. Afterwards I hardly dared look at my two Futura colleagues. I knew I should have been more firm in demanding mention was made of *Saffron's War* but my concern over the climax of the program had dominated my thoughts. To their credit they made no criticism or complaint, although we drove back over the Pennines in silence. For my part I was ashamed of my supineness and reminded again of the tricks and embossments the media can inflict on a man.

FIFTEEN

Rheumatoid arthritis had crippled my mother's hands in the mid Sixties and it hurt when I thought how beautifully she had once played the piano. Then, in the early Seventies, she lost her sight. Not totally — she was left with partial peripheral vision — but her direct vision went completely which meant she could neither read nor watch television. As she had enjoyed both, it was a crippling blow for her and meant her only entertainment now was the radio.

As always she bore her losses with little complaint but for a hardworking active woman, the growing restrictions of her life must have been hard to bear. She insisted on continuing to do her own housework and we felt that within reason it was wise to let her. We did, however, move her bedroom down to the same floor as her kitchen, and Shelagh, in her unobtrusive way, did the tasks my mother's limited vision made impossible.

To be honest, her loss was a loss to us too. We had never lived a hectic social life but we had friends with whom we shared the odd evening. Now it became very difficult for the two of us to go out together after dark. Although mother insisted we should go, the talk of rising crime on the radio had its effect on her and we both knew she was afraid of being left alone at night. We didn't like calling on our sons too often because of their youth and their youthful interests and one could hardly bother neighbours with such a request. In one way it was fortunate our tennis days were over.

As a consequence life became an uneventful round of work and evening television. The biggest problem of all were annual holidays. My brother had taken an early retirement and because he had received First Aid Training at work, he had offered his services to a London hospital. His work had proven so thorough and competent that he had been asked to continue and by this time, although he received no payment, he was working the same hours as the regular staff. In addition he had joined the St John's Ambulance Brigade and was going out nightly with its volunteers twice or three times a week.

It was all admirable work, which Shelagh and I appreciated, but the drawback from our viewpoint was it never gave him time to allow us a holiday. Year after year I would ask him to spend a mere fortnight in Bournemouth so that I could give Shelagh a break and always I would receive a somewhat impatient reply that the hospital needed him and it was too difficult to get away. If we needed a holiday so much, why did we not bring mother up to London to stay in his flat. That way he could continue with his work and she would have company in the evenings. The fact that mother was old and blind, dreaded journeys, disliked London, and was unhappy in his flat which was claustrophobic, was lost on him

In fairness to him this was probably because he had seen so little of her in recent years that he did not realize she was now a very fragile old lady. In addition, and truth demands it is said, I believe the family prejudices that his grandmother had inflicted on him when he was a child were still evident. To his great credit he had lived down most of them but perhaps it was inevitable that one or two would emerge at such a time.

Whatever the reason I was acutely aware how unfair it was that Shelagh was not getting the holidays she so richly deserved. Because of my perverse psyche the outcome was inevitable. Torn between my mother's needs and the life I was unable to give Shelagh, I became restless and irritable. I would phone my brother and when I obtained no satisfaction I would find myself taking my frustration out on the very people who were the victims of the situation. To make matters worse my mother, aware Raymond and I were quarrelling over her welfare, began feeling she was a burden to us all and wished she was at rest with my father. All this would leave me in a state of remorse that no apologies or assurances would ease. Once more my brother and I were not the best of friends.

However, shortly before I discovered I had diabetes, I had broken him down. With reluctance he agreed to spend a fortnight in Bournemouth on condition one of the boys looked after Saffron, whom we had just acquired. Peter agreed to do this and he and his girl friend made arrangements to move into the house for the current fortnight.

Although it was too late to book a package holiday, I contacted Ken Mennell. A year or two earlier Ken had piled up his belongings, his wife, his younger son Danny, and his dog into his old Jaguar and done a midnight flit to Southampton and Le Havre. From there he had driven down to Spain, sold his car, and taken the ferry to Majorca. Now he was living in Esporlas, a village some eight miles from Palma, and he had frequently suggested we took a holiday with him.

This seemed the appropriate time to accept his invitation and, because we still had money problems, he arranged for us to have one of the cheap flights available to ex-patriot residents. An additional advantage was that we could fly from our local airport at Hurn.

So on the surface all seemed set fair, and when my brother arrived we believed we were at last going to have a relaxing break from the stress and claustrophobia of the last few years. We hadn't the slightest idea of the absurd and sometimes hilarious events awaiting us.

It all began well enough. For some time I'd been ruminating on a plot for another *633 Squadron* novel and needed to remind myself how the estuary of the French river Loire looked from the air. As our route took us over it, I explained my need to the pilot beforehand and he invited me into his cockpit for the journey. This enabled me to take photographs which proved useful later when I wrote the novel.

Ken was waiting for us at Palma airport. To our surprise, instead of taking us to his home, he took us by bus to a small hostel in Esporlas, his reason being that he and his wife, Joan, believed we would be more comfortable in the hostel. As this was an expense I had not bargained for, he assured me that I need not worry about the tariff as he had 'seen to all that'. Puzzled now, we asked when we could call round and see Joan and he told us he would be bringing her round to the hostel as soon as we were settled in. At that he left us to unpack.

Although there were puzzling elements I could not fathom, I was not wholly surprised at this change of plan. Ken was well known among his friends for eccentric behaviour and although I liked him and respected him for his talent, I can't lie and say that all his ways met my approval. At the same time there was no turning back now and knowing Joan was a less complicated person, I consoled myself that all would be explained when we met her that evening.

So we unpacked and passed the time to dinner by taking a look at the village. It was no film set, being spread alongside a dusty road, but when we eventually sat down at a cafe table with a martini and watched the village life pass peacefully by, it seemed another world to the one we had known in recent years.

In this better frame of mind we went to dinner. It was served in a patio festooned by vines and fairy lights, and if the food wasn't exceptional, the ambience was pleasant enough. My only complaint was the noise of the children. In typical Latin style, the diners had brought their entire families with them and children were everywhere, some crying, some yelling, and some under one's feet. Shelagh thought it amusing but I was Yorkshire enough to believe that small children should be in bed no later that 8 p.m. By that time a man wants to do what a man wants to do, and that isn't to suffer the din and disruption that he has suffered all day.

However, as it was Saturday I consoled myself it wasn't likely to happen the following week. We finished our meal, had coffee, and were just wondering what to do with the rest of the evening when Ken and Joan arrived.

They took us to a small bar where we caught up with each other's news. They learned about my two recently published books and we learned that Ken had worked for a time on an English language newspaper based in Palma and was now writing comic scripts for a Dutch magazine. We also learned that their son, Danny, could now speak Spanish fluently and they had adopted a local dog. We learned everything about them except where they lived. When they told us they would visit us again in the morning, we finished the evening more perplexed than ever.

It was nearly midnight when we returned to our room and climbed into bed. We were on the third floor with the patio partially visible from our window. Sounds rising from it suggested it was still occupied but they were not loud and we were just drifting off to sleep when there was a sudden, heavy rumbling above us. It sounded exactly as if a huge tank had burst and water was crashing down on the roof.

I leapt out of bed and ran to the window expecting to see torrents cascading down to the patio below but there was nothing to see.

"Perhaps someone is moving furniture about," Shelagh suggested.

The rumbling grew in volume until it was shaking our room. "But it's past midnight," I said. "And we're on the top floor. There isn't a room above us."

The rumbling intensified, then ceased as suddenly as it had begun. We stared at one another, then gave up the mystery and tried to get some sleep.

A loud thump awakened me. As I listened I heard the sound of children. At first I thought the noise came from the patio but a moment later there was another loud thump and a loud yell of triumph from the corridor outside our bedroom.

I ran to the door and opened it. The corridor lights were on and I saw half a dozen children staring at me. One, the nearest, had a baseball bat in his hand and another, further down the corridor, was clutching a ball.

Shelagh's voice came from the bed. "What's happening?"

"What's happening? There's a crowd of kids playing baseball out here and using our door as their base or whatever they call it."

"But it's three o'clock in the morning!"

I waved my hand at the urchins. "Go away. Vamoose."

They all looked surprised. What was more natural than for children to play baseball in a hotel at three o' clock in the morning? What were they doing wrong? Why was I such a spoilsport?

When I told them to vamoose again they retreated to the far end of the corridor and went into a huddle. I waited a minute or so and when they made no move, I decided the war was over, closed the door, and climbed back into bed.

It was a short-lived victory. Not three minutes passed before there was another loud thump on the door and a yell of triumph. Breathing fire, I leapt out of bed again, threw open the door, and let out a roar of rage.

It had no effect whatever. The urchins had clearly decided right was on their side and their game would not be spoiled by a bad-tempered and inconsiderate Englishman. I could fume and protest as much as I liked but the game would continue as soon as I closed the door.

I tried to grab the ball but an urchin scampered off with it. The same thing happened to the bat. Fuming, I threw on a dressing gown and went looking for the proprietor but couldn't find his room. In the end I had to beat an ignominious retreat behind the closed door of our room.

There was no sniggering from the corridor when the game commenced again: the urchins were magnanimous in their victory. They simply went on playing ball until dawn came, which, no doubt, was their bedtime. We were left to catch what sleep we could before the summer heat made sleep impossible.

Ken and Joan came round soon after breakfast when we mentioned the night's events. Ken made light of them. The children probably belonged to Spaniards who were holidaying in the hostel and it was the Latin way to let the little pets enjoy themselves. And it had been

Saturday night. So let's get down to the beach and forget all about it.

But it did happen again, the very next night. Not the rumbling. We never found out the reason for that. But the baseball returned. Deciding enough was enough I found the proprietor and made a strong complaint. In return I received a sigh and a shrug. "What can I do, senor? The children's parents are guests like yourselves. Moreover they come to my hotel every year." A deprecating smile followed. "In any case, doesn't it make the senor happy to see children enjoying themselves? I cannot believe the senor or his beautiful wife want to take away their innocent pleasure."

We bore the innocent pleasure for one more night. By this time we were red-eyed from lack of sleep and I found myself swigging brandy for breakfast in order to face another day. As soon as Ken and Joan paid their morning visit, they received my ultimatum. We had come for a holiday, not to be playmates to a bunch of insomniac children. If they weren't prepared to put us up in their home, we would take the first plane home.

There was a long silence while Ken and Joan looked at one another. Then Ken gave a sigh and nodded his balding head. There was nothing else for it. We could share their home for the rest of our holiday.

Wondering why this was such a big deal, we packed our cases and gave our notice at the desk below. As we were about to follow Ken and Joan outside, the proprietor called me back with some embarrassment. "The bill, senor. You have forgotten, perhaps?"

I pointed at Ken, disappearing through the hostel door. "Mr Mennell has taken care of it, hasn't he?"

"No, senor. He only booked the room for you."

I glanced at Shelagh who looked as if she were going to have an attack of the giggles. "Then how much is three nights?"

"Not three nights, senor. Senor Mennell booked you for a week, with perhaps a second week to follow."

"But we're not staying a week. Your guests' goblins have driven us out."

"I'm sorry, senor, but I must ask for a week's payment. I have refused other guests to please Senor Mennell."

I paid for a week and went off after Ken with our suitcases. As we went Shelagh squeezed my arm. "Don't look so cross, darling. Perhaps Ken is short of money."

Tired and testy, I was in no mood for forgiveness. "Then why the hell didn't he tell us before we came? Why did he spin us a yarn like that?"

"Perhaps he was afraid you wouldn't come if you knew he was broke."

"That's even worse," I growled. "That's insulting."

She shushed me. "Never mind. He's doing his best now. Let's catch him up and see where he's taking us."

"I daren't think," I muttered. But because she was Shelagh and could never think ill of anyone, I gave in and did as she asked.

SIXTEEN

Still carrying our suitcases, we left the centre of the village and began climbing up a hillside covered with peasant cottages separated by narrow cobbled lanes. Ken led us up one of these lanes, paused by an unhinged wooden gate, and shoved it open. As he motioned us to follow him, there was a fusillade of barks and snarls and two dogs began leaping around us. One was the dog Ken had adopted and it took a shout from him to quieten it.

I shall never forget Shelagh's face when we entered the cottage. Her expression wasn't due to the accommodation itself. We had both lived under austerity long enough to take it in our stride. It was the state of sanitation that was the shock. With the windows merely holes in the wall, there was nothing to keep dust and dirt from blowing in and we left the imprint of our footsteps as we crossed the floor of the tiny kitchen.

I don't recollect Ken showing any embarrassment and so guessed it must have been Joan who, having given up trying to keep the cottage tidy, had suggested the hostel. We staggered with our cases up a narrow staircase, entered a bedroom, and passed through it into a second room. This, we were told, was normally Danny's bedroom but he would be sleeping with his parents for the rest of our stay. It was a tiny room and in the sunlight dust could be seen blowing in through the hole that served as its window.

Our bed boasted a thin mattress but the string base that supported it had stretched, causing it to sag in the centre. We lowered our suitcases and as clouds of dust arose from the floor, Shelagh glanced at me and then burst out laughing. Although afraid the Mennells would hear, we could not control ourselves and we dropped helplessly on the edge of the charpoy bed and laughed until tears poured down our cheeks. What excuse we made to the Mennells when they came upstairs to see what the joke was I can't remember.

What cannot be forgotten, however, was our first night in our bedroom. Being August, it was hot and sultry and the sagging bed slid us down to its centre. In a colder clime it might have been a bonus but not in the stifling heat of that bedroom. So we spent the first hour clinging like spiders to our respective sides of the charpoy bed in a vain effort to keep cool.

Then the coughing started. Some poor devil in the hovel opposite must have had bronchitis or worse and every few minutes his coughing would reach a paroxysm that ended with his spitting into the lane from his window. As the lane was so narrow we cringed at every expectoration in case the worst happened and our open window came within range.

Then I wanted to spend a penny. To put from my mind the trials ahead, I had shared a few beers with Ken that afternoon and now the price was demanding payment.

As I lay thinking about it, the task grew more formidable by the minute. To reach the toilet I had to pass through the main bedroom where not only Ken, Joan, and Danny were sleeping but their two dogs also. Thus I would not only awaken Shelagh, who had fallen asleep at last, but everyone else in the cottage.

Like a million men before me, I put off the moment, telling myself it was only a matter of will power and if I could get to sleep I would be able to last out until the morning. My bladder, however, had other ideas and the time came when its demands were imperative. Gritting my teeth, I lowered my bare feet to the dusty floor and tiptoed towards the door. Opening it, I heard heavy breathing from the Mennell's bed and began to hope I might be lucky after all.

I was soon disillusioned. Groping forward in the darkness, I stubbed my toe against some hard obstacle, and before I had the time to swallow my curse, pandemonium broke out. The two dogs leapt out from beneath the bed and began barking furiously, Joan gave a cry of alarm, and Ken, still half asleep, leapt out of bed and turned on the light, revealing me in my brief underpants.

I muttered something incoherent and fled down the stairs to the toilet. Pondering what would happen on my return, I almost stayed downstairs but then realized Shelagh would wonder what had happened to me. So I made the return trip, grateful that Ken had turned out the light again. But the dogs had not forgiven me for disturbing their sleep and they gave another salvo of indignant barks before I crept back into our room.

I found Shelagh sitting up in bed. "What on earth happened?"

I groaned and rolled down alongside her. "Don't ask me. Don't even think about it. Just try to get some sleep."

But neither of us slept again that night. The dogs had woken up half the lane and the coughing had started again in the hovel opposite. To make things worse, either my intake of beer or my nervous frustration made me want to tiddle again towards dawn but there was no way I could face running that gauntlet a second time. As the lane seemed to be used for everything else, I had wicked thoughts about the open window but somehow controlled them. There seemed nothing to do but sweat it out until voices and barking below told us we could leave that torture chamber at last.

We had another nine such nights to endure before the holiday was over and during each one I swore to take the next plane back to England. But the days, which we spent mostly on the beaches or climbing the mountain behind the village, were enjoyable enough, and for me it was a pleasure to talk to Ken about books again and to discuss new ideas with him. In addition neither of us wanted to hurt him or Joan because in their way they were doing their best for us. Ken was also very persuasive about the Esporlos fiesta due the following week. Ever since our arrival, posters all over the village had proclaimed it, and with guitars, mantillas, and luscious, heel-tapping senoritas in mind, I felt it a pity to miss it. So, after three hair raising trips around the island in an old car Ken persuaded me to hire and which proved an almost suicidal vehicle, and letting him have a loan from my rapidly emptying purse, we stayed on.

The opening night of the fiesta was on Friday, the day before our flight back to England. We were hoping to drive into Esporlas, the centre of the fiesta, but in accord with everything else of that holiday, the old car would not start and no tinkering with its engine would change its mind. So, denied my luscious heel-tapping senoritas, I had to be content to join the others in the cottage garden to see the fireworks and listen to the music.

It began at seven-thirty. A rocket that burst into a hundred stars in the sky and then the fiesta music. But not the strumming of guitars and the exciting rhythmical female voices I had romantically expected. Instead a hideous clamour erupting from a field only a short distance from our cottage. It sounded as if the portals of hell had suddenly been thrown open and a thousand banshees were howling to the moon. I turned to Ken. "What on earth is that?"

He grinned. "It's the fiesta starting up. They've put amplifiers all round the village. Don't you recognize the tune? It's Mohammed Ali."

I stared at him. "Amplifiers? Pop music? What about guitars, mantillas, and flamenco dancers?"

He eyed me almost pityingly. "What century are you in? There's no flamenco dancing these days. Pop music's the only thing these people like."

It was. And it went on all night, a howling cacophony of noise that drowned even the neighbour's coughing. As I clung to my side of the bed, I reflected that one more romantic dream was blowing away in the wind.

The holiday ended as it had begun. We arrived home to find the house in turmoil. According to Peter, Raymond had never stopped quarrelling with my mother and two days before had packed up his things and announced he'd had enough and was returning to London. In turn Peter's girl friend had told him that if he went, she and Peter would go too, leaving my mother on her own.

It had left Ray no option but to stay on but we had hardly put our luggage down in the hall than he was off to the railway station. Not surprisingly, Peter and Marion were not in the best of moods either, and mother was in tears when we went up to see her.

So ended the long-awaited holiday. It left us nothing else to do but laugh once the more pungent moments had lost their edge. Because one thing is certain about holidays. It is not the comfortable, easy days that one remembers but the days when everything goes wrong. As little had gone right during those two weeks, it remained one of the most memorable of our holidays.

SEVENTEEN

I went to see my editor at Corgi Books on our return. While we had been on Majorca, he had made me an offer for a third *633 Squadron* novel. The offer was only modest by present day standards but it was at lease an increase on what I had received for *Rhine Maiden* and it did mean that Cassell would produce a hardcover before the paperback came out. So I put the offer to my agent.

She was now Pat White of Deborah Rogers, a change caused by Innes's decision to retire. Pat thought the offer a reasonable one and so it was decided I would make the book my next work.

During this time Jerry Cassidy phoned me. Would I make an immediate trip to London as he had a film producer intensely interested in *The Tormented*. It must be that same day, as the producer was leaving for Frankfurt in the evening. Needless to say, I took the next train to London. There I met Jerry in a highly expensive restaurant and was introduced to the producer.

He was a youngish man called Michael Glass. From what Jerry had already told me, he was the son-in-law of a commercial tycoon. He had made a couple of films already, which, if they hadn't set the world on fire, had at least been widely distributed. The important thing was, as Jerry pointed out, he had the money to employ the best actors and the best background staff to make a major film of *The Tormented* which was his intention.

After all the disasters that had happened to the novel, I was in no mood to look a gift horse in the mouth and I greeted Glass with some enthusiasm. After our introduction, he told me he had been looking for a subject to film for some months now and among the books offered to him had been Frederick Forsyth's *The Dogs of War*. Then Jerry had given him *The Tormented* to read and, I quote his exact words, 'I found it in another league altogether'. So he wondered if he could do a deal with me.

As pleased as a cat with cream because the book was *The Tormented*, I drew up a contract with him there and then without consulting Pat White. He would pay me £500 for a six months option and a final l figure of £50,000. We each signed our bits of paper, we shook hands, and off he went by taxi to catch his plane to Frankfurt.

That left me to thank Jerry for bringing the book to Glass's attention and to insist he took 10% of any monies I made from the deal. Then I took the train back to Bournemouth, hugging myself all the way. Perhaps all those months and years of work on the novel hadn't been wasted after all.

Shelagh was waiting for me at the door when I arrived home and her delight on hearing the news wasn't only for the security the deal might bring us. After all the disappointments of late, I knew she had been worried about my health and it was a huge relief to see me in such good spirits. In fact I think we had a small celebration that night.

The author at Hengistbury Head, Bournemouth, Dorset

I gave all details to Pat White the following morning along with my apology for not consulting her first. She took it well and congratulated me on getting the deal. I then tried (without much success) to forget all about it while I worked on the third *633* novel, which I was eventually to call *Operation Crucible*.

I managed to get the first draft written by the spring of 1976 but then needed to go over to Brittany to get the topographical details. Before I left, *Rhine Maiden* was published in paperback and as part of its launch, Corgi obtained a slot for me in Open House, a popular radio program at that time. I remember it because Corgi had learned about the Queen Mother's letter to me during the war, and suggested it should be mentioned in my interview. I was hesitant that it might seem I was using her name as an advertising ploy, but both Corgi and the program controller assured me it would be brought up in a totally innocuous way. In truth it was and I received no adverse comment from any source.

I then made my trip to Normandy and while over there picked up radio transmissions about *Rhine Maiden* which Corgi Books were putting out on commercial stations. On returning home I found twelve author's copies waiting for me. I was somewhat disappointed with the cover picture, which I felt was rather wishy-washy, but nevertheless the book did well and was soon being reprinted. In all it went to three editions.

By the summer I had finished *Crucible* and Corgi must have liked it because I was asked by my editor if I would write three more in the series. I hesitated because of other novels I wanted to write. But I was also aware that if I signed such a contract, our security, if not our comfort, would be assured.

I had another reason for considering Corgi's offer. The next option payment from Michael Glass was now months overdue and although my agency kept trying to contact him, it was beginning to look as if yet another of life's golden promises was coming to naught.

I confess this hurt badly. I even began asking myself neurotic questions about why one's hopes were always being raised and then dashed in disappointment. But I like to believe my main complaint involved Shelagh. For over twenty years she had supported me through traumas and struggles and, if she were to be let down once again when so near to success, it seemed cruel beyond words.

It all meant that I had little choice but to accept the Corgi offer. At the same time I made a request that I might produce only one book every two years. This would give me time to fit in other novels that I might want to write.

This was agreed and left only payment to be settled. I suggested a percentage increase for each of the three books but my editor said he didn't want to begin a precedent which other authors might seize upon. Instead he suggested paying me a thousand pounds more for each book but paying these monies in two equal portions per year for X years until the total sum of the three books was paid off.

With inflation now a factor to consider, I was fully aware what was being done to me but at least it meant I would get an increase per book and two payments a year meant we would have security for seven years.

As security was something we hadn't yet known, and as Michael Glass now seemed to have gone from our lives, I agreed and signed the contract.

A footnote here is perhaps called for. Soon after I made this deal with Corgi, Jerry Cassidy phoned me. He could not confirm it but he had heard that Glass had been killed some time ago in a car accident. So perhaps this might explain why I'd heard no more about the film. It sounds absurd, but after Arthur Jacobs' involvement with *Hawks* and then his death, and now Glass's interest in *The Tormented* followed by his accident, I was left feeling almost guilty.

We had more sad, indeed tragic news, from South Africa at this time. Not only did Shelagh's father die but shortly afterwards Boy, Shelagh's brother, had lost his elder son, Terry, in a car accident. He had been a part-time drummer in a small semi-professional band and met his death on the mountainous road that runs from Cape Town to Hout Bay. We had barely got over this news when, almost unbelievably, Boy's second son, Roderick, was killed in a similar car accident only a few weeks later.

Such a sequence of tragedies would have been enough to destroy almost any man. Yet from our correspondence we heard that Boy had borne them with a simple faith and dignity that had in its turn helped his wife, Pat, to survive. Since working with Boy, I had always liked him. Now I found his courage both moving and inspiring.

His wife was to tell us later that it came from his religious faith. Although he seldom attended Mass, he was a Catholic by birth and inclination, and had a faith that was simple and unquestioning. Although I have often criticized those who follow their particular religion's tenets without question — with consequences that can sometimes lead to bigotry and even persecution — I have nothing but respect and envy for those who extract from their religion a nobility of spirit and a rocklike faith in divine intentions. Such a man was Boy, Shelagh's brother.

Operation Crucible was published by Cassell in 1977 and was featured by the Military Book Club. In fact it did well enough to fully justify more books in the series. In writing them I strove for verisimilitude by using true wartime situations. An example can be seen in the fourth novel, *Operation Valkyrie* which I began writing in 1977. As the series had now reached 1943 when the Norwegian heavy water saga had reached its second phase. I designed the story around the German attempt to obtain a second consignment of heavy water by using a ferry to reach a cruiser berthed at the mouth of the fjord.

As I had learned from my talks to Frederick Kayser, the Nazis had sent the second consignment in an armoured train to Tronso, where they put aboard the ferryboat Hydro. There it was to be shipped by fjord to the cruiser, where it would be delivered to Stettin.

Yet even these precautions hadn't saved it from the Norwegian Linge. Hearing of the plan, they obtained permission from the Norwegian Government in exile in Britain to sabotage the Hydro. One of them had then sneaked into the ferry and planted a timed explosive charge in the boat's bows which had destroyed the ferry at the deepest stretch of the fjord. As a result the Nazis had never obtained any heavy water which prevented their research into the atomic bomb.

As the original *633 Squadron* had dealt with the heavy water threat, I thought this second phase would make an ideal subject for the fourth book, particularly as I had inside knowledge from Kayser of the operation. It had problems, of course, as all fiction based on fact has. For one thing I couldn't contemplate taking away the slightest credit from the brave men I had met.

I puzzled over the problem for weeks before coming up with an answer. Surely after losing their heavy water stocks in the Norsk Hydro Plant, the Nazis should have hedged their bets by sending out two consignments in different directions. One armoured train would still go to the ferryboat but a second one could head along the line to the coast. This second fictitious one could be my squadron's target. It would in no way infringe my promise to Kayser because it would leave their feat and their heroism untouched.

But even here there were problems. There was no way the British could know when the consignment was due to start for the cruiser, and without that knowledge no squadron could fly all the way to Norway and launch a successful attack.

I overcame this problem by remembering that in 1940 a squadron of Gladiators, a heavy aircraft, had discovered they could operate successfully from frozen Norwegian lakes. As my action was taking place in winter, this could be the solution. I could fly my Mosquitoes into Norway at night and thus have them ready for take off the moment word came from Norwegian partisans that the rail consignment was on its way.

There were other problems to solve — a method to enable the Mosquitoes to land on ice at night was one — but they were all solved eventually and in ways that I believe were technically possible.

I feel safe in making this claim because by this time the books had become so popular with the RAF — to my unashamed delight one aviation critic said *633 Squadron* was now the best known squadron in the Service — and to date no one had complained that the technical proposals on which the stories were based were impossible or even suspect. I found this very satisfying.

But at this point in time I had only finished the first draft of *Valkyrie* and needed to scout out a suitable fjord in which to set my German cruiser. As this needed certain geographical aspects, I spent nearly two weeks driving up and down the west coast of Norway in my motor caravan searching for the right one. Finally I found it and was able to return home and complete the novel.

This was the pattern of all the *633 Squadron* books: they were all based on real-life events. *Rhine Maiden* used 'window' and the threat of German proximity rockets; *Crucible* featured an American newsman's criticism of the fighter cover the British were giving American bombers in 1942/43; *Valkyrie* as already stated; *Cobra* dealt with the German stocks of nerve gases, and *Titan* was written around the 1944 invasion of Europe, and so on to the end of the entire series.

I also kept the stories as true to life as possible by having major characters occasionally shot down or killed. This made extra work in introducing new ones but as I felt it emphasised the wastage of war and gave the books authenticity, it was well worthwhile.

By the time I completed them I liked to think they gave a realistic picture of life on an operational squadron during World War Two. I also believe they illustrated the obscenity of war. In this way I justified to myself the time spent in writing them.

EIGHTEEN

On completing *Valkyrie*, I had a year before I needed to write my next *633* novel and I approached my editor at Cassell with an idea gained from a meeting with an ex-Eighth Army Military Policeman in a London pub. He had told me that during the war in Italy one of his tasks had been searching for deserters. The mountainous spine of Italy had offered sanctuary to deserters of all armies and as their defection had put them outside military law, they tended to band together into groups that had no allegiance to either side. Germans and Italians would be found sharing the same caves or shelters with Americans, British or French in complete amity. When I heard this I could not avoid the capricious thought that perhaps they were the sanest of us who had fought in the war. Their attitude to one another had attractive anti-war symbolism.

As deserters needed food and clothing, some of the larger groups took their revenge on the armies that had conscripted them by raiding their supply convoys. These raids were often highly successful not only because the deserters were trained soldiers, but because in most cases they had taken their arms with them. As the raids increased in frequency, both the German and the Allied armies were forced to take action and began sending out heavily-armed patrols with the ironic order they should not fire on one another while both were engaged in the same search-and-kill operations.

Although it had always been my intention to write novels with a serious theme sandwiched between the *633* series, this true life situation had a whimsicality that appealed to me, and after sketching out a brief synopsis which made a German the leader of my band of deserters, I approached my editor at Cassell to see what he thought of the idea. He fell for it immediately and contacted Corgi Books who not only liked it but offered me the largest advance I had ever received for a book.

This advance had a significance I wasn't aware of at the time. It was the maximum amount the publishers could pay without their house rules forcing them to try to recoup the advance by giving the book national advertising. Without knowing it, I was still not going to receive the promotion that could turn average sales into good ones.

I started work on the novel almost immediately and worked on it for less than a week when a new and exciting idea struck me. As things stood at the moment, the theme of the book was merely escape and self-interest. But supposing I made my German leader an idealist who hated war and detested the destruction the Allied and German armies were inflicting on Italy. With men from many nationalities in his band, he would be in an ideal position to gain intelligence from both armies and so perhaps be able to counter their plans. Thus, if say the Germans were planning to blow up a dam to hold up the Allied advance, my leader could tip off the Allies so they could take counter measures. And vice versa. In other words my leader would be a man ahead of his time. He would be using his little army as an international police force against warring factions, a precedent for a United Nations Force that could one day keep peace in the world. As it was my belief then as it is now, that such a force could prevent tyrants and military adventurers from their destructive and murderous ways, it would give the novel a purpose it had not had before. And if at the end of the story I could contrive a situation in which my German and his band of criminals defended and saved an Italian village from destruction from both national armies, what an anti-war novel it could become!

This new theme excited me. I felt it lifted the book into an entirely different league from the mere adventure story it had been before. It also allowed a much deeper character study of the leader himself, and added a mystery element to some of his operations that would have been lacking in the first version.

Naturally it meant the original plot had to be completely re-written because almost every one of the partisans' actions needed a deeper motive than simple plunder. My German leader, whom I called Kessler, was also going to be a far more complicated character to portray. I did not expect, nor did I ask for, a higher advance to cover the extra work, but then no writer worth his salt will hesitate to make changes if he believes they will result in a book with a deeper and more satisfying theme.

I don't remember if I told my two editors about my new intention. Possibly not because, as they were both experienced men, I felt they should know that only hacks keep strictly to their outlines. The creative part of writing is in the actual writing itself and the true novelist almost always thinks of better ideas when he commences this work. I knew this new version would be every bit as exciting as the first and would in addition provide mystery and suspense that was lacking before. So with an enthusiasm I had not felt when writing them, I tore up my first few chapters and began again.

While working on this novel, which I was to call *The War God,* my Cassell editor recommended an American agent. To date I had used those linked to my English agents and they had done little or nothing for me. So when I was told that Arthur Pine was a high-powered agent who might do well with my work, I asked Pat White if she minded my moving my American affairs to him. She agreed without demur and I wrote Pine giving him my literary history. He replied he would be happy to take me on and I sent him copies of my recent work, including the published *633* novels.

It was 1978 before I finished the first draft of *The War God* and my need now was to go over to Italy to find the right site for my operations. As I knew hardly any Italian, I phoned up my old friend David Doig to ask if he would care to go with me. He had lost his wife two or three years earlier and was now retired. However, I knew that when he had edited the Thomson-Leng magazines, he had used Italian artists for illustrations and to ease his dealings with them had learned Italian.

His frequent trips over there had also netted him friends who would be of help in my research. Lastly, but by no means least, he was an excellent companion. This was important because in order to travel around Italy, I intended taking a newish motor caravan that I had recently bought. To avoid searching for night quarters and also to save money, I intended cooking and sleeping in it, and in confined quarters like that one needed an affable and convivial friend. David was such a person.

To my delight he agreed to go and we planned our trip. David, who had learned to cook since becoming a widower, would take care of the meals and I would do the driving. As yet unsure where to set my novel except it would be within the boundaries of Umbria and Marche and along the spine of the Apennines, I intended following my nose again. As I needed to give Shelagh some idea when I would return, we settled on six weeks. It was a long time to leave her caring for my mother but she agreed in her usual supportive way.

So, after packing into the caravan plenty of tinned food and beverages, we began our journey. We crossed the Channel on the Southampton/Le Havre ferry and made our way down towards Grenoble and the Col de Montgenevre. It proved to be a journey to remember. If David had a weakness it was for alcohol, and we had only to park in a village for him to search out its general store and to return with his arms full of bottles.

This made the early days of the journey pure comedy. Not only did inexpensive French wine affect David's culinary skills but they made him sleepy by mid afternoon. As by this time I had usually been driving for six or seven hours, on the third day in France I took the opportunity to have a rest myself and to continue in the late afternoon when it was cooler.

It was on our third day that I spotted a tract of common land just off the road and swung onto it. It was grassy, full of wild flowers, and looked the ideal place for an afternoon siesta. So I awoke David, we carried out our lilos and pillows, and before I could wink an eye David was fast asleep again.

For myself I could seldom sleep in the daytime but it was pleasant enough lying there stripped to the waist and enjoying the sunshine. Thirty to forty minutes passed and then a large coach pulled up on the road opposite. A moment later there was a loud chattering as the bus door opened and a crowd of women began pouring out. Most were middle aged, although there were a few younger women among them, and I guessed it was some firm's day out in the country. As I watched them, I noticed some were eyeing my motor caravan and its GB plate while others were laughing and pointing at us. Wondering at their interest I noticed a buxom, black-haired woman chatting to them and glancing our way as she spoke. Whatever she was saying, it brought nods and more laughter from them and half a minute later they began entering the field and forming a circle around us.

Puzzled and a little apprehensive, I watched the big buxom woman whom I guessed was their supervisor, walk into the centre of the circle. Beside me David was still snoring away on his lilo bed. As I sat upright to question the woman, she shouted some ribald comment, then turned to the giggling women and jabbed two fingers in the air. It was the signal for every woman in the circle to pull down her knickers, squat in the grass, and begin peeing.

As I shook my head in disbelief, screams of hilarity sent every bird in the area flying for its life. I turned to David but now the noise had awakened him. Lifting his head he saw the circle of squatting women and his eyes glazed. Still half asleep, he turned to me and tried to speak but words failed him. As his incredulous eyes turned back to the women, I began laughing myself. When the women saw David's expression, their salty amusement grew until some were weeping on their neighbours' shoulders.

Feeling we had to fight back in some way, I gave them a grin and a boxer's salute. They liked that, cheering and shouting jokes at me. Then they pulled up their knickers and led by the big woman started back to the coach where their driver, sharing the joke, was rocking with laughter.

David found his voice at last, although his Dundee accent was never so hoarse or pronounced. "For God's sake, lad, who were they?"

I wiped my eyes. "Women employees from some firm or another. Probably on a day's outing."

"But they were peeing, lad. Peeing! Right in front of us."

I grinned at him. "That's right. They saw two Englishmen, one with a posh military moustache, and thought they'd take the mickey out of them. They didn't do a bad job, did they?"

David was still in topsy-turvy land. "But how could they do it, lad? Right in front of two men?"

I clapped him on the back. "You're in France now, David. Take it as it comes and enjoy yourself. Come on, we've still a long way to go."

Events took a slightly grimmer turn after that when we reached the col that leads down to Turin. It was midday and midsummer, and as we'd been driving uphill most of the morning the engine was as hot as we were. Seeing our road took us down a long series of sharp hairpins before snaking down to the Turin plain, we stopped for a few minutes to stretch our legs and take a cool drink. Then we climbed back into the cab and began the long descent.

My shock was not long in coming. As we approached the first hairpin and I put my foot down on the brake nothing happened. I jammed my foot down again but still our speed increased. It meant I had to fight the wheel because the caravan was nine feet high and at that speed she tilted alarmingly as she swung round the first bend. As the tyres squealed their protest, I saw David glance at me. "Hang on," I yelled, somewhat unnecessarily. "The brakes have gone."

To his eternal credit, he barely flinched. "Can you get her into a lower gear?"

I tried but only heard a hideous grinding of cogs. With the first and second gears having a high ratio, I hadn't engaged them earlier, thinking we would have held up the traffic behind us. Now it was too late.

I pumped furiously on the brake pedal while trying to think of a way to save ourselves. I couldn't switch off the engine because the steering wheel had a lock that engaged as soon as the key was turned. Our only hope seemed to be a large truck that was descending the road a hairpin below us. If I could catch and run into her, her powerful pneumatic brakes might save us.

But first we had to reach her and our speed was increasing by the second. How I got her round the second hairpin, I'll never know. I felt the dormobile rolling and will swear she was on only two wheels as we turned. I know I could see the Turin plain swinging dizzyingly below us and believed that at any moment we would topple over the edge.

But with the engine screaming like a banshee and my pumping on the brake pedal we somehow rounded the hairpin and crashed down on all four wheels again. But it was now obvious to us both that we would never survive a third hairpin and our only chance was to collide with the truck ahead before she turned into it.

One's brain moves fast in crises like these and mine was telling me I must go for broke. I must slam down my clutch pedal and hope our increased speed would enable us to crash into the truck in time. It meant we would never survive the hairpin if we failed and even if we succeeded, the crash might still throw us over the edge. But it seemed our only chance and I was just about to disengage the clutch when I felt a sudden increase in pressure on the brake pedal. I pumped it even harder and began to notice a slackening in our speed. It wasn't much at first but it was enough to destroy our chance of reaching the truck in time. So it was a head or tails situation and I opted for heads. I would pump and pump and hope we could survive one more hairpin. If we did and the improvement continued, we might manage the descent without taking further drastic action.

We did round the hairpin safely although it proved nearly as scary as the earlier one. After that the brakes improved sufficiently to slow us and get us down to the plain, although I had to continue pumping until I was drenched in sweat and my leg was on fire.

We drew into the first garage we met and David tried to explain our problem to a mechanic. To our surprise he seemed totally uninterested in it. As David couldn't understand his behaviour, I assumed his Italian didn't lend itself to car maintenance and so drove on cautiously to the next garage. Here we found a mechanic who could communicate with David and what we heard astonished us both.

"It is nothing to worry about, signor. Your brakes are OK."

David looked as puzzled as I. "How can they be OK if they failed us like that?"

"It happens every year, signor." The mechanic made a dramatic gesture with his hands. "Cars run away with drivers. Every summer it happens."

"But why? What's the reason?"

The mechanic tried to explain but the technicalities defeated David. The only thing he could gather from the explanation was that now we were safely down from the high mountain our brakes would perform satisfactorily again.

This proved to be true although it was some days before I felt happy when descending a mountain road. Wanting an explanation I enquired at garage after garage on my return home but none of them gave me a satisfactory one. It took a former racing driver who lived nearby to solve the mystery. Had I changed the brake fluid before we set off on our journey? No, I hadn't. Then that was the reason. We had been at high altitude on a hot day and my brake fluid had contained water as brake fluid does if not changed at regular intervals. As water boils at a lower temperature at altitude, our water had turned into steam and rendered my brakes ineffective. That was what the Italian mechanics had been trying to tell us and why some tourists have accidents in summer time.

It all made sense and I believed him. What was more difficult to understand was why, after I wrote the leading motoring associations about our experiences, they did not stress in their overseas literature the dangers of driving in mountains with old brake fluid.

NINETEEN

Our first port of call in Italy after visiting the garages was Lucca where two generations of the Carreras family lived. These charming people were friends of David and made both of us welcome. Francesca, the wife of the younger couple, spoke excellent English, which was a help to me, and invited us to stay as long as we liked.

Her offer was tempting because the city of Lucca, with its numerous exquisite churches, is quite beautiful, as is the surrounding countryside. But we had a job to do and after two days of sipping good wine and chatting to the family, we were ready to leave. When Francesca asked our destination and I told her the mountains to the east, she looked concerned and conferred with her husband and family. She then told us that we must not think of going there without protection because there were bandits in the forests.

We both thought she had chosen the incorrect English word but then she told us that dozens of tourists had been attacked in recent months and some had lost their lives. We must choose another area to visit. This one was too dangerous.

Although we knew she meant well, we both thought she was indulging in a little Latin exaggeration. So we pacified her with some yarn or another and thanked her and her family for their kindness. Then, after promising to call again on our way back, we set off. We drove east to Pistola and then began climbing into the mountains.

As I had no idea where to look for a possible area of operations for my deserters, I found myself driving north, south, east and west during the next two days. The roads were steep and narrow and the mountainsides dense with trees. Sometimes we would drive for an hour without seeing a hamlet or a cottage, and I remember my surprise at finding such a sparsely populated district in Italy. With no possibility of finding a campsite, we spent our first night in a forest clearing.

We caught sight of a notice nailed to a tree the next day. Despite my non-existent Italian, it was not difficult to interpret. As I pulled up alongside it, David gave a whistle of surprise. "*Beware of robbers.* Then Francesca was right. There are some of the bastards in these parts."

We saw more warning notices as we drove on. Mixed with my surprise was the thought that, if thieves could ply their trade today without detection, my deserters during the war might have found the area highly suitable, particularly as one of the main coastal roads to the south was not far away. So I ear-marked it as a possible location for my novel.

We noticed a car following us later that afternoon. It was only a small convertible with the hood down but the two men inside looked tough and formidable. At first I had taken little notice of the car but when it failed to pass us every time the Dormobile struggled up a hillside, I became suspicious it was tailing us.

I turned to David. "I think we'd better stop while it's still daylight. Then we can see what those characters are up to. We don't want them creeping up on us at night."

As cool as when our brakes had failed, David shrugged. "If you think it's best it's all right with me."

We stopped near a bridge on the right-hand side of the road. As I expected, the convertible drew up some thirty yards behind. Otherwise the road was empty. We hadn't seen another car for fifteen minutes and the switchback road was deserted as far as the eye could see. As we stared through the rear window of the caravan we could see the two men gazing at us as they talked. Feeling certain they were debating whether or not to attack us there and then, I felt our best chance was to make the first move. So I turned to David "Let's look as if we don't give a damn. I'll sit on the step outside and you hand me a glass of wine."

I had my reasons for keeping David inside. Although as brave as a lion, he hardly had the physique to deter two tough thugs. For that matter I wasn't sure I had either, but without having James Bond in the Dormobile, it was the best we had. So I stripped off my shirt, opened the rear door, and sat on the step. There I yawned and flexed my arms as if enjoying the sunshine, at the same time hoping I hadn't forgotten my wartime unarmed combat training.

I then took the glass of wine David passed me. As I sipped at it, the two men threw open their doors and jumped out. Glancing back I asked David to pass me the shillelagh I always carried in the Dormobile. It took him a moment to find the knotted heavy stick and the thugs were no more than twenty paces away when he handed it to me.

I felt more confident now, particularly as neither seemed to be armed. As I laid the shillelagh across my knee, one of them called something in a gruff, threatening voice. "What does he say?" I asked David.

"He's got a hell of an accent. But I think he's saying he wants to talk to us but doesn't want any trouble."

"Tell him he won't get any trouble if he keeps his distance. Tell him it's up to him," I said.

David's reply brought more threatening scowls. Bluffing it to the end I stood up, swung the stick, and grinned at them. They conferred again, then both spat on the dusty road, and walked back to their car. A minute later it whizzed past us so close it nearly took off our wing mirror.

David was full of praise. "You did well, son. You scared 'em off."

I was too busy complaining to my Mr Hyde to listen to his compliments. In the past I had always relied on him to take over in situations like this, when I could sit back and be as big a coward as I liked. This time he hadn't even left his cave, much less offered his help. When he only yawned at my complaints and went to sleep again, I could only assume he hadn't thought the two thugs worthy of his attention. It was disdain that greatly deflated my sense of achievement.

After three weeks, during which time we visited other sites and towns and took many photographs for later reference, we returned to Lucca, where once again we were made welcome. While there I took the opportunity to phone home. Shelagh sounded very cheerful and after letting me know all was well with the family, told me a letter had arrived from Arthur Pine saying he had sold both *633 Squadron* and *Rhine Maiden* to Bantam Books.

The news delighted me. Until now I had feared that American parochialism would never allow novels of another nation's servicemen to penetrate their market. So this was a major breakthrough, particularly as Pine inferred that Bantam might take the remaining four books if these first two did well for them.

It was an occasion to celebrate and made more so by our being able to share it with the family who had been so kind to us. We stayed two days as before and then paid a visit to another family David was friendly with. On our arrival they embarrassed me by taking me for David's son but David took their mistake with his usual good humour. We stayed with them a day and night and then started back for France. As David didn't know France and we were well inside our scheduled six weeks, I allowed myself a couple of days to show him the Riviera with the intention of then driving north over the Massif Central to the Channel ports.

Our first campsite was in a deep valley near to the coast. I have forgotten its name but a huge railway viaduct ran over its entrance. Its massive stone pillars were deeply pitted, making us both believe the damage was caused by shell fire when the Allies had invaded France from the Mediterranean. I was to learn otherwise later.

Having done some hard driving during the last few days, we gave ourselves a day's rest and spent it on the campsite's private beach. It was full of lovelies of all nationalities and topless bathing was commonplace. One girl caught everyone's eye. As bronzed as a goddess, amazingly endowed and yet with a slim waist and hips, she spent the afternoon swimming the backstroke so that her breasts floated on the smooth water like two melons.

David made me a plea that evening. "Can't we stay another day or two, laddie? We're well ahead of time, aren't we?"

With Shelagh looking after the family I should not have agreed but driving the heavy Dormobile hundreds of miles in mountainous country hadn't been easy and a more pleasant place for a rest would have been hard to find.

So I gave in to temptation and we stayed two more days. During this time David became intrigued by a slim handsome woman in her early thirties who came down to the beach every day with a companion who might have been her mother. She, the younger one, had a two inch scar down her right cheek which instead of disfiguring her good looks seemed only to add a mystery to them.

David was enthusiastic. "I'd like to know more about her. She'd make a marvelous character for that novel I keep saying I'll write."

Why don't you tell her?" I asked. "She might be thrilled."

"But what if she's French? I'd make a fool of myself if I couldn't talk to her."

"You're never going to make any progress if you don't try."

David tried to solve his problem by moving close to the couple the next time they visited the beach but although we both strained our ears, neither of us could hear their conversation. David was deflated that night. "I caught her eyes a couple of times but there wasn't a response. I wonder if she thinks we're a couple of gays."

"Gays? With you drooling like a starving bloodhound every time you look at her. Go over and talk to her tomorrow. What can you lose?"

He never did. His woman with the scar remained a mystery as we drove away. But he never forgot her and years later he told me how he'd tried but failed to write a novel about her.

So, after a detour to Mont St Jean and the invasion beaches in Normandy, we returned to Britain. David stayed with us a couple of days and then took the train back to Dundee but not before he had a final word with me. "That was bloody marvellous, lad. Bloody marvellous. Let's do it again sometime. Promise?"

It was no hardship to tell him I would do my best. He had been the perfect companion and I had and still have happy memories of that journey.

TWENTY

Shortly after my return an extraordinary thing happened. A letter from South Africa arrived from Shelagh's first son, Barry. It told her his father was in a Cape Town hospital dying of a brain tumour, and while visiting him Barry had remembered his grandmother lived in the city and had searched out her address.

This was necessary because after Shelagh had left for England, her ex-husband had barely mentioned her name to the boy and he had grown into manhood knowing next to nothing about her or her whereabouts. But his visit to the city had made him curious and on discovering Mrs. Mac's address, he had visited her and learned where his mother lived. The outcome was this letter, in which he told her how much he hoped they would meet in the near future.

As can be imagined it was a marvellous surprise for Shelagh. Although she had hardly ever spoken about it, she must have believed she had lost her first son for ever. Instead she read that he was happily married, had three children, and they all wanted to see her. It could only mean one thing. We would have to make the trip to South Africa as soon as we could afford it.

I had more good news about my *633* novels at this time. The Deborah Rogers agency said they were debating the possibility of selling two of them to a large American legal corporation. It seemed that under American law a corporation was excused certain revenue taxation on money invested in foreign works of art, providing those works met certain conditions. As a consequence three representatives of this corporation were visiting Britain and going round the agencies to see what was available in the literary world.

The books they were seeking had to be well known, and the author had to be prepared to sell his copyright for nine years. After that period the new owner could either buy the copyright outright for a huge sum or it would revert back to its original owner.

Somewhat puzzled I asked where I came in and they told me they wanted to offer *Rhine Maiden* and *Crucible* to the corporation if I were agreeable. Should the corporation take them, I would receive a handsome sum for each book. However, I must realize that if the deal went through, the corporation would take fifty per cent of any sale made on the books after the contract was signed. This arrangement would last for the full contractual nine years.

At first it seemed a deal too good to be true until I realized that if any film company came up with an offer I would probably be well out of pocket, and, from the way things went with me, it was quite possible an offer would come immediately after a deal was finalized. On the other hand *Rhine Maiden*'s American and foreign sales were almost completed; *Crucible*'s were halfway through, and I wouldn't have to pay the corporation a share of such monies earned before the contract was signed. Deciding a bird in hand is worth two in the bush, I told Deborah Rogers to go ahead.

I was in her offices when the three lawyers paid their visit to consider the two books. I was introduced to them, then retired to another office while Deborah Rogers argued her case. Conscious the money would make our South African trip possible, I found the next half hour dragged interminably but when Pat White appeared her expression told me the deal was agreed. Somewhat stunned that the two books should be considered works of art, I signed the contract and returned home jubilant. I felt we had turned the corner at last.

Cassell published *Valkyrie* in hardback a couple of weeks later. To my relief its reviews were every bit as favourable as those received by its predecessors. They were still coming in when I had another letter from Arthur Pine. He had succeeded in selling *Valkyrie* and *Crucible* to Bantam for three times the figure received for the first two books. (If the thought struck me that *Crucible* had sold only because I would now receive only half the sale, I pushed it aside as ungrateful). Even better news was that Bantam were prepared to commission the final two books as Corgi had done. I decided *633* Squadron and its sons were doing very well for me.

Although 1978 was proving a good year financially, I still hadn't taken Shelagh on holiday since our Majorcan experience. So once again I asked Ray if he would relieve us for a couple of weeks. The usual bickerings and delays followed and it wasn't until late August that he agreed to come down. As it was too late to arrange a European holiday and we couldn't leave the dog with him, we had little choice but to take another holiday in the Dormobile.

We spent a couple of days with friends in a village north of Bristol and then decided to drive up to the Lake District. As we had never been there before without the heavens opening up, we took the decision with some hesitation but our friends had been there only a couple of weeks earlier and their enthusiasm persuaded us to try again.

Never was a worse decision made. It began raining cats and dogs the moment we arrived and jet black clouds suggested the day of judgement was near. Waterfalls cascaded down the fells and waterlogged trees bowed their heads in prayer. We endured it for three days and nights and then fled eastwards across the Pennines.

For all the good it did us, we might as well have stayed put. The drenching rain followed us, swelling the streams and making a quagmire of the valleys. When we tried to take the poor dog for a walk, he would slither almost to his belly in mud. Desperate, we continued our flight eastwards but the diabolical weather followed us right to the coast.

By this time we had given up staying in campsites. All seemed to be waterlogged and in one we had needed a tractor to put us back on the road. Instead we parked wherever there was a hard standing, and on our seventh night, when we were heading south in the hope of escaping the weather, we found a gravelled lay-by a mile or two south of the huge domes of the Fylingdales Tracking Station. Thankfully we pulled into it.

It was dark and still raining but I had to stretch my legs, so the dog and I walked down a path that led into a wood at the back of the lay-by. After a few minutes we came to a notice and there was just enough light remaining for me to read it. Black Bog was its inscription and, although the name seemed appropriate, one's mind reeled at the thought of its present condition. Hurriedly we turned and went back to the Dormobile.

The night that followed was one of those nights all campers will recognize. We were wet and had no way of drying our clothes. We hadn't found any shops open that afternoon and so were lacking bread and milk. Our gas bottle ran out when Shelagh was cooking our dinner and I found the thread on its replacement was crossed. We put on our small portable television to cheer us up but either the weather or the interference from the tracking station hopelessly distorted its pictures. We tried the radio but it only buzzed and crackled. All of which only left bed and we huddled into it and tried to ignore the sound of the wind and the driving rain.

A deep growl from Saffron awakened me. I reached out and tried to calm him but he pulled away and growled again. By this time Shelagh was awake. "What is it?"

I climbed out of bed and put on the light. The dog was standing at the rear door with all his hackles up. I went over to him. "What is it, old lad? What's worrying you?"

Normally he would have answered by wagging his tail but he was listening intently. As he let out another series of snarls and barks, Shelagh turned to me. "This isn't like him. There must be someone out there."

I dragged on a pair of slacks and opened the door. It was pitch black outside with the rain still drenching down. I peered out but could see nothing. When Saffron let out another blood-curdling series of yelps and snarls, I gave him a push. "All right, if you can see something, go and frighten it away."

He wouldn't go. Still snarling and trembling, he backed away. I closed the door and locked it. "It must be a sheep or a cow that's wandered past," I said. "Anyway, it seems to have gone now."

But Saffron didn't think so. It must have been an hour before he settled down and even then he kept twitching and making frightened noises in his sleep.

We drove off the next morning. As it was still raining, I took Shelagh into a pub for lunch. While ordering it, I got talking to the barman and asked him if he found the television reception poor in those parts. When he asked where I'd spent the night, I told him about the lay-by. He gave a chuckle. "I don't wonder you couldn't get anything there. Don't you know what they call that corner?" When I shook my head, he gave another chuckle. "That's The Devil's Elbow. They say he walks about there on certain nights when the weather's black and evil. Maybe it was him who buggered up your reception and frightened your dog."

The rain ceased when we reached Bridlington and we decided to call on my old friend Blanche Appleby. When we reached her bungalow the sun was shining and as our spirits lightened with it, we decided to spend the remaining week in East Yorkshire.

Now the weather had improved, we should have known better. Until then I had been phoning home every second day to ensure all was well, and although Ray had not sounded happy, at least there had been nothing to disturb us unduly. When I phoned him from Blanche's, however, he sounded almost hysterical, saying my mother was driving him crazy, he couldn't bear it any longer, and if he didn't get away soon, he didn't know what he would do.

We felt little sympathy for him but were only too aware what my mother would be going through. So we had little choice but to say goodbye to Blanche and to drive straight back to Bournemouth.

After all that had happened, I wasn't in the mood to spare him and before he left for London I told him point blank that the following February I intended giving Shelagh a proper holiday by taking her to South Africa to see her son and relatives and he had better prepare for it because we were definitely going, come hell or high water.

It was all unpleasant and unsavoury and I could only hope my mother heard nothing of it or her feelings of being a burden would be worsened. Once again I regretted the way my grandmother had divided our family.

I worked on *The War God* right through that winter but hadn't completed the first draft when February arrived. There was a time when I wouldn't have dreamed of taking a holiday until a work was finished but the circumstances gave me little choice. After a winter of argument and counter argument Ray had agreed to take care of mother for the month of February but only if she stayed with him in London. I knew she hated the idea but I couldn't always sacrifice Shelagh's interests for my family.

Nor was I being altruistic. I badly needed a holiday myself and although my dislike of apartheid was as strong as ever, I was looking forward immensely to taking Shelagh to Barry, to seeing Clifton again, and to walking once more in that golden sunshine.

But there were problems and at the time we couldn't estimate their gravity. Would I receive a visa, and, if I did, how would I be received on my arrival? I wasn't worried about the death threats I'd received after the publication of *Laws*. Twenty-three years had passed and the cranks who had made the threats must have long ago transferred their venom elsewhere. But governments have longer memories and if I were seen as an undesirable alien for my criticisms of apartheid, it would be easy enough for immigration officials to either deny me a visa, or send me straight back to England on the next plane, leaving Shelagh to travel round the country herself.

We could only hope for the best and this we did. We joined a travel club, I obtained a visa, we made our arrangements, and finally I drove my mother to Ray's flat in London. Although she made no complaint, I thought she looked very pale and strained when she kissed us goodbye and I left her hoping she wouldn't be too unhappy. I remember wondering as I drove back to Bournemouth if it were ever possible in this life to enjoy anything without remorse or some other negative emotion spoiling it.

We left for Heathrow two days later, leaving Kevan and his girl friend to take care of the house and Saffron. They had volunteered, which was a relief to us both because we did not fancy the idea of putting the dog into kennels.

Because of the travel club, we flew to the Union on South African Airways. This proved a disadvantage because, with no African country at that time allowing South African aircraft landing rights, we had to refuel in the middle of the night at an airfield in the Cape Verde islands. Dark and windy, with armed guards everywhere, we were allowed out of the 747 only to have coffee and a snack in a rundown restaurant, and then the guards shepherded us back to the aircraft. To be guarded this way was an uncomfortable reminder of the general dislike felt at that time for all things South African.

We landed at Johannesburg and I admit holding my breath when we passed through immigration. However the official who handled me was a a portly cheerful soul who, on seeing from my passport that I was an author, asked if I was Wilbur Smith in disguise. When I said I'd love to have his royalties, he gave a belly laugh, handed back my passport, and wished me a happy holiday in the Union.

An old school friend of mine, Roy Cowling, was waiting for us. Roy, an accountant, had emigrated to the Union some eight years earlier and we had put up his family for a few days before they followed him. We had kept in correspondence ever since and we spent three days with them before flying on to Cape Town. There, Shelagh's sister, Monica, and a friend 'Bubbles' Nolan, met us. Monica drove us to Clifton, where Mrs. Mac was waiting for us. It was a happy, if nostalgic meeting, which was not lessened by our seeing the rented bungalow where twenty-seven years before we had spent two of the happiest years of our marriage. After chatting for an hour with Mac and Monica and giving them the latest news, Shelagh and I walked along the promontory to Big Rock at its far end. There we stood gazing at the panorama of Lions Head, the Twelve Apostles, and the four sunlit beaches. As we turned and watched the waves lapping into the rocky coves and the cormorants skimming over the blue sea, I knew I had never lost my love for this beautiful and enchanted place.

TWENTY-ONE

We spent a week in Cape Town and then began our journey to see Barry who lived over one thousand, four hundred miles away in a town called Sabie. As Monica was taking her summer holidays, she suggested going with us to see Barry and driving up in her car instead of taking the train. We liked the idea and we left at dawn two days later.

Some moments in life are unforgettable and that morning was one. As we left the suburbs and the road began climbing towards the Hex River Pass, the city below us was caught in early morning sunlight and lay pink and tranquil in its cradle of mountains. It reminded me of the mornings during the war when I had risen early at Clifton to return to my airfield and of the many times I had flown over it with pupils.

Our destination, Sabie, lay in the north-eastern Transvaal, so we had a long drive ahead of us. The first hundred miles were over the Hex River mountains and then through the fertile vineyards of Paarl and Worcester, then the less fertile plains of the Little and Great Karoos. As it was the middle of summer, the heat was severe and before long the little car began to suffer. Twice we had to stop to fill up the radiator but, although we found a garage mechanic in the hamlet of Three Sisters, he couldn't find the cause of the trouble and we had no option but to continue.

We spent the next two nights in small 'dorps' that lay at intervals along our route. Because of the distance to Sabie, we decided to start each day soon after dawn. As I am no lark in early mornings we solved the problem by letting Monica drive for the first two hours and I taking over when the morning mist had cleared from my eyes.

Our route took us through the Cape Province to Colesberg where we entered the Orange Free State and then on to the massive Vaaldam on the border of the Transvaal. Always alive when seeing new places, I was enjoying myself until we began the last leg of our journey through the north-eastern Transvaal. Then my misgivings about meeting Barry began to assert themselves again.

How were he and his wife going to receive me? I knew from Barry's letter that Shelagh would be made welcome but surely I, who had been the initial cause of the thirty-two year separation between mother and son, would fall into a different category. Toleration was surely the most I could expect, and if Barry was the kind of man who bore a grudge, even that reception might worsen before the end of our stay. I don't think I said much to Shelagh and Monica about my misgivings but they grew in inverse ratio as the miles to Sabie grew fewer.

Sabie proved to be a beautiful little town and we soon found Barry's house. He and his wife, Rita, must have been looking out for us because as I pulled up outside they both ran out to the car. While Shelagh and Monica climbed out to enjoy their greeting, I sat and waited.

A most moving scene followed. Barry had been a child and Shelagh a young woman when they had last met. Now, three decades later, they were meeting with Barry now a grown man with a family and Shelagh now a grandmother.

Barry (Shelagh's son) and Rita (Barry's wife)

I don't remember what they said to one another: I was too moved by the meeting. Nor do I remember what I said or what was said to me when I was introduced. I was too astonished at the warmth of Barry's greeting. He hugged my shoulder as if I were a long lost friend and when his wife reached up and kissed me, all my misgivings fell away.

They proved a delightful family. Barry, a good looking man in his late thirties, was slightly below average height but as strong as an ox. He was a forester by profession and at that time was working for the South Africa Forestry Commission. Rita was a slim, beautiful girl with black hair who taught at a local school. Their three children were named Vincent, Barry, and Lisa. Although initially shy at meeting their grandmother for the first time, they soon accepted both of us as part of the family.

Rita's brothers, whom we met later, were as huge as she was petite. One of them was an engineer who worked at the airfield in Nelspruit, a larger town some fifteen miles from Sabie, and it was he who arranged a flight for me to Jo'burg. The South African Broadcasting Corporation wanted an interview with me and the request came during our week with Barry. After talking it over with Shelagh, I decided to accept.

So, borrowing Monica's car, I drove to Nelspruit the next day. It was hot and humid and the weather news forecast one of the storms prevalent in the Transvaal during the summer months. Nevertheless I had a trouble-free flight to Jo'burg where Roy Cowling was waiting for me. We had phoned him the previous day about my interview and he had offered to take me to the SABC studios. This he did, where I was introduced to a glamorous creature wearing an off shoulder dress and plunging neckline who was something of a celebrity on radio and television but whose name I have forgotten. I had believed the interview was only to discuss my latest book, but she had done some homework on me because soon I found myself being questioned about *Laws*, why I had written it, and what were my present views about the Union. Didn't I find an improvement in the country's race relations? Wouldn't I like to come back to live there again? etc, etc. Conscious such a public grilling might revive old antipathies, I began to wish I had never agreed to the interview. However, as I always found it difficult to avoid direct challenges, I said what I still thought about apartheid and hoped nothing more would come of it.

Roy took me to his home for lunch and then ran me back to the airport. By this time the sky was heavily clouded and thunder could be heard rumbling in the distance. I noticed when I boarded the small commuter aircraft that there was only one pilot instead of the two present on our outward journey but gave it little thought at the time. I found a seat behind the pilot and settled down for the forty minute flight to Nelspruit.

As we crossed the Reef and flew eastwards, the storm broke with a vengeance. Lightning could be seen jagging down on mountain tops below us. It was exciting and exhilarating as such things can be, but on the debit side the gale force winds were throwing the small aircraft round like a cockleshell and I could see the pilot in front of me struggling to hold her steady.

We flew like this for about fifteen minutes and then a sudden vivid flash appeared to strike the aircraft's starboard wing. As a woman passenger gave a cry of shock, I noticed the pilot's head drop forward.

Knowing lightning seldom strikes aircraft or harms passengers, I thought at first the pilot was searching for something on the floor. But as the plane began to yaw and he sagged against his straps, I realized he was unconscious.

How oddly the mind works at such moments. I was fully aware of the danger we were in but my initial thought was fear of making a scene or looking foolish in front of the other passengers who as yet seemed unaware of what was happening. So it was a couple of seconds before I unfastened my seat belt and leaned forward to take a closer look at the pilot.

There was no doubt about it. He had passed out and the aircraft was pilotless. Nor was the automatic pilot engaged. We were swinging about helplessly and as the aircraft tilted forward, passengers began to shout and scream.

Clinging to the pilot's seat, I tried to decide what to do. If I could get the pilot out of his seat, could I fly the plane? With my past experience of flying I felt I might be able to hold it steady but without knowledge of its instrumentation, I knew it was unlikely I could do much more than that. Yet something had to be done and I turned round to the passengers. I wanted someone to come forward and hold me while I tried to get the pilot out of his harness but the one man who moved forward was thrown helplessly across the cabin. As I struggled to reach the harness buckles, I thought I saw the pilot's eyelids flicker.

Without thinking, I struck him hard across the face. When his vacant eyes opened, I struck him again. It was drastic but it worked. I yelled as loudly as I could in his ear. "Get her under control! Hurry up, for God's sake!"

Realizing at last what was happening, he grabbed the controls and we began to level out, although not before we were perilously close to the mountaintops. When finally we landed and the passengers had either made their complaints or dispersed, he drew me aside and thanked me for what I had done.

"I didn't do anything but slap your face," I told him. "But why didn't you have a co-pilot? I thought two pilots were obligatory under commercial flight regulations."

He confessed they were but told me his co-pilot's wife was ill in a Jo'burg hospital and the man had asked permission to visit her. It wouldn't happen again if I would be decent enough not to file a complaint.

I felt he'd had a big enough fright already and in any case I didn't want our holiday spoiled by an enquiry. So I left it there and drove back to Sabie but not before I had a long talk with my gremlin. Why, I asked him, did he always give me these problems and adventures when other people were allowed to enjoy quiet and peaceful lives? But even as I lectured and admonished him, I had little hope he would curtail his tricks in the future.

Barry and Rita did everything possible to make our stay a memorable one. They drove us about the beautiful countryside, took us to the old mining town of Pilgrim's Rest, and finally took us to a caravan in the nearby Kruger National Park that they had booked for our visit.

It was very hot the day Barry drove us into the vast park and when we reached the campsite and opened the door of the caravan, it was like opening the door of an oven. The air cooling system had broken down and although Barry phoned for a mechanic, he was told repairs could not be made until the following day. So a hot night awaited us.

Both Shelagh and I had to laugh at what followed. Although the temperature in the early evening was still in the nineties, Barry began preparing for a 'braiflesch'. Barbecues as they are known in England and America are a way of life in South Africa and it takes more than a heat wave to cancel them. Although it was uncomfortable to get within ten feet of the glowing charcoal, Barry manfully produced burnt offerings for the four of us. Afterwards he and Rita insisted we used the only room in the caravan that had an electric fan.

We spent the next day driving around the park searching for animals.

We saw no elephants, which disappointed me because I've always liked the huge creatures, but giraffes were plentiful and we were lucky in coming across a pride of lions. Although I was told there were about two thousand lions in the park, that is not a high density in an area that covers some six hundred square miles, and it encourages motorists who find them to tip off others of their presence. Our pride seemed to be an entire family and as I had brought a movie camera with me I was able to get excellent shots of them and of other animals we saw later.

Our week in Sabie passed only too quickly. Barry wanted us to stay longer but there was still Shelagh's brother to see in Durban and so we were forced to make an emotional goodbye. Rita openly wept and even Shelagh, who usually contains her feelings well, was seen wiping tears from her eyes. Goodbyes are seldom easy to make and this one contained so much loss and grief from the past that my own throat caught as Barry wrung my hand and made me promise to return again soon.

So we drove south to Natal. Durban was looking superb when we arrived. In the bright sunlight everything seemed in bloom, the glittering tiposheena, the purple heliotrope, the red and white oleanders: the entire city seemed a cosmorama of light and colour. As we drove through the suburbs and the red flames of bougainvillaea swept past, I was reminded of my time in the city during the war when Shelagh and I had been torn apart and I was waiting there for my posting to the Far East. A young man worried sick about Shelagh and her divorce, I had thought it the loneliest city on earth as I had wandered through its streets and seen civilians making their way home. But now I was with the woman I had thought I would never see again, and Durban was transformed into a place of magic.

Boy and his wife Pat were living in a flat out at Umshlanga Rocks. Although Boy was suffering from diabetes and restricted circulation in one leg, he made us welcome and did his best to see we enjoyed our stay. Shelagh, Monica and I went swimming a few times in the pleasantly warm Indian Ocean and spent a couple of nights sightseeing in the city. By this time nearly three weeks of our holiday was over and we had to say our good byes and start back for Cape Town. Shelagh and I wanted to drive back through Lesotho but Monica, carrying a South African passport, was concerned at the reception she might get in the black protectorate and so we took the longer route around it.

On our way we passed Ischwanghana where a British regiment had been wiped out during the 19th Century Zulu Wars. A film unit was present at the time and we were told a film of the encounter would be in the cinemas the following year. But although I watched for it on our return to England, we never saw or heard of it again.

Our last week was spent in Cape Town with Shelagh's mother who was now looking very frail. One of my ambitions before making the trip had been to see my old airfield again and to make another ascent up my beloved Table Mountain. But although Monica lent us her car for the rest of our stay, we never got to the airfield, driving instead to Cape Point. As for Table Mountain, we did go up in the cable car but the weather was poor that week and hid from us the superb view of Clifton and Camps Bay that had lasted in my memory throughout the years.

However, we did spend those last few days in Clifton and had to be grateful for that. At the same time its beauty disturbed me. I could never forget that it was I who had taken Shelagh from it and on the last night before our return I asked her to walk with me to Big Rock again. We stood for a long moment gazing at the necklaces of lights above the beaches, at the moonlit mountains, and the sea breaking in phosphorescent waves among the rocks, before I turned to her and put my question. "Now you are back, would you like to live here again?"

She paused for a moment, then shook her head. "No. It's not the same as it used to be. They've made too many changes."

It wasn't the answer I wanted. "Even so, it's still beautiful. Don't you ever regret leaving it to go to England? I had hoped my writing would give you a good life there but it hasn't worked out that way, has it? It's just been one disappointment after another."

She understood then and turned to me. "I've no regrets, darling. Not a single one."

I still wouldn't be consoled. "But you had such a good life here. Are you sure you don't miss it?"

At that she lost patience with my soul-searching. "I've a good life over there, so stop talking rubbish. I've enjoyed the holiday but now I'm ready to go home."

It was a moment I shall never forget. Too choked to speak, I could only thank God for giving me such a loving and devoted companion.

TWENTY-TWO

We arrived back in Bournemouth to find Kevan and Ann had taken good care of the house and the dog but were concerned about my mother in London. During the few phone calls they had made, they thought Ray had sounded terse and fraught.

I thought the same when I phoned to say we were home, so wasted no time in driving to London to collect mother. Shelagh went with me and we were shocked when we entered Ray's flat. Before a word was spoken between any of us, the tension between him and my mother could be felt. She burst out sobbing and begged to be taken home as soon as possible, while Ray barely spoke to either of us as she prepared to leave.

We learned later that quarrelling had broken out between them only a day or two after her arrival. To be as fair as possible, I am not suggesting all the fault lay with my brother. The flat was claustrophobic and my mother, in the way of her generation, liked to take over domestic tasks herself. As she was very old and her sight was so bad, this could cause accidents and be an irritation to a younger person.

At the same time she meant well. She needed patience but no matter how he tried, it seemed my brother could not forgive her for what had happened in his childhood. It wasn't that he lacked love for her: future events were to prove that. His emotions were ambivalent and when he was left with her for any time, the negative side of the relationship always seemed to emerge.

So we took her home, where it was weeks before she ceased fretting about the things Ray had said to her. Why couldn't he understand she had only been trying to help him? Why couldn't he see she loved her two sons equally? I found it very distressing and can't deny it took some of the gloss off the holiday.

Although I had sinned against my own disciplines in taking a holiday before completing a novel, it seemed to have done me good because I returned to *The War God* with renewed energy and problems of its structure were now solved as if they never had existed. Within three months I was able to send the completed novel to my Cassell editor.

Previous to this he had asked to see my first draft, something I hated doing because I tend to omit alterations which I make later. But as he and Corgi had jointly commissioned the novel, I could hardly object, and, as I feared, he had found faults which I knew myself needed correction.

Now it seemed all his doubts were dispelled. He told me he couldn't fault the book in any way and felt certain it would do well.

This proved to be true, certainly as far as the United States went. I airmailed a manuscript copy over to Arthur Pine and six weeks later received a letter saying he had sold the novel to Bantam Books, his seventh sale for me within a year.

With that large work finished, I took the opportunity to pay a quick visit to the States. My editor at Bantam had said he would like to meet me and I felt it was also time I met Arthur Pine who had been so successful with sales. When I told Tom Carlile of my intentions, he invited me to spend a few days at his house on Long Island.

I would have liked to take Shelagh with me but she couldn't take another holiday off work that year, nor was she particularly keen to visit New York. At this time its high crime statistics had gained it an unsavoury reputation in Europe.

Tom met me in at Kennedy Airport and took me to his house where I met his young and attractive English born wife, Ann, and their two children John and Helen. As it was my first visit to the States, Tom, who had worked for a New York newspaper in his youth, spent the first two days taking me round some of his old haunts as well as to some of the city's most celebrated places.

In some ways I was disappointed by New York, although I soon realized the reason. Brought up like so many of my generation on films like *42nd Street* and *The Lullaby of Broadway,* it was a disappointment if not a surprise to find how tawdry 5th Avenue and Broadway were with their strip clubs and shady cinemas. I was also disappointed by the skyscrapers. I had expected them to dominate with their massive presence but I found myself hardly noticing them as Tom and I trod the sidewalks.

Perhaps the heat had a debilitating effect on the spirit. It was August and the heat wave we had experienced in Africa seemed to have followed me. The streets were sweltering and every morning and evening warnings were given on the radio and television for diabetics and heart sufferers not to travel in the subways. Physically it didn't seem to affect me but Tom looked quite grey on the days we spent in the city. It became easy to understand why New York had so many homicides, and the evening news provided grisly details of the murders that had been committed that day.

I phoned to make an appointment to see Arthur Pine and Tom asked if he might come with me. In his role as a film publicity agent, he was in contact with many of the leading stars of the day and one of them whose name I have forgotten had given him permission to write a series on her life. As he needed an agent to handle the work, Tom wanted me to introduce him to Pine.

With his help, I found Pine's offices in Broadway. Pine was a stocky, balding man with what I understood was a Brooklyn accent. His son, who came into the office to meet me, was very different in appearance, being tall, slim, and good looking. They both congratulated me on the sales my books had made in the States and asked what I was working on at the moment. When these pleasantries were over, Tom was invited into the office. I introduced him and then sat back for Tom to put his case.

What followed fascinated me. All the time I had known Tom I had found him a modest, unassuming Texan who impressed by his height but never by his self-esteem. But when Pine senior enquired about his role in the film world, Tom told him without batting an eye that he was the leading publicity agent in the film business.

It was probably true but it wasn't the kind of remark an Englishman would make. Astonished, I watched for Pine to show the reaction a London agent might have shown. Instead I noticed immediate respect and interest. It taught me a lesson I have never forgotten. In America self-esteem is everything and so enables one to understand why it is the extroverts who become the celebrities. Modesty gets one nowhere. If one doubts this, watch and listen to the so-called celebrities featured today on our television screens.

I met my Bantam executive editor the following afternoon. Named Roger Cooper, he was a youngish man who appeared full of drive and enthusiasm and seemed genuinely glad to meet me. He told me he liked my work very much and intended to push it hard until my name was known internationally.

It was not the first time I had heard such a promise and at first I took it with a grain of salt. But from the time Cooper spent with me and the interest he showed on aspects of my life not related to my books, I began to believe I had met an editor, and a highly important one at that, who intended to keep to his word. I felt my American trip had been worthwhile when I finally left his office.

Tom had to fly to Los Angeles to publicise a new film on the day of my return flight so I had to make my own way to the airport. There I was told my flight, by Laker Airways, was delayed for nine hours. As this was a long time to fill in, I had a meal and then went for a walk.

It was still very hot and there were few people on the sidewalks. As I approached an overhead bridge, two young men approached me and one asked me for a light. Aware this was often a mugger's ploy to put a man off guard, I tucked my briefcase more firmly beneath my arm when I told them I did not smoke.

My reason for this caution was the package of dollars inside the briefcase. Before I had left England my accountant, who needed dollars for one of his clients, had asked if I would bring back the cash from my Bantam sales when he would then make conversion into sterling. As currency exchange of this nature had recently been made legal, I had seen no reason to refuse and so I was carrying the dollars with me.

This gave me no wish to be mugged. So I gave my two characters a smile and made to move on. But then the larger one stood in front of me and asked what I had in my briefcase. Wondering if he had X-ray eyes, I said only a few papers and documents but in any case they had nothing to do with him. At that the smaller one drew out a knife and made a menacing gesture.

That was all Mr Hyde needed. Until then he had allowed his better half to be more cautious and perhaps more civilized in handling the situation. But if there was one way to bring Hyde from his cave it was a threat. What he said to them I don't know but it was enough to make the one with the knife back away.

What Hyde would have done then I have no idea but fortunately the howl of a police car settled the issue. I never saw the car but with a curse the would-be muggers turned and ran away. Muttering my thanks to Hyde I wasted no time in getting back to the airport where I still had seven boring hours to wait before my flight home arrived.

The news of my Bantam interview delighted Shelagh. "The one thing you've needed but never had," she said. "An enthusiastic editor to market your books. Now you've got one in the biggest paperback publisher in the world. This is the turning point. You'll see."

I wanted very much to believe her and as the weeks went by and letters from Roger Cooper about *The War God*, which he was editing, expressed his enthusiasm I think I succeeded. Life became lighter and every effort seemed worthwhile again.

That is until the 26th October when I received another letter from Roger Cooper. It began innocuously enough with complimentary comments on some changes I had made to *The War God* and his second paragraph, beginning with the words 'I have some important news to tell you' made it seem something exciting was happening in the promotion campaign I believed he was waging for me.

I read on and then words seemed to freeze on the page. I quote them verbatim: 'As from November 5th I will be joining Berkley (another, though much smaller mass market paperback company) as Vice-President and Editorial director. The decision was a difficult as well as a sad one but I am very excited about the opportunities for me at Berkley.'

That was not all. He went on to assure me *The War God* and the *633* titles would still be handled with 'great care' by his successors. Although dismayed by the news, Shelagh tried to console me by this assurance but by this time I knew too much about publishers and their politics. New editors seldom showed enthusiasm for the books of their forebears. Empire building is the name of the game and new men bring in their pet authors and squeeze out their forebear's protégés in a dozen subtle ways, not least by denying them attention and publicity.

So once again a dream bubble had burst. I think this time it hurt Shelagh more than me. Perhaps I had already decided one could defeat anything but the stars. So I poured us both a drink, then took her in my arms. I think I said to hell with it all, but I knew full well that on the morrow I would begin another novel.

TWENTY-THREE

The War God suffered precisely the same editorial fate in England as in America, although in the English case three editors came and mishandled it before it was published. By the time the final man took over, all the promises I had been made that it would be treated as a major novel and be given bestseller status had been long forgotten.

Evidence of this came when I was shown a jacket design of the book. It featured a jeep tearing past a burning building with an enlarged soldier, standing above it with a semi-automatic weapon in his hands. Its juvenile effect horrified me and I made an immediate complaint to Cassell via Pat White, my agent. She was equally dismayed by the juvenile image and said so. In return we were told our complaints would be noted and then heard no more. The reason was precisely the one I believed would happen in America. The new editors had their own favourites and past acceptances received only minimum attention.

I received my courtesy copy of the book just before Christmas and found it was wrapped in that same dreadful jacket. I sent a copy to Pat White and she wrote a long and critical letter to Jeremy Greenwood, who was the new editor handling me. To avoid sounding as if I am exaggerating my case, I quote parts of it verbatim below.

'Having been present at a lunch with the author, Alan Earney of Corgi, and Mike Legat, I know that *The War God* was to have been treated as a major book, and, upon its delivery, proved it deserves to be. When Frederick E Smith's earlier book, *The Tormented* was published, both Mike Legat and Michael Catt acknowledged that they had misjudged the book in their promotion and that the author could fully expect the promotion of his next major book would, providing it met editorial standards, be given the bestseller status which, lamentably, *The Tormented* was not. That included national advertising, an Australian publicity tour, etc, etc. . . .

'In the summer the author was shown a jacket design for *The War God,* but clearly no notice was taken of his comments because the jacket hasn't changed at all since the design stage. In my view, and I am not alone in this, this is simply the wrong jacket for the book. The main figure bears no resemblance to the central character, and appears rather weak-faced, even in the wrong military cap. This jacket makes the book look like a war comic.'

Pat went on to comment: 'Sarah Saugman's letter to Fred Smith, having assumed responsibility for the "seeing through" of publication of *The War God*, alas, only arouses fears of a good deal less in the way of advertising and promotion than was promised him theretofore ...there is no mention of non-trade advertising of *The War God*, promotion, etc.... I cannot believe that an incredibly readable novel about the manipulation of war, by an established writer, won't sell — but it won't sell if there is no national advertising, nor public push for it.

'Surely we are all in this together — you have a marvellous and very saleable novel which at the moment looks as if it is being published anonymously ... the promises made by directors of the company aren't being honoured. What a loss for us all if the stops aren't pulled out for *The War God*.'

The stops never were pulled out although Pat, Alan Earney, and myself went together to Jeremy Greenwood's office in a final attempt to have the jacket design changed and the book given the promotion it had been promised. Alan Earney, of course, was concerned that the jacket and the lack of publicity would drastically limit Corgi's paperback sales, which proved to be the case.

It was all in vain. Although I personally obtained a few radio broadcasts, including a quiz programme, *The War God* was left by Cassell to languish under its appalling jacket and without public promotion its sales in 1980 reached little more than 3,500 copies. Moreover, although the reviews it did receive were superlative, with one critic describing it as the only war book he had read with a moral and others saying what a film it would make, it soon became clear that the jacket had prevented many serious critics from reading it.

In other words Cassell had done exactly the same thing for me as they had done for *The Tormented*, and lost me another bestseller both as a hardcover book and a paperback, as well as two more years of my writing life.

It was the last time I believed in the promises of princes. Although it gives me no pleasure to say it, I was left without a modicum of trust in the honour of editors or the publishing houses that employ them.

By the summer of 1980 I had finished the first draft of *Operation Titan*, the sixth and last book in the *633* series, and needed to visit the river Loire in France. Remembering how David had enjoyed our trip to

Italy, I asked if he would care to come along and he accepted with enthusiasm.

A comment or two about this sixth book might be of interest. I had now reached the time in the war when the invasion of Europe was imminent and I wanted to involve my squadron in that titanic operation. My plan was to give them the task of destroying a certain bridge over the Loire after the invasion had begun.

This could not be done earlier because the interdiction air raids that destroyed bridges, railheads, and other transport facilities prior to the invasion had to be carefully spaced out so that the Germans could gain no hint from them where the attack would come. Thus while most of the bridges over the Loire were destroyed, one large bridge that could carry the massive Tiger tanks was left standing. As there were two divisions of Tigers south of the Loire, it was hoped this bridge's immunity would fool the Germans into believing the attack was coming elsewhere.

However, once the invasion was launched, it was imperative this bridge was destroyed before the huge Tigers could cross it or they would destroy the lighter skinned Allied tanks that were landing on the beachheads.

Such was the task, based on fact, that I set my squadron. But how could they be certain of success? In those days bridges were notoriously difficult to hit from the air and many had required numerous missions before being destroyed. The viaduct over the camping site where David and I had spent those pleasant days was a good example, as I discovered in my research. It had been visited by 617 Squadron but even the earthquake bomb dropped nearby had not brought it down.

My bridge couldn't afford the luxury of numerous visits. It had to be destroyed in one attack or the invasion might fail.

I racked my brains for a long time on this until I remembered Barnes Wallis's second weapon, the Highball. Designed to spin as it fell from an aircraft, its purpose was to crawl down the side of a ship and explode below the waterline where protective armour was thin. However, after it completed its trials and went into production, someone pointed out that we had more ships than the Germans and if it were used against them, they would soon gain its secrets and use it against us, whence it would do far greater damage. So it was put into mothballs until Germany was defeated and it could be used against Japan.

As a Mosquito could carry two of these bombs, my plan went as follows. I would arm ninety per cent of my squadron with inert Highballs (that is bombs that were not fused). These would be dropped on the river, would bounce over the torpedo booms, and crawl down to the base of the bridge. This would continue until the concentration of the bombs was sufficient to destroy one of the piers. On my estimation this would require a total charge of 19,000lbs of Torpex. Then a fused bomb or two would be dropped to detonate this charge and the combined blast would bring down the bridge.

The idea seemed sound enough but as always the solving of one problem brought another in its wake. To drop these Highballs accurately and also to avoid the worst of the flak, my aircraft would have to approach the bridge at river level and almost certainly the Germans would have barrage balloons anchored nearby to prevent such an attack. How could the Mosquitoes pass through lethal balloon cables?

The only answer was to fit cable cutters on the leading edges of their wings but a Mosquito's wing was made of wood and would never withstand the initial impact of a cable before it slid into the cutter. The obvious answer was to fit a metal strip to the wing's leading edge but could this be done on a Mosquito? Would the wings stand it, or, alternatively, would it slow the aircraft down to a dangerous degree?

Here I was helped by my old friend, Stewart Cottingham, who worked at that time for British Aerospace. He knew Frank Jeffrey, who had been a wartime colleague of Barnes Wallis, and he arranged a meeting for me.

Jeffrey was an elderly man by this time but was as bright and alert as a squirrel. At first I had the impression he saw me as a frivolous novelist playing with a subject I knew little about, but when he learned I had served nearly seven years in the wartime RAF and one of my subjects had been armament, he began taking me more seriously.

As I was interested in his dealings with Barnes Wallis, I persuaded him to tell me about them before asking my questions. One of the things I remember vividly dealt with their ground testing of Highballs. He and Wallis had rigged up a gadget inside a factory that spun the giant circular bombs at great speed and I didn't need Jeffery's laugh to tell me the risks they had taken. Had one of the huge bombs broken free, its gyroscopic spinning would have sent it bounding and crashing through the factory and God knows what else outside. Such were the chances taken in wartime.

Seeing he was enjoying his memoirs, I ventured my first question. "You worked on Mosquitoes with the Highball. In your opinion, could their wings have taken a metal leading edge without seriously affecting their performance?"

His glance was sharp. "How do you know about that?"

I was puzzled. "About what?"

"How did you know we'd put metal strips on their wings?"

I gave a start. "Are you saying you did?"

"Yes. I can't remember why but it was done."

I was hugging myself. "How did it affect them?"

"From memory, very little. They lost a few knots in speed but it wasn't significant." His voice turned curious. "Why do you want to know that?"

I now explained my story line. For a moment I thought he looked excited but when I finished, he shook his head. "It wouldn't work. Your crews couldn't guarantee to hit the bridge piers and even if they did, the Highballs would squirt off and go through the arches. You'd never build up a sufficient concentration to bring a bridge down."

I hope I didn't sound too triumphant. "No, that wouldn't happen. To prevent saboteurs moving along the rivers, the Germans strung steel nets between bridge piers. It was done before torpedo booms were set up but afterwards they were left as a second line of defence. As they were made of heavy steel mesh to resist wire cutters, they'd have taken the impact of an inert bomb striking them. Your Highballs would have worked their way down the nets and settled together on the river bed."

He gazed at me, then his eyes suddenly shone. "You're right. I think it would have worked. My God, why didn't anyone think of it? We'd put in all that work on the damned things and nobody thought of this."

Before I left he gave me photographs of the experiments he and Wallis had carried out and which I still possess. Then, feeling like one of Churchill's secret boffins, I returned home and made preparations for our trip to the Loire.

In all David and I were away a fortnight. It hadn't any of the exciting moments of our Italian journey but was enjoyable enough, although it did rain for the first three days. Nevertheless, it cleared when we reached the Loire and we spent the remaining days cruising around the valley examining each bridge in turn. It wasn't easy finding one that met all my requirements but eventually I settled on one and took my photographs and made my notes.

On our way back we stopped at the small French town of Chateau Renault to see Joe Wilkinson, my friend and one-time neighbour with whom we had shared family holidays in Spain. Joe had told me earlier that he would be staying there that week on some business venture and if we were in the vicinity to call on him.

This we did and spent a happy evening with him in one of the local estaminets. Then we said our farewells and started back for England.

For once it had been an uneventful trip and although David and I shared many laughs together, my foremost memories are of the evenings in the Dormobile after supper and wine. David's bed was the one that ran across the caravan and he would lie there in the mellow lamplight, puffing his pipe and listening to the tapes I had brought with me. Bing Crosby and Perry Como singing the old songs were his favourites and I can't think how many times he asked me to play them. After all the storms and disappointments life had thrown up, there was a simple tranquillity about those moments that I remember with nostalgia, more so perhaps because this was the last trip we made together.

TWENTY-FOUR

That same year I had a letter from Mike Legat asking me if I would give a talk at the Writers' Summer School at Swanwick. Now retired from publishing, he was chairing the conference and thought a talk about the things that had happened to me while researching my novels might be of interest to the assembly. From memory the talk was titled The Adventures of a Novelist.

I agreed and in August made my way to the Hayes Conference Centre. Set in spacious grounds it was an impressive complex and at first I was surprised such a large venue had been chosen for a writers' conference.

I soon realized the reason as cars and bus loads of writers and would-be writers began arriving. Although it might seem difficult to believe, until then I had known nothing about such conferences or that so many people wanted to write, and was astonished to learn that meetings of this kind were commonplace all over the country.

Nevertheless, with a guest list of over four hundred, Swanwick seemed to be the queen of them all and I learned that applications to attend were always in excess of the rooms available. It was also soon obvious that it was mainly women who wanted to write, because they outnumbered men ten to one, and without being sexist I have to admit that the sound of hundreds of excited women in full fortissimo in the huge dining room that evening was somewhat unnerving. Certainly it made me wonder what madness had prompted me to accept Mike Legat's invitation.

To make things worse my talk came towards the end of the week so I had four days to browse on it. But it did give me time to study the various courses on writing that the school provided. It also enabled me to meet other writers, and I found this a real pleasure.

I gave my talk in the main hall in front of what seemed the entire multitude and to my relief it seemed to go quite well. Afterwards, a number of people approached me to say how much they liked my books.

To a non-writer it might seem strange to hear the thrill this gives an author but in simple truth writing is one of the loneliest professions on earth and unlike other artistic pursuits, it has next to no feedback. A playwright or an actor will know immediately whether he or she is a success by the reaction of the audience but a novelist has no such response. Apart from the year or two he has to wait before his book is published, the reaction it receives is usually impersonal. Good reviews might come in but there is nothing to take the place of one sincere human being expressing his or her pleasure. For the first time in my life I experienced this from people I had never met before, and when one lady librarian told me my books were the most popular in her library, I was like a cat with a bowl of cream. While I had no idea at the time that this introduction to literary conferences was going to open a new chapter in my life, I did know I wanted to attend Swanwick again in 1981.

The Cassell saga ended dismally the following year. A letter dated 3rd February from Jeremy Greenwood announced that the company was phasing out its general publishing activities. In effect this meant that back list books would be remaindered except a selected few from authors such as Winston Churchill and Robert Graves. Current books would continue to be handled until their momentum ran out. New fiction would no longer be accepted.

It was a double blow for me. Not only did it mean my four published *633 Squadron* novels would be remaindered but it also meant there was no longer a hardcover house for the last two in the series, *Cobra* and *Titan*. 1979 had been a false dawn indeed.

Although it was promised that *The War God,* being a current book, would receive normal attention, in my view this promise was not kept. Early in the year Tyne Tees Television invited me to take part in a literary programme called 'A Good Read'. As this particular programme was devoted to novels about war, this seemed to me an ideal opportunity to advance the cause of *The War God* which until then had been so ineptly handled. As the programme was to appear on each of the commercial stations in turn, my suggestion was that bookshops in each catchment area should be alerted and offered books on sale or return during the week of the broadcast. In turn I would make certain the book was well featured during the programme.

I could hardly believe it when Cassell turned down my suggestion. In the past when I had suggested television advertising to publishers, their answer had always been: "We would love to do it but can't afford the cost." Now here was an offer of half an hour free time, worth thousands of pounds, and no one was interested. The only excuse I received was that bookshops were unlikely to stock a book that had been published the previous year. The word unlikely should be noted. No one had the business acumen to ask booksellers if they minded making a profit out of a last year's book. The bookshops' interests as well as the author's were totally ignored.

I took the train up to Newcastle and took part in the TV programme. It was dominated by a man named Cooper who was billed as a publisher of factual military books. He prepared the scene beautifully for me by stressing he greatly disliked war novels and would never dream of touching them. I don't remember if I made the point that only fiction could slice through the lying propaganda that war produced and tell the truth. Perhaps not because I was still simmering at the opportunities lost.

I flew back on a commuter aircraft which damaged its undercarriage and had to have running repairs before I arrived back in Bournemouth. When we finally touched down I wondered if for the sake of air travellers everywhere I ought to put a flight embargo on myself.

I now had to decide whether to let all my printed titles be remaindered or whether to buy them and try to dispose of them myself. As I had never had my books remaindered before, I took a deep breath and ordered them all.

A couple of weeks later a huge lorry and trailer drew up outside our house. As Shelagh gave me a puzzled look, I tried to look nonchalant. "It's probably my books," I said. Leaving her to faint, I ran out and began helping the driver to carry the parcels inside. There were dozens of them, each containing forty hardbacks. When we finished unloading them, our large room at the rear of the house was stacked from floor to ceiling. Staring at the piles, Shelagh nearly fainted again. "What are we going to do with them all?"

"We're going to do what the publisher didn't do," I told her. "We're going to sell them."

"But how?"

"We're going to offer them to shops and to public libraries all over the country. I'm told my books are popular in libraries. Well, now we'll find out. I'll seek out all the addresses and markets and we'll canvass for orders."

This we did and although it took us two years we eventually sold every copy. The irony was that we made far more money out of the transactions than if the sales had been made through the normal trade procedures. I found it highly satisfying, feeling that I had proven how inept and inefficient so many publishers are.

Operation Cobra had been scheduled for hardcover publication in 1981. As it no longer had Cassell for a home, Severn House publishers made a bid for it and Corgi accepted. This meant that both hardcover and paperback versions came out that same year.

While these things were happening my mother was beginning to fail. At first she had no specific ailment, instead a series of complaints that in a person of ninety years might or might not be serious.

As anyone will know who has lived with an old person, this caused medical difficulties. Neither Shelagh nor I had ever been people who called on doctors without good reason, but by this time there was no way my mother could be taken to a doctor and await her turn in his surgery. If she needed a doctor, we had to send for one, and as we never knew if any of her ailments were serious or not, we found ourselves calling for one more and more often.

At this time our doctor was a young man and clearly felt his calls were wasted on someone so old. Sensing this, my mother urged me not to bother him and I did try to cut our calls down to the minimum. At the same time she was my mother, who in the past had worked herself to the bone for us, and the last thing I wanted was something to happen to her because I was too inhibited to ask for help.

The affair came to a head when we heard a bump one morning and found mother lying on the floor beside her bed. It seemed that in trying to reach the toilet, she had suffered a severe pain around her heart that had caused her to collapse. We helped her back into bed and then phoned for the doctor.

He was a long time coming and pushed past me without a word when he arrived. After examining her, he left her room without speaking, then waited for me at the foot of the stairs. "Why did you call me? Your mother's heart's as good as can be expected in someone of her age."

I thought it was one of the most ridiculous things I'd ever heard. "How could I know that? She collapsed and complained of severe pain."

He made a gesture of contempt. "It was probably hysteria. Old people often panic when they get a pain."

I thought of that dear old lady who had suffered more hardship, suffering, and pain in her life than this little brat could even visualize, and the Hyde in me began to bristle. "My mother doesn't panic. She's one of the bravest people I've ever known. She's always telling us how sorry she is for causing us so much trouble and she always apologizes to you when you come. If she said she'd suffered a pain, it was a hell of a pain."

He then said the thing that makes all authors' hackles rise. "I think you tend to exaggerate these things. Perhaps it has something to do with your profession."

That was all Mr Hyde needed. It was something of a miracle he didn't pick the brat up and throw him straight through the door. "Now I'll tell you something. If you were half a doctor, I wouldn't have to keep calling you to see that old lady. You'd do what doctors used to do when they were real doctors: You'd pay a call every week to see if she is all right. I'm not even sure you're not supposed to do so under the National Health Charter."

Hyde must have looked more than angry because the brat went pale and almost ran from the house. The next morning an envelope was pushed into our letter box. Inside it was a terse note telling us he no longer wanted us on his panel and we would have to find another doctor.

Shelagh found me sitting on the bottom of the stairs with the letter in my hand. She gazed down at me, "What is it, darling?"

I showed her the letter. She shook her head. "What an obnoxious little man. But why are you laughing?"

I don't remember if I was able to tell her. It just seemed to me that there is only one way you can win in this topsy-turvy world and that is to treat it with the derision it deserves.

All this happened during the late Seventies. In 1980 mother began passing blood and we feared her kidneys were breaking down. However, on investigation it was discovered she had tumours in her bladder that needed surgical treatment.

This was carried out successfully but I was warned on hearing she would need an investigative cystoscopy and possibly a similar operation every six months. This proved to be true but as she needed an anaesthetic each time, the third one almost proved too much because the surgeon found it difficult to resuscitate her. As a consequence he asked if we wanted to continue the treatments.

I contacted my brother for his opinion but he couldn't make up his mind and left the decision to me. In fairness it was a difficult decision to make because we did not know what the long term implications might be. Yet at the same time there seemed little point in her having treatment that in itself seemed likely to kill her.

I agonized about it for weeks before asking for the treatment to cease. Time proved it to be the right decision but not in the way I would have wished because that Christmas she suffered another attack of chest pains. It so happened that Ray was with us that Christmas and because she had suffered these chest pains before, for once Ray and I were in accord. She needed to see a heart specialist without delay.

By this time we had a more sympathetic doctor and she was admitted into hospital. Our relief turned into dismay, however, on our first hospital visit. Some bureaucratic administrator, no doubt because of her age, had put her into a geriatric ward. Nor was she in bed. When we entered the ward she was sitting in a chair among a group of senile old people facing a television screen. From their expressions it was clear most were under drugs and among them my mother looked lost and terrified.

Her face lit up when she saw us and she begged to be taken home. When we spoke to the ward sister, she told us a heart specialist had not yet seen her but her condition was being monitored in the meantime. When I asked why she was in a geriatric ward when her faculties were still unimpaired, I was told it was no such thing. It was just a ward for people with the similar health problems. I remember my dreams that night were full of senile old faces with my mother looking terrified among them.

It all ended in the deepest irony, a finale not unknown to us. The heart specialist declared her heart was not too bad for a person of her age and prescribed drugs to ease her attacks. But before she could return home, she caught a cross infection that gave her a form of bronchial pneumonia.

Her last days make me flinch to record them. Although heavily sedated and so unable to recognize us at her bedside, she must have been suffering agony because all her feverish cries were for God to take away her pain. This from a woman who had endured pain without complaint from conditions too personal to record. My guilt at that time seemed almost as severe as her pain. I had wanted her to go into hospital and this suffering was the result.

To his credit, my brother came to stay with us at this time and we shared the bedside vigils. For the hours I wasn't there, I told the nurses to phone me immediately if her condition deteriorated and I would be there within a quarter of an hour.

Ray returned to London for a couple of days but returned on the Sunday. It was a day when my two sons, as well as Ray, went with us to the hospital.

I went into the room first and to my horror saw her lying with her dead eyes staring at the ceiling. After all our visits and all I had told the nurses, she had still died alone with no one to hold her hand.

We had the cremation the following week. I remember Shelagh whispering to me to let Ray walk between us as we entered the chapel and this I did.

The last act was the opening of my father's grave and her urn being laid alongside his. As I stood beside the chaplain and watched a dead leaf flutter down and lie on her urn, my thoughts had never been more bitter. There were the two people who had suffered two wars, depressions, heartbreaks, and yet whose love, faith, and courage had never faltered. People whose rewards were deaths of mutilation and intense pain and were now just dust in two little boxes. Once again I wanted to understand the ways of the God my mother had taught me to love and worship as I walked with Ray and Shelagh away from that pathetic little grave.

TWENTY-FIVE

There is no doubt that some of my negative emotions at this time were due to remorse. Although I had tried to give my parents care and attention, it had consumed a large amount of my life and, with human nature being what it is, there had been times when I had resented the handicap it had imposed on both Shelagh and myself.

This was the case during my mother's last year. After the disaster of losing my deal with Corgi Books and Cassell, I particularly wanted to visit America because Tom wanted to introduce me to a film director who had shown interest in my work. He, the director, was engaged in some project in New York at this time and Tom had kept urging me to come over quickly before the opportunity was lost. In addition there were American writers whom I had met at Swanwick who offered me both accommodation and introductions that might prove useful.

Worried that I might lose everything I had fought for over the years, such thoughts made me feel I was resenting my mother's dying days and filled me with shame.

This was my state of mind when I visited the States shortly after her death. To make matters worse I had missed the film director who was now filming in the Bahamas or some such far off place, and the other introductions promised me came to naught.

I was helped by friends giving me accommodation for a few days in a small village near Milleton in upper New York State. The village was opposite the woods of the Tatonic Reservation and for some days I roamed about them in the snow — spring had still to appear — and gradually the exercise and the clean air began to put life into some kind of order and sense again.

I was further helped by being driven to Cape Cod for a weekend. On the way my gremlin played one of his smaller, more comical tricks. The driver of the huge car I was travelling in had borrowed it from a friend and she didn't know how to dip its headlights. So when dusk came she told me she would need to stop and examine the dashboard. As the road was busy at the time, we waited until we saw a garage forecourt and pulled into it.

It turned out the garage was closed, so we had no help there. Unable to find the right switch myself I told my driver to stay in her seat while

I jumped out and stood in the headlights beam to check when the beam dipped.

She was still trying to find the right switch when a siren suddenly began screaming. A few seconds later a police car swung into the forecourt and two policemen leapt out, each with a drawn revolver. As I stood paralysed in the headlight beam, another car swung in and disgorged two more policemen. We were surrounded.

The largest policeman of them all, gun pointed as if he expected me to draw on him at any moment, demanded what I was doing. As I was trying to tell him, the second policeman closed on me. I had clearly committed some heinous crime.

I was ordered back to the car where my driver was also being held at gunpoint. In the meantime the huge policeman told his colleague to put in a call to the stolen car register.

Understanding now the reason for the alarm, I began to laugh. At first I received only scowls. "What's so funny, bud?"

I tried to explain. But they had clearly heard it all before because the guns remained trained on us. Then the huge policeman moved closer. "You English?"

"Yes," I said. "I'm over here on business."

As he glanced at his colleagues I felt the tension slacken. "What kind of business?"

"I'm a writer," I told him. "A novelist."

That didn't help at all because their suspicious looks returned. But then the second policeman returned from the car radio. "It's OK, Mike. The car's clean."

The atmosphere changed. Guns were shoved back into holsters and scowls turned into grins. "Sorry, folks, but we had to check. You guys looked suspicious with one of you prancing about in those headlights."

I could see their point of view now as well as the funny side of it but my driver couldn't. Like many other Americans she had no great love for her police force, although to be fair I think the incident had frightened her. I gave the huge policeman a wink and he, grinning back, leaned into the car and showed us the right switch to press. Then he and his colleagues took off and we were free to resume our journey.

Although my friend remained unimpressed, I couldn't help breaking into laughter every time I remembered the incident. After all, it isn't every day that a man and his friend are mistaken for Bonnie and Clyde.

I finished the trip with a visit to the United Nations Headquarters. A friend of a friend held an administrative post there and obtained permission to take me round. I attended one of the daily press conferences and was then shown the main assembly halls where the propaganda for world consumption is handed out. Then I was taken round the smaller rooms where the real wheeling and dealing is done. It finished my trip on a high note and although none of it had furthered my career, by the time I flew back to England I felt more able to cope with life's vicissitudes again.

Before returning home, I stopped in London to see how my brother was faring. He was out when I arrived but a young woman who shared the adjacent flat told me he had only gone shopping and should be back soon. Would I care to have a cup of tea with her while I waited?

I accepted and while we sipped tea the girl told me she was worried about Ray. Prior to my mother's death, he had been a good neighbour and always willing to help those around him. Now he had become morose and reticent and one night the girl believed she had heard him weeping as she passed by his door.

At the same time she had often heard him quarrelling with my mother when she had stayed with him. Did I think he was suffering from remorse? If so, would I do my best to help him? He had always been kind to her and she hated to see him distressed like this.

Ray arrived back fifteen minutes later and I saw a change in him immediately. He seemed pleased to see me, however, and he made me welcome. But although he did his best to hide his grief (and he had been an actor) it still hung over him like a cloud. As undoubtedly some of it was due to remorse, I felt a fellow sympathy, and as we discussed my mother and all that had happened, I felt we hadn't been so close for years. I remember thinking how sad and ironic it was that it took my mother's death to do this.

I left after gaining his promise that he would keep in touch and come and see us at his earliest opportunity. As he had told me he'd been having a number of insulin comas of late (in all likelihood due to stress) I was genuinely worried about him but even so I had no idea what the outcome of his grief would be. That shock was to come later.

My last commissioned *633* novel, *Operation Titan*, was published by Severn House, Corgi, and Bantam in 1982. It ended my contract with Corgi and although the books had done well for us both — *633* was in its twenty-sixth edition — Corgi told me that, in general, World War Two novels were going through a 'down' period and were no longer as popular as they had been, not even anti-war novels as I believed my *633 Squadron* novels to be.

Not that my mail bore out this fading interest. Every week I was receiving letters asking when I was going to write more books in the series. But without Corgi's interest and with Cassell no longer taking fiction, there was little point in my writing another.

Instead I was involved in a different kind of novel. It had come about from a conversation I'd had with Alan Earney in 1977. Aware I was writing 'straight' novels between the *633* ones, he had asked if I would care to write a love story for him. He wouldn't be able to pay me anything like as much as he'd paid for the *633s*, but if I fancied the change of genre, he would commission the book.

I accepted for a number of reasons. Even before the offer I had been thinking of writing a novel dealing entirely with the complexity of human relationships. I also had the notes I had made of my father's death, which could find their way into the story. In addition I felt that such a novel would help to liberate emotions that were still locked within me.

So a contract was drawn up. Knowing about my other work and conscious how small the advance was, Alan Earney left out a completion date, which allowed me to write the book as circumstances allowed.

I have forgotten when I completed it, although it was possibly 1982. I do remember feeling satisfied with it, however. As I have already said, fiction is emotion and I doubt if I had written a page of that book without an emotion of one kind or another gripping me. Often I had a lump in my throat and on one or two occasions I'm not ashamed to admit that I couldn't see the typewriter keyboard for tears. There was so much of a story behind the story, and the writing of it drained me. I called it *The Obsession*.

But it wasn't published. Alan Earney liked it but believed the sales wouldn't meet costs in its present form. His reason was the unhappy ending I had given it. If I would change the ending he could publish and felt the book would do well. If I didn't, it would become my only unpublished novel.

I couldn't make such a change. Every instinct in me said the ending was right for the story. I tried to convince him of this but no doubt under pressure from his Board, he wouldn't publish, although he did honour his contract and pay the final instalment of the commission. It was a heartbreak because the novel contained so much I wanted to publish.

However, Corgi had money tied up in the book and so they tried to interest a hardcover publisher whose offer would help offset their advance. They soon found two who liked the novel, Judy Piatkus and Severn House. The Piatkus offer topped that of Severn House and so she obtained the publishing rights.

Although I received no money from this sale, I was delighted that the book was to be published at last. At almost the same time Arthur Pine in America sold it to St Martin's Press. Such is the way the pendulum swings in an author's life.

Before the book appeared Shelagh and I went to South Africa again. As this time Monica wasn't free to holiday with us, we decided to travel round the Union by air and made such arrangements before leaving England.

This time we flew by British Airways and as there was no overflight ban on British aircraft, we had a journey down the east coast of Africa. After re-fuelling at Nairobi, we landed at Jo'burg, where we spent four days with Joan Cowling, Roy having sadly died since our last visit. Barry then collected us by car and took us to Nelspruit, where he and his family were now living.

As we had arranged to be away for six weeks this time, we were able to spend two weeks in Nelspruit, during which time Barry and Rita took us to the Kruger Park again. It was enjoyable but even hotter than the last time. The North Eastern Transvaal was having a heat wave and the thermometer needle was hovering around 45 degrees centigrade most of the time. In the Park the drought conditions were so bad that water was being brought in to save the animals.

Barry was no longer working for the South African Forestry Commission. He and Rita's brother had formed their own timber company. Nevertheless he took time off to show us the beauty spots and Rita couldn't have been more hospitable.

After a farewell dinner in town, we said our goodbyes and took a train back to Jo'berg. Here we caught a plane to our next stop, Durban. It was good to see Boy again although we were both distressed to see how he was failing. His leg was so bad now that he could barely walk across the room. Shelagh felt he should use it more and try to go for short walks but he only gave her his wry, patient smile and told us to use his car and go down to the beach, which we did on most days.

He cheered us up by seeing us off at the airport and we flew back feeling that perhaps his leg was on the mend and he would stage a recovery. We were not to know that was the last time we would see him.

The author in South Africa

We flew on to Cape Town, where Monica met us and took us to the bungalow. Mrs Mac was no longer there, being resident in a rest home. Monica took us to see her the following day and we were shocked to find she was now suffering dementia. It was particularly distressing for Shelagh, who felt her mother did not recognize her. I told her I believed she was wrong and that for a few lucid moments Mac had recognized us all.

For some reason we never took the cable way up my beloved Table Mountain that week. Instead, Shelagh and I walked the beautiful beaches, visited relations in Hout Bay, and I was taken by a friend to see my old airfield again. It had changed so much I barely recognized it, reminding me once again that it isn't always wise to walk back down one's memory lane.

Monica drove us to see Mrs Mac once more before we left. Knowing that Shelagh would believe it was unlikely she would ever see her mother again, my heart bled for her when we finally drove away. But as ever she bore her sadness with the courage I loved so much in her. Then Monica took us to the airport and we were on our way home. It had been a strange kind of holiday, leaving one unsure whether we had enjoyed it or whether its sad moments had outweighed the rest.

TWENTY-SIX

I had a spate of jury duties at this time, which not only forced me to cancel a series of talks but also did nothing to improve my opinion of our adversarial legal system. On the other hand there was encouraging news about the Public Lending Rights position. The argument that authors should be entitled to some financial reward for their books borrowed from public libraries had been going on for over twenty years and until the previous year few if any of us had believed we would live to see justice done. Nevertheless, authors had fought on and as in general they are not equipped for militant action, some of their efforts to influence public opinion had been hilarious.

I had attended one of these affairs three years earlier. I hadn't wanted to go, because, with newspapers giving prominence to a few mass-market authors and their huge advances, and making no mention of the pitiful payments made to more serious writers, I believed the general public would show little sympathy to the cause. But with the Writers' Guild asking all its members to attend, I had gone in spite of my reservations.

The venue was Grosvenor Square and a number of well-known names had promised to lend their august presence, among them Antonia Fraser, Kingsley Amis, and Frank Muir. My train to London had lost half an hour on the journey and so the rally was in full swing when I arrived. Our three celebrities were already addressing a huddle of authors while other writers were parading round the square carrying poles on which fluttered the plea: SUPPORT PLR.

I shouldn't have laughed but I did. It was all so civilized and self-conscious that a blind man could have seen it was useless. Francis Clifford, a lovely writer with a delightful sense of humour, saw my amusement and came over to me. "Are you thinking what I'm thinking, Smithy?"

"I'm certain I am," I told him.

His eyes moved to the well-meaning trio with their loud-hailer. "It's the public we need to reach, not the converted. I can't see this doing that, can you?"

"Let's find out," I said. As a celebrated lady author carrying her banner came opposite us, I checked her. "Excuse me, but do you think the general public know that PLR means Public Lending Rights?"

She gave me a cold glance. "Of course they do. Everyone in the country knows by this time."

"But do they?" I insisted. "Shouldn't we find out first? Otherwise we'll all be wasting our shoe leather walking round the square."

Her stare was an attempt to wither me. "I've never heard anything so ridiculous. Everyone who reads a newspaper knows what PLR means."

"Everyone who reads the Daily Telegraph, the Times, and The Guardian," I said. "But don't more people read the Sun and The Daily Mirror?"

As she gave a contemptuous snort, Francis made his gentle suggestion. "Why don't we ask a few passers-by? It won't take more than a minute or two."

She hesitated, then flung her head impatiently. "Oh, all right. I suppose it can't do any harm."

The word had gone around by this time and two or three dozen writers broke away from the main group and followed us. Francis, looking wickedly amused, stood alongside me as I asked the question to the first passer-by, a man.

At first he looked blank. Then he recovered and said he hadn't a clue. I asked the next one, a woman, and she only shook her head and walked on. I got similar negative replies from the next five but the sixth, an old lady, showed promise. "Oh, yes, I know what it stands for."

My lady celebrity, whose pole had been drooping more and more at the answers, now showed signs of rallying. "Yes," she said eagerly. "What does it stand for?"

The old lady hesitated. "Mind you, I can't pronounce Greek. I'm not a scholar."

My lady celebrity stared at her. "Greek? What are you talking about, Greek?"

The old lady's face cleared. "Now I remember. It's Greek and means Aid for the Armenians. How silly of me to forget."

Of course it was naughty of me to spoil such a self-satisfied rally but all the exhortations can't have been in vain because at long last a bill was passed and in 1982 authors were invited to submit to a PLR office set up in Stockton-on-Tees a list of all their published books. With reprints and paperbacks, I had over sixty titles to send in but I had no idea what payment I would receive.

In fact, I was agreeably surprised. While not receiving the top limit of £5000, my share did put me among the top thirty or so writers out of the many hundreds who received payment. I remember receiving it with a certain wryness as well as gratitude. I couldn't help thinking what a godsend it would have been during those first twenty years when every penny had to be counted. It does seem that life gives its bounty either too early or too late, although when I put the cheque in the bank I thought it was still better late than never.

I was compelled to change my literary agency around this time. The fault did not lie with Deborah Rogers, with whom I'd had a happy and successful relationship. It came about because at that time they dispensed with their film agent. As in the past a substantial part of my income had been derived from film sales or film options, I couldn't afford to allow this side of my career to languish. So I had a long talk with Pat White, who was most understanding, and my affairs were amicably withdrawn.

Consequently, while I looked for an agent who had good screen contacts, my affairs were in my own hands. It was during this time that I had lunch with Judy Piatkus who was shortly to publish *The Obsession*. Prepared for her to ask what book I intended to write next, I passed over to her a piece of paper containing eight lines. They announced my intention to write a family saga based on the lives of my parents. I had always seen them as members of the bravest and most enduring generation this country has borne, and after all that had happened recently I wanted to pay my tribute to them.

They must have been reasonably well written lines because there and then Judy offered to commission two books for quite a reasonable advance. Perhaps she was also influenced by the style and content of *The Obsession* and hoped I would produce two other books like it.

I made it clear from the onset that it was not my intention to write cliché-ridden, stylised stories of the rich and famous and their often dubious dealings. I intended them to be books about real people in real life, struggling to survive and live decently. For this reason, although I hoped I would be wrong, I wasn't too optimistic they would sell in America, where the general standards of fiction had fallen even lower than in Britain, with lust, greed, wealth and exploitation almost obligatory elements.

The truth was they were going to be family books I had long wanted to write but time and money had prevented me. Now after my parents' demise, and with capital we had not squandered, I felt the time had come. It would be work that would bring pain as well as well as pleasure in the writing, but that is the price any work of intimacy demands.

By this time an agent had been recommended to me and after having lunch with him, I felt we could work together. So although I had made the deal with Piatkus myself, I felt it would put us on a good footing if I let the publisher send her draft contract to him so that he could vet it and obtain his commission.

I could have kicked myself when he passed that contract on to me. He couldn't possibly have checked it because there were omissions and clauses that might have seriously penalized me. So now I found myself paying him commission for work I had obtained myself and commission for vetting a contract I was now compelled to re-write myself. It seemed one was punished even for one's sense of fair play in this crazy profession.

The Obsession was published in 1984 both by Piatkus and St Martin's Press. Both used the same jacket design, a photograph of Robin Hood's Bay in Yorkshire with a Victoria Cross lying over it. Although I had not been consulted about it, I liked the design and said so.

Piatkus's publicity manager, Jana Somerblad, was one I had worked with at Cassell. Very efficient, she produced an itinerary of fifteen or more radio stations ready to give me interviews. As the book had a Yorkshire setting, the stations were mostly in the North and Midlands and so I stayed with my old friends, the Ellises and the Barrs, while completing them.

As some interviews were in the mornings, I often found myself rising at five a.m. to reach the cities on time. On other occasions I might have an interview in Manchester in the morning and another in Leeds or Birmingham in the early afternoon, which meant a mad rush by car or between railway stations. It was a taxing fortnight but it was good to have another book out and I enjoyed seeing my old haunts again.

The reaction to *The Obsession* was pleasing. Its reviews were excellent and quite a number of people thanked me for writing it, saying that among other things it was a book that would help an understanding between children and parents and so ought to be on the school reading list.

But I was irritated when people suggested the main character in the story was drawn on myself. It embarrassed me because its character, Tom Reid, had won a V.C. and apart from a war wound medal or two I hadn't won more than a stick of rock. It is true that I had used certain elements from my own life in the book — perhaps more than was wise — but never at any time had I related Tom Reid, even distantly, to myself. It was a misconception that worried me in case it was thought I had tried to glamorise myself through one of my own characters.

It was around this time that my Corgi editor invited me to lunch. Thinking as one does on such occasions that he had a book in mind, I went up to London very willingly. But to my surprise he made no mention of books during the meal. Only when we were driving back to his office did he give his reason for our meeting. He disliked saying it but I would be wise if I began looking for another paperback publisher.

As I had been with Corgi Books since *633 Squadron* in 1964 and they had done quite well out of me, it was a bombshell. I was told that Bantam, the parent company, had instituted a new policy regarding promotional budgets. A much higher percentage of the annual outlay was to be spent on half a dozen big names, whose work was to be hyped to the skies. The other authors, the middle-of-the-list and new ones, would receive diminished budgets and so were likely to wither on the vine. Hence the advice for me to look elsewhere.

At first I found it hard to believe. If other authors than a few big names were to be starved of the little promotion they already received, how could they survive? How would new ones, the seed corn, emerge?

He made no attempt to explain. Perhaps he was as baffled by the policy as I was. Whatever the reason, I had lost a publisher to whom I had been providing books for over twenty years and so perhaps once again my feelings toward publishers are best left unrecorded.

It was not an auspicious beginning for the first novel of my family saga, but by this time I was case-hardened to any blow that might fall. If on some mornings I felt depressed, I would run over my credits. In spite of everything publishers had done to me, I had still published every novel I had written, I'd had a highly successful film made from my work, I had won a literary award; I was published in twenty-four countries, I had filled a dozen scrap books with excellent reviews; and I had at last put away enough in the bank to keep us in old age even if I never sold another work. So who was having the last laugh, I asked myself?

Although most of this self-congratulation was to keep my spirits up, there were one or two other facts that comforted me. For one I had never appeased the market by writing the same kind of book over and over again. For another I had never curried favour with publishers by changing a word or a sentiment I believed in. I felt there couldn't be that many fiction writers who could make the same claims.

Such were my feelings when I began to construct my first saga book based on the lives of my parents. Almost immediately I ran into a problem. One of the main themes of the saga was my grandmother's persecution of my parents, and the way she had alienated my brother from his natural family. To do this successfully I had to show the destructive effects her possessiveness had wrought on us all.

There was no problem in showing the effect on me but what about Ray? He was highly sensitive to criticism and yet since my mother's death he and I had been closer than for many years. I knew he was as pleased by this as I was, and the last thing I wanted was to make him feel I blamed him for the past, particularly now that he was missing mother so much.

My answer was to make him a girl in the story, in the hope he would not recognize himself. Perhaps it was a thin hope but he was not a great reader, and although he supported me by buying my novels, I doubted that he read them in any detail.

With no other option open to me I began the work, which was to begin when my parents were children. To help me I had a few notes from my father about his war experiences and an autobiography of some 40,000 words from my mother which she had courageously written just before her eyesight failed. For the rest of my research I immersed myself in books about the 1890's, the turn of the century, and the First World War. I re-shaped my synopsis half a dozen times, as was my way, and finally produced one that I felt was adequate to work from, although I knew I would make changes as soon as I began to write the novel. Finally I took a deep breath, slid a sheet of paper into my typewriter, and began.

I had little difficulty with the first few chapters but as soon as my major characters became adults I struck problems. Somehow I could not make them read like real people.

At first this seemed quite ridiculous. No people I had ever written about before had been so real to me: they were my parents with whom I had spent so many years of my life. I thought I knew them better than anyone on earth except my wife, and yet here I was tearing up sheet after sheet of paper in frustration.

I had another problem. No one's life is a perfect novel, no matter what they might believe. Like a war, life goes in fits and starts. Between moments of high emotion there are often long periods of inactivity and boredom. Illness intervenes at awkward times. Resolutions are often unsatisfactory. The disciplines of drama are blatantly disregarded.

I was lucky in that my parents' lives were more dramatic than most, but I still needed some changes and embellishments, and these proved surprisingly difficult to make.

The reason, I soon realized, came from my very involvement in their lives. The things that had happened to them in my lifetime had been imprinted on my mind like the grooves on a record, and whenever I tried to change track, my mental needle rebelled and slid back into the original groove.

Of course changes could and were made but the effort to fit them into the natural progression of their true lives was far more difficult than if I had been writing a book with fictitious characters and an invented story line.

But the real problem was the characterization. No matter how I tried, my characters would not come into life, and my frustration grew. Without warm, flesh and blood characters enjoying their youth and young love, and then suffering pain and separation, the entire purpose of the books was destroyed.

I was given the solution when talking the problem over with Val Manning, a writer friend, at a conference. "I had the same trouble when writing about my late husband," she told me. "He was still too close for me to see him in perspective. The tip I was given was to try to see him as a fictitious character. It wasn't easy at first, but once I'd succeeded, everything else fell into place."

I knew immediately she was right and wondered why I hadn't thought of it myself. I made myself stand back from the story and to see its every element as my own creation. The moment I did that, the characters came into sharp focus and the new situations I needed dropped neatly into their allotted places.

The book took me the rest of that year and almost the whole of 1985. Obsessed by it, I neglected to give Shelagh a holiday but I promised we would both have a good one in 1986. The only breaks we had were a couple of weekends and the odd day in the motor caravan — marriage to an author is not for the hedonist — and I spent three days at a writers' conference in Scarborough and another week at Swanwick. I had no option about the Swanwick week because the previous year I'd been voted onto its committee. Both events proved worthwhile, however, because through them I met a fellow writer named Moe Sherrard-Smith who liked my novels and offered to copy edit for me. Her friendship and the spontaneous and generous help she has given me since our meeting have left me hopelessly in her debt.

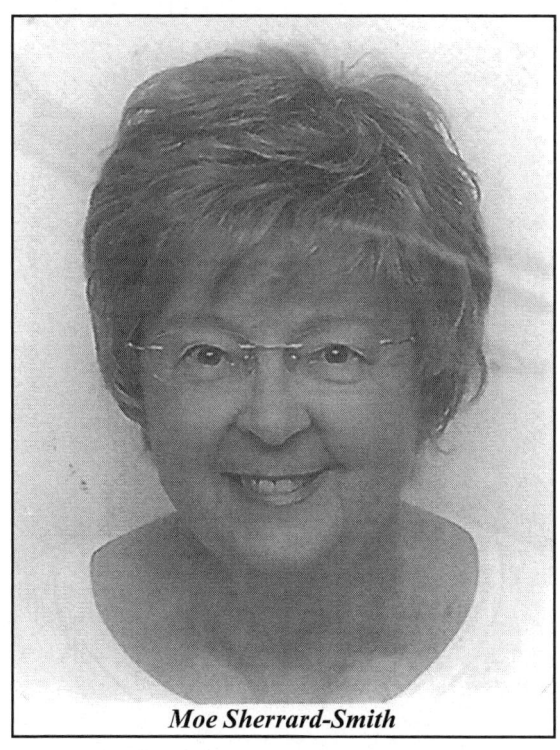

Moe Sherrard-Smith

The Saga book ran to over 100,000 words. Although never satisfied with my own work — and in this case being particularly critical because of its subject matter — I still felt it was as good as anything I had written. But to be certain of it, I edited it three times and re-wrote the final chapter over twenty times before I finally closed the story down and sent it to Moe for copy-editing.

She returned it within a week but I couldn't submit it yet because I couldn't think of a suitable title. I wrote dozens down over a period of a fortnight but none satisfied me. Then, with the deadline only two weeks away, I had to attend a funeral of a friend of one of my sons. Having known him only slightly, I wasn't emotionally involved and to my shame was thinking more about my problem than the service. This showed when we were singing the 23rd Psalm and my eyes fixed on the line 'In the presence of my foes'. To me it was exactly right for the book and I posted the manuscript off to Piatkus under this title the following day.

I had her reply three weeks later. She liked the novel but not the title. Would I give her another? I racked my brain for another week and finally came up with *Rage of the Innocent*. This she accepted and the book went into production.

TWENTY-SEVEN

1986 began with no hint of what was to follow. Judy Piatkus seemed to be full of enthusiasm for *Rage* and had it scheduled for publication in April. I had already started writing the sequel and it was going well. And to add cream to the chocolate cake, Shelagh and I had made provisional arrangements with our close friends, Peggy and Stewart Cottingham, to accompany them to America in May.

So I was optimistic enough to believe it might be a good year. I was to learn otherwise in the most dramatic fashion. On the morning of the 14th March, while Shelagh was out shopping, the telephone rang. It was Blanche Appelby in Bridlington, who had always been a close friend of my brother. Greatly distressed, she told me Ray was dead.

I stood speechless as she told me his flat caretaker had found him lying unconscious on the floor beside his bed. He had been rushed to hospital where he had died at 3 a.m. Death was due to hypothermia and a ketoacidotic (diabetic) coma. It was believed he had been lying on the floor for twenty-four hours before he had been discovered. Blanche had been informed because her address was the first one found in the flat.

I remember putting down the phone and sinking into a chair. I felt numb and slightly nauseous. I was still sitting there when Shelagh arrived home. Like myself, she found it hard to believe. "But what happened? Why was he found on the floor like that?"

I had no idea. "I'll have to go up to London right away," I told her.

Shelagh and Peter, my elder son, went with me. The flat was in an unbelievable state when we arrived. With papers strewn all over the floor and items of clothes draped across pieces of furniture, it looked as if a bomb had burst within it. As the caretaker told us it had happened after the police and the ambulance staff had been there, we could only assume it had been subsequently burgled.

We went to the hospital where his body was being held. A young woman doctor confirmed his death was due to bronchial pneumonia and diabetic ketoacidosis, the former being caused by his lying unprotected on the floor through a bitterly cold night. Wanting to know why he had been lying there unconscious in the first place, I made enquiries at the hospital where he had worked for so many years and reluctantly the facts came out.

It seemed he had at last approached the hospital's diabetic clinic for advice and help. I say at last because for many years he had suffered from hypoglycaemia comas. To those unacquainted with diabetes, these are comas induced by an overbalance of insulin in the bloodstream. The victim stumbles about, sometimes talks gibberish, and is often thought to be drunk. The treatment is to give him or her sugar or some such easily absorbed carbohydrate and recovery is usually speedy.

As I have said, Ray had been having such attacks for years, and they had worried us all because accidents could easily happen during them. Indeed we knew he had had at least two hypos when outdoors in London and in both cases needed hospital treatment. With his living alone, it was a worry for us and we had urged him many times to go to a diabetic clinic and have his condition monitored. I felt his daily intake of insulin was too high and a proper investigation would establish this. But Ray was not an easy person to advise and for years he had taken no notice.

However, it seemed he had done so at last and seen the diabetic clinic at the hospital where he was working. From what I could gather this clinic had first reduced his insulin intake and then decided to stop it altogether. What the doctors had done next was to my mind unbelievably irresponsible. They had given him diabetic tablets to take in place of insulin and then allowed him to go home to an empty flat.

It had been the height of folly. Most laymen know that a change in diabetic medication should always be monitored by keeping the patient under close observation. To be sent away after such a drastic change in treatment was almost asking for disaster.

This had been Ray's fate. That night he had fallen into a diabetic ketoacidosis (sugar coma), fallen out of bed in his unconscious state, and with no one to aid him he had lain there for over twenty-four hours until he had suffered fatal bronchial pneumonia.

To me it was the nearest thing to a criminal act that one could imagine, particularly as it was known Ray was an 'unstable' diabetic i.e. one whose own production of insulin varies from day to day and therefore requires more careful monitoring than the average patient. Although it was hard to find excuses for such behaviour, it might have had some mitigating element if the hospital hadn't known he lived alone. But he had been working there for over nine years and everyone knew his circumstances.

His body was brought to Bournemouth and six members of his St John's Ambulance Section came from London to be funeral bearers. Afterwards they told us how respected he had been among his colleagues. For three years he had won the St John's Ambulance Cup and only that year the Commissioner had congratulated him on his loyal and dedicated service. He was cremated and his urn was later buried in the grave with our parents. I was immensely relieved that his will had not requested a burial with his grandmother.

After the service, one of his colleagues from the hospital who had also made the journey, hinted that I ought to complain about his medical treatment to the local Community Health Council whose function was to monitor cases of malpractice. This I did after first writing a strong letter of complaint to his hospital, which produced only unsatisfactory excuses. The Health Council promised to take up the matter with the hospital and some two or three weeks later I was told that both the doctors involved would be willing to come down to Bournemouth to 'put my mind at rest', as near an admission of culpability as one could expect.

I replied that I had no intention of suffering hours of excuses and medical jargon. I wanted to know what steps were being taken against two doctors whose irresponsible conduct had led to the death of my brother.

As I might have guessed, this caused an immediate closing of professional ranks. From then on my letters from the Health Council made it clear (although, of course, without saying so) that they were either not prepared to fight the establishment or that they had no brief to do so. Unless I was prepared to fight the case alone, the affair was closed. I believed, and still believe, that I had a case for litigation but it had never been my wish to make a claim for money. Money would not bring my brother back. What I wanted was a written assurance from these two doctors that they would never again treat diabetics in such an irresponsible fashion. Losing all faith in the Health Council I made this request in a letter I wrote to them.

Of course I never received this assurance. But by the time I finished with them, I doubted that either doctor would behave in such a way again.

It was an embittering experience. In effect, after working for nine years at the hospital, passing a number of nursing examinations, and putting in over ten thousand unpaid hours in that time — hours confirmed by a posthumous tribute sent to us by the hospital — that same hospital had contributed to his death. Once more I was witnessing the incompetence of the professional classes and the alliances that disguise it.

If that were not ironical enough, it will be noted that I was one of the people who had urged my brother to seek medical advice. It really does seem at such times as if there is no way one can win in this world.

Only a few days after my brother's death I received a transparency of the photograph intended to be used on the jacket of *Rage*. Because of my past experiences with jackets, I had asked for an assurance I would be consulted, and I hold a letter from Judy Piatkus saying: 'I confirm that we will be glad to consult with the author about the jacket and about the presentation of his name in conjunction with the title'.

I had felt safe with this, although the production manager's request that the transparency be sent back to him by return hardly suggested I was being given much of a chance to file a complaint. Certainly a complaint was needed because the photograph chosen to illustrate a book about a young, ardent Englishman and his wife was that of a grizzled French poilu in his nation's battle order. (I was told later that the mistake came about because the production manager, coming from an ethnic minority, hadn't known the difference between the uniforms of British and French soldiers!)

I ought to have gone immediately to the publisher and made a vigorous complaint. But like everything else in life, disasters are relative, and the fact that such a jacket might destroy the book and the eighteen months of work involved in it, seemed an almost unimportant item beside my brother's death. I did write a letter of complaint, but when I read it today it seems almost innocuous. All my energies were being consumed elsewhere.

I admit it was not an easy book to design a jacket for, because history demanded that half the novel was set in the years prior to 1914 and the second half in the war years up to and including the Battle of the Somme. But this could have been overcome by the use of a split design, one scene depicting peacetime and the other war, and this was the design I suggested. I also felt the strap line 'A Family Saga of Love and War' should be included. Apart from the catastrophic effect of a French soldier depicting a very English book, I felt a purely war scene would put off potential woman readers.

I made these points in the full expectation they would be taken and then had to return to my brother's affairs. We had hoped to take our holiday in May but on learning the book was scheduled for publication that month, it had to be cancelled. As we didn't want to upset our friends' plans a second time, we opted for September, thinking everything concerned with the book would be over by that time.

We were almost proven wrong. Firstly the publication date was changed to June, then to July, and then to August, all of which meant the unnecessary cancellation of lecture dates. August could hardly have been worse for me because I had to be at Swanwick between the 15th and the 22nd, and our flight to America was scheduled for the 3rd of September. This left precious little time to fit in a promotion tour.

I received my advance copy of the book on the 6th July. In spite of all my protests, my grizzled French poilu remained on the cover to promulgate a book about a Yorkshire family. The only concession to my complaints was the strap line across the bottom of the picture. There and then I knew the book was effectively destroyed. Even worse, the effect would spread on to the sequel that was to follow.

I did the promotion tour that was expected of me and tried without success to fend off interviewers' questions about the mysterious French soldier. I was helped by Moe Sherrard-Smith going with me to some of the radio stations and taping some of the favourable comments made about the book. I did this because I felt certain the jacket would destroy my chances of getting many book reviews.

I sent copies of these reviews to Piatkus Books in the hope they would include some on the jacket of Book 2. After that appalling jacket of *Rage*, I felt it needed all the help it could get. Then Shelagh and I packed our bags and flew off with our friends to America. I for one was glad to go.

After all that had happened that year I had my doubts about the trip, but in fact it was a success. We needed a complete change of environment and this we found. After two nights in New York our Greyhound coach arrived and took us to nigh every city and landmark of interest in the northern U.S.A and Canada. We visited Washington and the Smithsonian Institute, we rang the Liberty Bell in Philadelphia, we examined the old cannon at Gettysburg, we sped up to Niagara Falls, to Toronto, Chicago, The Great Plains, The Yellowstone Park, Salt Lake City, The Grand Canyon, Lake Powell, The Hoover Dam, Las Vegas, Death Valley, Hollywood. It was a tour that only ended after 5,300 miles of travel when we reached San Francisco. I know Shelagh enjoyed it, which delighted me, and my only problem was a dull ache that I kept getting in my lower abdomen. Thinking it was perhaps caused by the jolting of the coach I tried to put it out of mind.

Not a little punch drunk from our three weeks on the road, we spent a couple of days with an old friend, Bernard Phillips, who was now living with his American wife Patty in the Golden City. Then Barnard drove us to the airport and twenty hours later we were receiving a frenzied welcome by Saffron on our return to Bournemouth. The feeling of warmth and pleasure gained from that welcome and from our two sons was proof enough that, long though the journey had been, it had served its purpose and we were ready and glad to be home again.

TWENTY-EIGHT

I had to plunge into the sequel of *Rage* as soon as we returned. It was due at the publisher the following spring, and although I had worked on it between interruptions for some months before our holiday, it was still a long way from completion.

One problem stemmed from my brother's death. Although I had portrayed him as a girl in my story line, the change had affected the real life story in dozens of ways, and now that he was dead, I seemed completely disorientated. I kept trying to keep on the tracks laid down by the earlier chapters but the motivation and words would not come.

This went on for weeks and for almost the first time in my writing life I began to feel despair. Had I been writing any other kind of novel I wouldn't have been affected in this way. Writing can be therapeutic in taking one's mind off one's loss, but I was writing about my lost family, and every day was reminded about the unfortunate ways they had died.

Nevertheless, there are few problems that cannot be solved by persistence. I kept at my typewriter and gradually the book took shape again. By working through the Christmas holidays I had it finished by early March 1987 which was still within its contractual deadline of the 31st.

This time I had no problem with a title. I believed *In Presence Of My Foes* was even more appropriate to this book than to the first, and this was the title I gave it before posting it off with a sense of relief.

It was now the gremlin began playing his games again. Judy Piatkus acknowledged the manuscript's arrival but warned me she was leaving for America on the 29th and so might not be able to read it before her return two weeks later. During this time I learned, not to my surprise, that Arthur Pine had failed to sell *Rage* in America. Although most of the rejection slips he sent me praised the period and atmosphere of the book, the general complaint was that the book was 'too English' in content.

I found this complaint parochial. Every week books came into this country as American as blueberry pie and we were expected to put up with scenes and situations totally alien to our culture. Yet send the USA a book about an English provincial town and immediately the cry goes up that Americans could not possibly identify with such distant places and characters. Apart from reminding American publishers that human behaviour is much the same whether in Barnsley or Beverly Hills, I would also point out that they are doing no favours to their readers and countrymen by making them all sound like uneducated morons who know nothing about the big world they shared with the rest of us.

May arrived and I was still waiting to hear from Piatkus. Frustrated by such a wait, I began work on a book about pioneer flyers and none were closer to me than Amy Johnson who had once been educated at my own private school.

My plan was not to write a book about her — plenty of those existed already — it was to write a novel about a girl like her whose feats and character tried to fill the gaps missing in her biographies. In other words, to use fiction to illustrate fact, as I had done with the *633* novels.

I don't want to make too much of this project. Its main aim was to be a readable story of high endeavour and turbulent human relationships. With my family saga now looking unlikely to cover my costs, I needed a healthy sale both here and in America to top up our finances.

So I constructed a synopsis with a charismatic American who would become my heroine's lover, picked myself an historic aircraft capable of flying across the Atlantic, gave the two main characters plenty of strife and incidents all linked with the factual happenings of the day, and began work on the book. It went well and helped to ease the frustration of waiting to hear from Piatkus about *Foes*.

Nine weeks passed before I decided it was an absurd time to wait for news of a commissioned novel and penned an impatient letter. When I received no reply in the next fortnight, I wrote again and still heard nothing. By this time I was completely baffled but just when the situation was becoming totally unreal, I received a letter of explanation. It seemed my gremlin had been having the time of his life at Piatkus Books. Firstly the manuscript had been sent to a copy editor who had mistakenly thrown it on the slush pile (rejected and unsolicited manuscript pile) where it had languished for weeks while the staff had struggled to find it.

That was bad enough but worse was yet to come. The copy editor wanted changes both in the writing and the structure as well as the book lengthening, and the manuscript was being sent back to me with her letter explaining these requests.

I confess I was both surprised and aggrieved. Apart from my Bantam editor, who had asked for one or two Americanisms to be included in my last two *633* novels, I had hardly ever been asked to make changes in my novels. Indeed until I began to meet other writers, I had never imagined one would be asked to make the kind of constructional changes now been demanded of me. Whether this meant I'd had a succession of lazy editors or that I had learned to construct soundly myself is not for me to say. But it did and does seem to me that an author should have the skill and professionalism to structure a novel correctly himself. If he needs an editor to do this, then should not that editor have been given credit within the book? (If any editors are still burning at my earlier criticisms, please note that for once I am your advocate.)

In the case of *Foes* I was being asked to make changes that I was certain would harm the novel. Apart from structural alterations, I was being asked to re-write dozens of sentences with adjectives and adverbs that I felt would give an amateurish flavour to the characters.

This was particularly irritating because before posting the manuscript to Piatkus Books I had taken the trouble to send it to Moe Sherrard-Smith, whom I had found to be an excellent copy editor, and she had found no faults whatever in the dialogue or structure.

Nor did I feel the novel was too short. In fact it was 10,000 words longer than its contractual minimum. On top of all this, with over sixteen weeks since its submission, the novel had gone cold on me.

I was feeling even more aggrieved when the manuscript failed to arrive. I phoned the publisher's office and was told it had definitely been posted. I waited a few more days and then made enquiries at the Post Office. A week or two later a parcel looking the worse for wear arrived. One glance at the label explained all. Some typist with anything on her mind but her job had addressed the parcel to me in Eastbourne. In all, five wasted months had passed since I sent the manuscript to the publisher and it was now back in my hands without moving an inch further along the production line. By this time I felt it was quite impossible to deal with publishing houses in any sane and orderly way. One entered into an Alice in Wonderland world where inefficiency was the norm and commonsense was considered a liability.

I made only one major change to the book: I re-located its first chapter. Regarding the rest of the changes, I asked to see Judy Piatkus in person and it was then the truth came out. Her copy editor had previously worked for a woman's magazine, which explained why she wanted a novel of family life to read like romantic fiction. Judy fully agreed my novel fell into an entirely different category and agreed the novel should remain as written. But because of all the confusion and delays, publication had now to be rescheduled for March 1988.

During this time I had finished my book on pioneer flyers, which I called *A Clash of Stars*. As Piatkus Books weren't interested in books on flying, it was eventually published in two volumes by Robert Hale.

During this time, while writing the two family books, I had discovered I needed a third to complete the full story. As Piatkus Books had insisted on a 10% share of any monies received from America, and as neither novel had sold there, I felt it unlikely they would commission a third on the same terms as the others. Consequently I offered to write one for half the previous advances. As the book would take at least a year to write, I knew I would be out of pocket but the project had an importance to me beyond profit or loss. Judy very graciously saw my need for a third book and so accepted my offer. We exchanged contracts in January 1988, and I began work on the third book right away.

We had a happy event in July that year. Barry and Rita flew over from South Africa and stayed with us for two weeks. It was the first time Barry had met his two half-brothers and to our delight the three of them and their wives struck up an excellent relationship on their very first meeting. I remember thinking how happy Shelagh must have felt seeing her three sons laughing and chatting together for the first time.

As I had a few lectures and broadcasts to do during the fortnight, I was able to take Shelagh and the two of them with me and show them something of the country. One weekend stands out in my mind. I had to tutor a course on short story writing at Dartington in Devon and obtained accommodation for them along with Shelagh and myself. The weather was poor — drizzle fell the entire weekend — and yet Rita could be seen running around the grounds in a thin dress and bare feet with Saffron barking alongside her. She had left a heat wave in South

Africa and she loved the feel of rain.

Their fortnight passed only too quickly before they flew over to Europe to complete the rest of their month's tour. Afterwards Rita wrote to say their days in England had been far the most enjoyable, and they would come again as soon as possible. It was good to hear.

While waiting for order to emerge from all the confusion involving *Foes*, I made a quick trip to Germany in October. From my childhood I'd always been fascinated by the Zeppelins the Germans had built before the First World War and from studying their history I had learned about an epic journey one of them had once made. But I needed more information before I could think of handling the story and so I had written the burgomaster of Friedrichshafen, where the Zeppelin museum was based, to ask if he would be so kind as to provide me with an interpreter on my arrival. He agreed and three weeks later I packed up the Dormobile and headed for Lake Constance.

From a fact-finding point of view, the journey wasn't a success. The museum at Friedrichshafen provided me only with information I already possessed. The facts I needed about the epic flight were at Koblenz and I hadn't the time left to go there. But the journey was extremely pleasant and did much to erase the frustration I had been feeling about my work that year.

TWENTY-NINE

In Presence of my Foes was published in 1988. This time the jacket had some link with the story inside and carried two comments from newspapers. One, from the Hull Daily Mail read: *'A telling commentary on class and military warfare'*, and the other, from the Yorkshire Post: *'Beautifully and graphically told.'* With these, of the many reviews the book obtained, I had to be content.

I had a talk to give to the Women's Institute in Bournemouth on publication day, so couldn't begin my tour of radio stations until the morrow. Naturally I made mention of the book and a dozen or so of the ladies made a note of its name and told me they would be buying copies when the talk was over. To ensure there were copies available I went afterwards to the city's two largest bookshops and discovered that not only was there not a copy of the book in either shop but neither manager had heard of it. On making enquiries I discovered the local rep had forgotten I was resident there!

Although by this time I had long ago abandoned any hope of finding my books handled efficiently, my desire to finish the series was as strong as ever and I worked hard on the third book for the rest of that year.

Saffron died in August. For a couple of years his back legs had been troubling him and we had been forced to take him on shorter and shorter walks. By the late summer he could barely reach the park which was only a hundred yards away.

Although he was now thirteen, he never looked an old dog. His body still retained its shape and at times he looked almost youthful. This made the thought of having him put down that much more difficult. Dreading the prospect, we fed him analgesics the vet gave us but one day his bowels gave in and it was obvious the end was near.

When the vet came I told Shelagh not to stay in the room while the deed was done, but I should have known her better than that. "Saffron has been faithful to us all his life," she said. "The least we can do is be with him at the end." So she stayed with me while the needle was inserted. Saffron gave one low cry — the only time in his life I ever heard him cry in pain — and then he was gone.

We had to go out of the house that evening. But what walks were there nearby that Saffron had not shared with us? Finally we took the car and drove miles away. We felt we had lost one of the family.

Shelagh with Saffron (c. 1975-76)

I wrote the third saga novel, which I called *Years of the Fury,* on my first word processor. Although no expert on it, I found its word processing facilities a huge benefit.

This time, to my great relief, there was no quibbling about the book's contents (perhaps the copy editor had moved on to new pastures). Nor, as its time scale took it to 1934 which made it as long as *Rage*, could anyone complain about its length. It could go into production without the hassle that I had suffered previously.

So the family trilogy was completed. In all it had taken me over four years and in purely financial terms I estimate I could have made twice as much if I had spent that time sweeping the roads.

But I had no serious regrets. I had suspected from the beginning that the odds were heavily stacked against large sales, although even in nightmares I had never dreamt the book would be given such a crippling start as that French soldier had given it.

My only real regrets were that relatively few people had heard about the trilogy and so had not been reminded of the courage and steadfastness my parents' generation had shown. But writers must be optimists to survive and I retained the hope that one day the books would reach a wider audience than they had reached so far. I retain that hope to this day.

With the saga finished I entered on an entirely new project. Since my first visit to Swanwick, I had started to give talks and lectures to various universities and colleges on novel writing, and in nearly every venue students had asked if I had written a book on the subject as they would like to buy copies if any were available.

I had done nothing about this until I came into contact with Moe Sherrard-Smith. Needing an agent after my Saga problems, I had asked if she would consider handling my novels and although it was a new role for her she had agreed.

Time was to prove this one of the best moves I ever made because, being highly intelligent, she quickly worked out the best ways of handling an author's work and in the years to follow my novels were published in markets all over the world. She even sold a couple of my *633 Squadron* novels to Japan: a sale I found hard to believe.

However, these sales were to come later. At the present time Moe, who tutored creative writing herself, had also received requests about a book, and she suggested we wrote one together, she asking the kind of questions students often asked us and I attempting to answer them.

The idea appealed to me, not only because she was a patient and pleasant colleague to work with but because her contribution, her questions, were creative in themselves. After receiving my answers to them, she then produced an index and attractive layout which we then sent to a publisher.

It was accepted but less than a month later the firm was taken over and all new acceptances cancelled. We sent it to a second publisher and to our disbelief they were also taken over before a contract was signed. Losing patience we decided to take the risk and publish the book ourselves. So we put up an equal sum of money together and gave the manuscript to a firm in Bournemouth to print. Using the name of Escreet Publications and entitling the book *Write a Successful Novel,* we published it in 1991.

Our next task was to get the book known. Here I was fortunate enough to know a goodly number of radio stations who had featured my earlier books and so we had no difficulty in obtaining interviews that discussed the manual. We also circulated letters to newspapers and magazine that had reviewed my novels,

The reviews that followed delighted us. All were excellent with the one from the Writer's Guild, which had allowed us to include its ideal literary contract in our pages, topping them all. It read: 'Questions are answered with great clarity ... very enlightening to tyro writers but just as interesting to those with a long track record. It is often said that struggling writers can't be helped by seminars on how to write novels, that technical jargon about writing stultifies the pure act itself. That does not apply to this book. The jargon is noticeably absent.'

It was my one and only venture into the self-publication market, but with thanks to Moe it was a success. In the end the manual went to four large editions before our other work prevented our spending more time on its affairs.

Thus 1991 was a good year and not least because Shelagh and I found ourselves another dog. Taking a day off work I took her into the New Forest to have a picnic lunch. As we found a clearing and drove our motor caravan into it, a car from the local RSPCA drew up alongside us and its woman driver asked if we intended to take a walk. When we said it was our intention, she told us to be careful as a German Shepherd had been abandoned in the woods and left to survive as best it could. As so far it had evaded capture and was now hungry and wild, we must not go near it but should notify the RSPCA of its whereabouts.

We had our walk but saw no German Shepherd. But as Shelagh was unpacking our lunch, I spotted a large dog moving at the other side of the clearing. Grabbing up some food I ran across the clearing and threw some of it at the animal. As it snatched it up, I backed towards our motor caravan, throwing food to entice it to follow me. As I reached the caravan I asked Shelagh to open its rear door and after she obeyed I threw more food into the vehicle.

As I had hoped, the half-starved dog jumped in after the food and I slammed the door to keep it inside. Telling Shelagh to wait for me, I was about to enter the driver's seat when she demanded to come with me.

Telling her it was far too dangerous as the snarling dog might attack her, I tried again to drive off but she would have none of it. If the dog were so dangerous it might attack me when I was driving and that might cause a major accident. So she would accompany me.

Before I could argue she pulled open the rear door and jumped inside, slamming the door closed before the dog could escape. Terrified for her, I was about to scramble back when I saw she was talking to the dog whose growling had ceased. A moment later she called out, telling me there was nothing to worry about and I could now drive away.

To cut the story short we never took the dog to the RSPCA. Instead we took it home, where it followed us into the hall and sat gazing at me while I phoned the RSPCA and told them what had happened. Shocked, they said they would pick up the dog at once as it was highly dangerous. Asking what they would then do, I was told it would have to be put down because of its history. When I told this to Shelagh she pointed at the half-starved creature sitting harmlessly in a corner of the hall, and we both knew we couldn't allow this. So I told the RSPCA not to come as we would take care of the dog ourselves.

This we did and after a few weeks of grooming and good food it became as obedient and impressive as Saffron had been. As it was female and we did not know its name, I tried alphabetic ones and when I reached the Ts its ears pricked up and so we called her Tess. From that day onwards we had a dog that would have died for us and particularly for Shelagh. All it had needed was a home and it lived with us for the next seven years.

In all it was a good year until I had a sudden breakdown in health. My heart began fluttering alarmingly and the abdominal pains I had felt during our American trip grew worse until I was forced to seek medical advice.

I won't dwell on the two complaints because illness is a negative subject, but although the heart problem was believed to be caused by excessive work and eventually cured itself, the abdominal pains were caused by a similar tumour that my mother had suffered from and for which I needed immediate surgery. Here I was lucky because it was discovered the tumour had not spread and so could be removed before further complications developed.

In all I was in hospital for ten days and a bedridden patient at home for another three weeks before I was on my feet again. As the growth could have killed me had it eaten through my bladder, I consider myself a fortunate man and must this time pay tribute to the profession and the surgeons who saved me. As in all walks of life there are good men as well as shoddy ones, and it is an unforgiving and ungracious person who cannot make the admission.

Frederick with Tess c. 1980

THIRTY

It was shortly after the publication of *Write a Successful Novel* that I decided on a new project. Whether it was my illness with its intimation of mortality I cannot say but I decided to write my autobiography. I had been asked to write it as far back as my days with Pan Books, but had fought shy of it for a number of reasons, one being the belief there were many other writers with more to say. That belief still held but after all the memories that had been conjured up in writing the trilogy I now felt the urgent need not only to acknowledge my debt to my parents but also my immeasurable debt to Shelagh who had made so many sacrifices for me.

Not that one can claim an autobiography depicts every major incident in a man's life. There are confidences that cannot be betrayed, an occasional change of name to avoid embarrassment to its owner, there are loved ones who cannot be hurt, there are personal misdeeds that, being human, one feels too cowardly to record, and, even more regrettably, there are one or two entrepreneurs who cannot be exposed for their perfidy because the proof is not available.

Nevertheless, I could only hope there was enough material to show the love and support I was given by my family, the generous help given by my friends and colleagues, and the almost unbelievable loyalty and inspiration given me by Shelagh. I make this point because otherwise I might be accused of making too much of my mishaps and disappointments.

Regarding publishers and other agents in the literary and entertainment professions, I had other reasons for mentioning my traumas because I felt the most likely readers of my memoirs would be those interested in writing either as a hobby or a career, and after a lifetime in the profession, it seems almost a duty to depict its heights and its lows. I also felt, with my tongue in my cheek, that I ought to remind publishers, radio and film producers, and all the other characters involved with them, that, in general, novels are written by sensitive people and so their work should not be treated like frying pans or electric kettles. I also wanted to give would-be authors the warning expressed in an earlier chapter, that before sending their work out into the business world, it is more than wise to exchange their smoking jacket for a flak jacket and a tin helmet.

Does all this mean that if I had my time again, I would not try to become a full-time writer? No, I cannot say that. I had many things I wanted to say and novels seemed and still seem the best medium in which to say them. So for myself I hold no regrets but for my parents and my dear uncomplaining Shelagh, it would have been such a joy if the profession had allowed me to give them the rewards they had so richly deserved. But the choice had been made, the die had been cast, and all I could do in my memoirs was to acknowledge my fervent gratitude for the sacrifices they had made. I could only hope I could do it adequately.

Such were the thoughts and emotions I had put into my autobiography while working on two more novels. Consequently it took much longer than I had planned. After its completion I handed it over to Moe, and although she liked and agreed its contents, she did not think it the right time for its negotiation and so, after its completion, I laid it aside and returned to my novels.

With Moe handling them they sold as never before, and were widely published until the Nineties when a sickening blow fell. Shelagh had a stroke while I was away giving a talk and when I dashed back home I found her in bed with a friend taking care of her. It seemed she had suffered with high blood pressure for years but because of her belief in her health and her refusal to see a doctor, it had gone undetected. To my intense relief she recovered quickly and suffered no physical handicap that any of us could detect. Yet she told me she could no longer handle words and speech with her earlier fluency, and although I assured her this belief was only in her imagination, from that day onwards she avoided social occasions, parties and festivities with anyone but our closest friends.

As I believed it was to avoid causing me any embarrassment, I and our two sons did everything in our power to assure her she was the same endearing person she had always been, but she remained unconvinced and remained socially inhibited for the rest of her life. I found it desperately wasteful and desperately sad.

Not long after this came another blow. Moe developed a serious illness and with regret had to give up her agency work. Her message was that I must get another agent as soon as possible.

But after all she had done for me, how could I? Loyalty demanded that I must wait until she recovered and so I continued to write novels in the hope that soon she would be herself again and resume our partnership.

So the final decades of the 20th Century were not our happiest. To Shelagh's distress both our sons were divorced during this time. We never knew the reasons because neither Shelagh nor I had ever pried into their private lives, and so both breakdowns came as a shock to us. Shelagh was particularly distressed because of the grandchildren involved. At that time Peter had two daughters and a son and Kevan one girl and one boy. During her earlier working years Shelagh had laid money aside for all five of them, and when each had reached the age of eighteen she had given them the money and the relevant pass books. Now, although Peter's grandchildren remained in close touch, Kevan's children took the money from Shelagh but neither contacted us again. Obviously their mother had turned them against us as well as against their father. Neither Shelagh nor I could understand the reason for this because neither of us had intervened in any way in the divorce. With Shelagh having a deep love for her family, I found it painful to see her distress.

As a final touch to the century, even our lovely Tess left us without warning. I was having my breakfast one morning when she entered the room, approached me at the table and laid a paw on my leg. Surprised by the act because German Shepherds are not demonstrative dogs, I leaned down and patted her. "What is it, old girl? Are you feeling lonely this morning?"

She removed her paw and then padded into the kitchen where Shelagh was working. I don't know what the dog did there but I heard Shelagh say: "What is it, Tess? Do you want to go outside?"

I heard the door open, there was silence for perhaps half a minute, then a cry of pain. I ran outside with Shelagh to find Tess lying dead on the path. I know it sounds fanciful and perhaps sentimental but Shelagh felt the same way. The dog seemed to have known her death was nigh and had come to say goodbye.

Thus the century did not end well for us. Shelagh, as supportive and helpful as ever, was living under the misapprehension that she had a speech handicap, our two sons were divorced, Tess had gone, and I had two novels written but un-negotiated. One could only hope the new millennium would bring better tidings.

THIRTY-ONE

In its beginning the century began well, although in a totally unexpected way. It began with a phone call from the USA. I cannot remember the caller's name but he wanted to know if I were the author of a short story called *The Devil Doll*. When I told him I was, he referred me to a certain Richard Gordon, the producer of the film, who wanted to contact me.

I made the contact and discovered Gordon was an Englishman who had made many films in the States and, now that he had discovered my whereabouts, wondered if I would care to attend a major Fantasy Film Competition that was being held in Manchester in 2002. As *The Devil Doll* was his entry among the many films that were being shown, he would be making the trip over to England himself and would be delighted to make me his guest.

I wanted Shelagh to go with me but for some reason I cannot remember she decided against it and so I drove up to Moe and her husband's house in Millington, E. Yorks, and the next day over to a large Manchester hotel where the exhibition was being held for the next four days. As I was allowed a guest and Shelagh had not come with me, I invited a fellow writer as a companion.

Richard Gordon proved to be a charming and generous host and was soon introducing me to film producers and directors from all over the world, some of whom were fascinating characters. A few were as out-of-this-world as the films they had made, and as most could speak English there were not many dull moments in the days that followed.

Wondering when *The Devil Doll* was to be shown, I learned from Richard that it was scheduled for the last day of the competition, which gave us three days to watch other films or chat with the competitors.

The last day arrived and *The Devil Doll* proved to be the final showing of the day. When the projector broke down halfway through the performance and minutes passed before the action began again, I felt no surprise. With my case history I would have been amazed if nothing had gone wrong. When the last scene was shown and the judges began comparing their notes over the many films they had seen, I was about to suggest we all went out and had a drink when Richard caught my arm. Although I don't think he was too optimistic himself, he felt I should wait for the winning announcement to be made.

It came and I could not believe my ears. *The Devil Doll* had won the award. The little short story that I had written nearly fifty years ago had ended up in a film that had won a major international competition. Half-dazed and unbelieving, I was led to a stage where in front of heaven knows how many entrants and producers I had to make my winning speech. Totally unprepared, I tried to remember when and how the idea had come to me. Heaven only knows what I said but as I jabbered on I suddenly realized the opportunity it offered to strike a blow for authors everywhere. So I told them how a magazine publisher had obtained the film rights from his authors by making them surrender copyright when he bought their stories. When someone asked what I had received for *The Devil Doll* I dropped my bombshell. Ten pounds. £10-00! Not a penny more. From the horrified gasp from the audience I knew my point had been well and truly made.

I never felt able to ask Richard what he had paid the magazine publisher for the rights. Instead I received from the Competition Committee my award: a statue with my name inscribed on it. It stands on my mantelpiece to this day. I call it my Oscar. I value it because of the pleasure it gave Shelagh when I returned home and handed it to her. Apart from my American Mark Twain literary award, it remains to this day the only recognition I was ever able to give her for her faith and devotion to my sixty years of writing.

During this time Peter and Kevan had now found new partners and to our relief seemed happy with them. As a result, with our finances secure at last, we held hopes that the years left us would bring us some measure of tranquility. Indeed we took a few holidays that we would never have allowed ourselves earlier, including a couple of coaching tours round Scotland and Wales.

By this time I had completed three novels which awaited agency handling. I should, of course, have sought another agent, but good ones are difficult to find and I still had hopes of Moe's recovery. As money was no longer a necessity, I placed the manuscripts in a drawer, consoling myself that even if they remained unpublished in my lifetime, they might be of help to our sons.

In 2002, by virtue of a local magazine to which I had contributed short stories and articles, I was invited to give a lecture course on the Queen Elizabth 2 while she toured the Mediterranean. As Shelagh was included in the invitation I accepted it and in June we joined the awaiting passengers in Southampton.

It was then our gremlin awoke and began his tricks again. On ascending a gangway to enter the ship, Shelagh lost her footing and I had to catch hold of her as she fell. At first she assured me no harm had been done but later that day I could see her lower back was hurting her. The pain grew worse until she was unable to walk to the dining room or to lie in her bed. As a result I had to take her to the ship doctor and after diagnosing a bad sprain, he detailed a nurse to visit her daily and to assess her condition

My course was no great success either. Prior to accepting it I had been told I was to instruct on novel writing. Yet when I met my members on our second day of sailing I found to my dismay that they had all been given entirely different versions of the syllabus. Some had been told it was a course on play writing, some on short story writing, and others on writing autobiographies. As they had all paid for the course on top of their tourist fare, they were not pleased. Nor was I for that matter because having been told I was to lecture on novel writing I had only brought that course with me.

As if that were not enough for one journey, the Mistral blew for the entire fortnight, leaving only one day fit for sun bathing. Moreover the ship lost a full day through some navigation error which affected the passengers' days ashore. Not that this delay affected us. Shelagh's pain was so severe that we could only go ashore at Gibralter on our way back to England.

In other words the holiday was not a huge success. Yet I try to remember the best of its days because it was our last real holiday together.

An amusing thing happened during this time. Years ago, at the request of a research engineer, who had the ambition to build a full size replica of the Haviland Mosquito aircraft featured in my *633* novels, I had copyrighted the title because he intended to give it the *633* emblem. Now a renewal of this patent became due, so to please him and also to protect the title in case I decided to write any further novels under it, I applied and paid for a renewal.

But less than a week later I had an indignant phone call from a lawyer of the Ministry of Defence. What on earth was I doing patenting the name of an RAF squadron? Did I not know it was an offence to register the name of a unit of the Queen's Armed Forces?

Unable to believe what I was hearing, I told him there was no such squadron in the RAF and the title was legitimately mine. Clearly thinking I was some kind of a shyster, he would not listen until I told him I had a letter from the Air Ministry giving me permission to use the title. At that he demanded to see the letter and I posted a copy to him. I received no reply or apology in return, and so was left pondering what would happen if some international crisis occurred and the MOD called on 633 Squadron to resolve it! The mind boggles at the thought.

The warning, had we recognized it, that my sixty year relationship with Shelagh was nearing its end came one evening when she complained about needing new spectacles because she was now finding it difficult to read. As reading was one of her great pleasures, we saw our local optician the next day but instead of recommending new glasses he sent her to an eye specialist who told her she was suffering the onset of dry macular degeneration. As to date there was nothing that could be done for the affliction, she soon found it impossible to read at all.

It was only a few months later that she awoke feeling nauseous and had some difficulty in swallowing. I wanted her to see our doctor but after her eye fiasco she dismissed the nausea as 'just one of those things'. But it became worse towards the end of 2005 until she retched every time she tried to swallow. I took her to a specialist who could find no cause for it, but when the symptoms worsened she was compelled to go into hospital over the Christmas holidays.

There she was put on drips, which eased her eating problems, while tests were carried out to identify their cause. Our sons and I visited her every day only to be told no cause had yet been found. After a week I asked to see a doctor but each time was told we should wait until the full routine of tests were carried out.

After X rays were taken and still no cause detected, I asked again to see a doctor but was now told they were too busy. As the Christmas holidays were now in full swing, I had my private thoughts about this, but after Christmas came and went and still no cause was found, I was told by the ward sister that Shelagh was being given a clean bill of health and as beds were in short supply she would now need to return home.

Although the accusation was not made, I had the impression it was thought Shelagh had been exaggerating her symptoms. I wanted to tell everyone concerned that no person on earth was less likely to act the hypochondriac than my wife, but as she looked much healthier after a fortnight on nourishing drips, I could do nothing more than take her home and hope she would soon be her old self again.

Instead a month of hell followed. As soon as she tried to take food by mouth the pain and the vomiting began again. She could absorb nothing: not even the pills I had been told to give her. Alone in the house with her, my helplessness and frustration grew until I was finally compelled to seek medical help again.

This time a young woman doctor paid a visit. After she told me she could find nothing wrong either, my twisted psyche began to take over and in the days that followed my anguish at seeing her distress turned into frustration and anger and I became afraid she would think I was blaming her for my impotence.

This hell went on for a month until, on my frantic insistence, she was taken into hospital again, although this time into one for rehabilitated patients, which made me believe yet again that the seriousness of her condition was not recognized.

For a short while she seemed to improve, although, as I realized later, this was because, being put on drips again, she had not needed to swallow or absorb food. But after a couple of weeks a specialist said he wanted a private word with me.

The short interview that followed was like the roll of drums before an execution. "I am sorry, Mr Smith, but we have at last discovered your wife's problem. She has pancreatic cancer and I am afraid it has progressed too far for it to be removed."

I have no idea what I replied. Because of my diabetes I had always believed I would be the first to go, and I had not only wished it but planned for it too. Now the worst possible thing was happening and my thoughts and feelings were indescribable.

A day or two later Shelagh was taken into the nearby Macmillan Unit where she behaved as bravely as ever, although she must have guessed what the move signified. To my relief and gratitude, Barry in South Africa responded immediately to my cable and flew over to be at her bedside. He was here ten days and stayed with my elder son, Peter, and his partner. I lent him my car and every day we drove to the cancer unit. Shelagh was in a private ward and from her courageous behaviour no one who visited her could believe she was near to death.

I shall not try to express my feelings when I lost her a couple of weeks later or my thoughts when in the Chapel of Rest I kissed her for the last time. One knew one had reached life's last major crossroad. The left turn would be the acceptance that I would never see that loving face again. To turn right would take one along the path of faith which held the promise of reunion. As I had lost the greatest gift life had ever given me I was left with no choice whatsoever. From that moment on, my daily prayers have been that in another place and another time a merciful God will ensure that reunion.

How many thousands of others must have taken that route, I wonder, and how many have continued living in the hope their faith will not be betrayed. As undying love is perhaps the only human virtue without a stain or blemish, one feels it is the one request that deserves its reward.

As I write these memoirs today I find only two things keep me sane: my hope of that reunion and my work. Sitting in my study writing, I can sometimes deceive myself that Shelagh is still with me. I also know that the last thing she would want of me is an abandonment of the work she has supported and inspired for so many years.

So I have to date written two more novels since her death, all of which were put into the drawer with the others. But during a visit of my dear friend, Val Kemp, who is now a publisher, she read one of the novels entitled *The Mysterious Affair*, and said she would love to publish it. At the same time, because of its theme, she felt it stemmed from the early part of my life, and so wanted to publish both works in tandem.

The offer appealed to me because I realized the wartime details of the memoirs include my first meeting with Shelagh. So I sought out the earlier work I had done and began its re-writing. I then began this second part of my memoirs in the hope that Val Kemp would publish it later.

I also know, in her loyal and unselfish way, that Shelagh would want less about herself in my memoirs than the views and aspects of the world that a long life has given me. So today, while wanting these memoirs to be my tribute to Shelagh, I move to my last chapter with the hope that readers will find within it a few thoughts, ideas, and beliefs that do not make these ninety-one years totally without purpose.

THIRTY-TWO

I cannot say it has been easy. Only a year after I lost Shelagh I developed the same dry macular degeneration that had afflicted her, and so lost the ability to read normal print, and only the computer, which enables one to enlarge the font, has made it possible for me to continue writing. At the same time, the desire to pay my tribute to Shelagh, and the urging of my friend Val Kemp, have given me the incentive to go on living and to complete the task. Indeed the work has been a godsend because it has not only helped to ease the sight of that empty armchair but also to speed the passing of the days.

The problem of being unable to read or watch similar pleasures has perhaps one advantage: it leaves the mind free to contemplate the many things life has taught one. Such subjects range from an analysis of one's character, thoughts of one's friends past and present, opinions of the present world of professionalism, commerce, and politics, and the random thoughts one has at various times and in certain moods.

The first and easiest is oneself. I know to my shame that I am a mass of contradictions. I enjoy the company of like-minded friends one day and yet am perfectly happy to spend the next one alone. I dislike vulgarity, not because I am a prude but because I find it ugly and it debases emotions that I like to keep unsoiled. I need melody in my music and believe the trained human voice is the most beautiful musical instrument of them all. I deplore the decline of good manners because I believe courtesy is the very oil of civilisation. I like style in women and not for them to look like scruffy schoolboys with short hair and shirt-tails dangling out of unflattering jeans. I detest bullies and their political equivalents, and although my action towards them has often been forceful and even violent and so has betrayed my credo of non-violence, I cannot claim it comes from courage because I do not see myself a brave man. Instead it stems from the paranoia induced by my school days. And while it is true that I have often confounded myself by going ice cold and under complete control when in extreme danger, the explanation is simple enough. As I have never thought highly of myself, my threatened demise has never seemed a great loss to me or to the world. Lastly but not least, I am ambivalent about the Internet and its associate items because while I appreciate their encyclopaedic values, I also fear they have opened wide gateways for a new breed of crooks and predators.

If all this makes me seem like an Old Grumpy, I dispute the assertion because I have studied my passing years with a detached interest. It has fascinated me to see how time refines one's judgements. One begins with the impatience and aggression of youth, but then, as the years pass by, a modicum of tolerance enters into one's arguments and conflicts until old age completes the refinement. Then one can sit back with a bottle of wine and talk over the pros and cons with an opponent without the resentment and distaste that one would have felt in youth. This is the reason no politician should be allowed his role until age has mellowed him. The world would then be saved from many of its trials, riots and wars if such an embargo were imposed internationally.

I like to think I have reached this mellow stage and can claim a couple of virtues with my faults. My first, if it is one, is perseverance. I am dogged. I grumble and complain at misfortune but I come back and try again. And again. And again. I unashamedly hate defeat, although in sport I believe I accept it graciously. But in other roles my instinct is to continue the fight until it is won.

My second is a hatred of cruelty, mental or physical. Indeed I sometimes wonder if kindness and cruelty are not the only true virtues and vices and the rest are only social offences. If this sounds a simplistic philosophy, I would ask a reader to consider the manifold aspects of kindness and cruelty before he makes his judgement.

But enough analysis about my character, which in any case is probably well wide of the mark. The thoughts about one's friends are far more compelling. Sadly, as the years pass by, one hears more and more about their demise. In my case I will never again be able to put the world to rights with Johnnie Gemmell, Frank Holland and Stewart Cottingham. Nor will David Doig smoke his pipe and listen to Bing Crosby in the caravan again, for he died a few years ago.

Indeed, to me, who had always seen friends as family, the loss of them is one of the worst penalties of old age. At times it seems not a month passes when one does not hear about the demise of yet another. Among the many who have favoured me with friendship, I must mention here my long term friend, Peter Skipworth, who died only a couple of years ago at the premature age of sixty-two. Although our friendship began soon after our move to Bournemouth, after I lost Shelagh he unfailingly visited me twice a week. Indeed it is no exaggeration to say he has been my lifeline during these last six barren years. To my death I shall always be grateful for his understanding and companionship.

At the same time I do still have a few friends left from the old days and others gained more recently. I am tempted to give their names but am afraid that by accident I might omit one or two and so give the impression of not caring. As nothing could be further from the truth, I feel it is safer just to raise my glass high to them and let them all know how grateful I am for their friendship and their enrichment of my life.

At the same time I feel none of them will mind my mentioning Moe Sherrard-Smith. This highly-talented friend and colleague, who became my agent in 1988, sold my novels in countries who previously had never heard of me, wrote a text book with me in the Nineties, and did so much to improve and consolidate my sales and finances that she became a veritable nonpareil of friends. Even after circumstances forced her to give up her agency work, she has continued to help me in ways far too numerous to mention. Moe has extended the very boundaries of friendship and my debt to her is immeasurable.

I must also pay tribute to my dear friend, Val Kemp, who has chosen to publish these jottings of mine in case some might find interest in the experiences of authors. I can only hope for her sake that she is right.

I must also thank from the bottom of my heart my kind neighbours, the Gruners, June, Debbie and Irene, as well as old and precious friends like Kay Braddick, Margaret, Sapphire, Gill, and Dorothy Bennett, all precious friends who have kept my spirits up by regularly phoning me or in some cases paying me visits. I cannot exaggerate the comfort they bring me by their friendship. Dorothy Bennett has also been a huge help to me in my present situation, checking my new work for literals and recommending my trustworthy home help, Sonia, and my secretary, Angela Clarke, whose efficiency and love of books gives me the hope she might one day become my new agent.

So now we move into the wider world that is manipulated by our professional classes, our businessmen, and our politicians. What have I learned about them as the years have rolled on? Too much, I am afraid. When very young I believed in the wisdom of our leaders. I did not think of them as being cleverer than I. If I thought about them at all, I saw them as a breed apart, set on this planet to control and administer our affairs.

It did not take a war to destroy that image, although it certainly completed it. As my powers of observation and perception grew, I began to realize that our mandarins suffer the same frailties as ourselves, which means they should always be watched. While in fairness some desire leadership in a belief they can improve the lot of their fellow men, far too many have backgrounds and natures that make them believe in their superiority, and such men are always suspect.

For, being creatures like ourselves, they will often behave like us, and if their consciences ever prick them for their transgressions, they will find little difficulty in convincing themselves it was all done for our benefit. Man is perhaps the only animal with the power of self-deception but by the Lord Harry how he makes up for the rest. Moreover, his self-deception increases in inverse ratio to his wealth and power. When lackeys crawl at the feet of the wealthy, the Midas men swell up like barrage balloons and their misdemeanors grow apace. When a people worship a political leader, that leader soon believes he is Christ and in no time at all is behaving like Anti-Christ. The 20th Century provided us with more than its share of such characters.

The same arrogance applies to the professional classes, as my earlier chapters have shown. While one cannot blame them for their occasional mistake, they should be ashamed of the speedy way they close their ranks and discuss those errors in secret. Mistakes and their redress should always be open to public scrutiny, or otherwise they are open to suspicion and distrust. The same rule should apply to the mistakes of big business and politics or we cannot claim to be a true democracy.

As it is seldom done, our only answer is to have eternal vigilance. Every piece of advice, every statement, every promulgation, every new law being prepared for the Statute Book, should be combed through again and again like a mother searching her child's hair for lice. Power in politics, power in the professions, power in business, are all part of the same heady drug that distorts a man's integrity and judgement.

That is why rebels are hated by these mandarins. Rebels probe, irritate, and sometimes even manage to frustrate their leaders' schemes, although sadly, because their role is that of an agitator, they often irritate the very public who gain from their cussedness. Nevertheless, at all costs rebels must be allowed to flourish. They are the cathartic that saves a clogged-up system from poison and decay.

Indeed, do not our religious leaders need criticism too? In most of the many religions to which we humans claim allegiance, do they not all believe in a God of mercy and beneficence? Yet what have our clerics and ourselves done with such beliefs over the centuries? Have we shown forgiveness to those with a different faith and given them tolerance and charity? Instead, throughout the centuries, we have sanctioned the slaughter of one another in hideous ways, and today some of us are even committing suicide to murder those with different cultures and ideologies. Can anything show more the insane way we allow our prejudices to overcome our tolerance? Even as I have been writing these memoirs, a number of Armenian and Greek monks in the Chapel of the Holy Sepulchre, the very site where Christ is supposed to have been buried, have been seen arguing fiercely and exchanging blows.

It cannot be denied. Religious fanaticism is causing death and misery in a dozen countries at this very moment in time by the very people whose venerated prophets ordered them to love, tolerate, and to forgive. If there is a God above all this mayhem, He must surely shake his head in despair over the sick creature He has created. Why, He must ask, do they not all sit together, smoke the pipe of peace, and unite as brothers under my ministry?

We do not even keep our intolerance limited to religion. In our sexual relationships we are influenced not by common sense but by primitive instincts of possession. Our dictionaries state the word love means endearment and devotion, but precious little of either is shown when one party of a union finds happiness outside it. A rutting animal would be envious of the rage and fury often shown by the dispossessed lover. He or she ignores or does not realize that love is an emotion outside the boundaries of flesh and time. It is, or should be, a bottomless well that cannot be drained dry by its users. Yet from our behaviour one would think it a mere cupful of water to be drained by the first thirsty traveller our spouse encounters. How many eons must pass before we find ways of controlling the primitive sub-human within us that turns us into fools and the world into a primeval jungle

Does not the same irrational prejudice stain our attitude to nationality? Like the one-time pride of our clan, we toast ourselves for being English, American, Chinese, Indian, Japanese, Bulgarian or whatever. Without giving thought to it, we see peoples of other nations as unfortunate foreigners.

We do this while at the same time our scientists tell us we all come from the same basic stock. But are we taught this at school? Instead, are we not given lessons on our national virtues, our military victories, and our achievements? Being told nothing about our sins or failings, we are led to believe we stand head and shoulders above the other less fortunate races.

Not that we are alone in being fed this propaganda. All races praise their nation's achievements and ignore their inequities. The result gives an imbalance of emotions that prevents our seeing one another as part of the brotherhood of man. It also keeps old resentments alive that should be long forgotten, and often taints present day negotiations. Why on earth don't we all come clean and call a world conference in which every nation confesses its sins of the past? It could be organized by the United Nations and be called The Contrition Conference. It might not stop future conflicts but at least it would ensure they were not products of the unhappy past.

Then one's mind slips into another mode and reflects on the world of business and commerce. To any thinker it has always seemed patently obvious that if the Western World continued to use a commercial system that impoverishes the Third World, the outcome must one day be disastrous if only because nature abhors a vacuum. Yet even today, when a recession exposes the inequities of the system, we are still reverting to the old selfish ways. Will we never live up to our democratic claims of goodwill and fraternity? Or are we basically unable to suppress our avarice until our planet loses patience with us and makes us pay the price of all exploiters?

What we will never admit is that we like our Mr Hydes. War taught me this. Without effort we can sink into depths of cruelty that no other animal can reach by instinct or persuasion. Every now and then one of us lifts himself up from the mire, but swiftly the rest of us sense the danger of the apostate and drag him back. What we need more than anything else is a pill that frees us from our primitive roots. Why don't our drug companies make such a drug their priority?

As things stand I truly believe that if creatures from an alien planet were to circle our globe and study us, they would decide we are both insane and dangerous. Such a threat indeed to other aliens who might discover us, that a cordon sanitaire should be erected around us to keep them from contamination. How could they think otherwise when they discover that our entire financial system is based not on social justice but instead on the very offence that many of our religions condemn as a mortal sin. It is, of course, usury, the lending of money for personal profit. Yet almost daily television and commercial radio urge us to borrow more and more money to buy possessions we do not need.

Then there are our hungry millions in Africa and the Far East. Apart from our selfish business methods, why does not the United Nations organize a world birth control scheme? We already know that in less than twenty years we shall have another billion children crying for food from a planet that already cannot feed its millions today. Rats and other animals restrict breeding when their food supply diminishes. Then how can we be so stupid not to do the same?

There is also the factor of creation and invention. In many aspects of our business culture, the man or woman who invents, produces, or grows an item receives far less reward for it than the middle man who buys and then sells it for profit. How can any intelligent species accept such an absurd injustice that inhibits invention and progress?

And if that were not enough, what will our aliens think when they discover that although we suffer from diseases that kill millions of us every year, we spend ten times more of our time and wealth on weapons designed to kill one another than on medical research that might keep us alive. What other creature in the universe could be so insane?

It is not as if we do not know how to change ourselves. Nazi Germany proved that millions of citizens could be programmed into aggression and genocide. Logic tells us the converse must be true and could be achieved if we wanted a sane and moral world. Then why do we not firstly give a course on ethics to our school children? At present we hand them knowledge without guidelines to determine its usage. Thus a man may grow up and without a qualm of conscience use his knowledge to invent a new weapon of destruction. He will even seek praise and reward for it, and in all likelihood will receive both.

To me, giving knowledge without firstly giving ethical training is as stupid and dangerous as giving a loaded machine gun to an untrained chimpanzee. Yet to suggest giving it in schools, as I did in my novels *The Sin and the Sinners* and *The Tormented,* is to raise the outcry that it would be brainwashing. Yet every day our consumer-orientated society brainwashes us into wanting more and more possessions from a world that is already groaning under their weight. We are even taught by our financial experts that any system that does not cater to our possessive instincts will not be successful. On that premise do we allow our other basic instincts the same freedoms? Do we allow polygamy or theft or murder?

The truth is that none of our financiers, businessmen or politicians want an ethical society. What would then happen to the carrots they dangle before our eyes? They promote our cupidity and they benefit from it. The loveless circle is complete.

So thoughts come and go, sometimes inspired by items heard on the radio. There was a case the other day involving hard drugs that made me wonder if our present approach to them is sane and sensible. In my younger days, when the Nazi fascists were massing on the shoreline of France with the intention of invading us and poisoning the minds of our children, there were no doubts about our duty. The threat had to be stopped at all costs and we were mobilized, armed, and trained to fight it. Yet, even so, it was still on the other side of the Channel. Today the threat is here, in our streets, in our clubs and in our work places. Sold to us by characters who make millions out of a trade that causes family strife, traffic accidents, hospital emergencies, and an untold number of crimes and unwanted pregnancies. In addition to all that, such a deterioration in our Western culture that many believe it will cause its collapse. Is it therefore sufficient to give such purveyors of decline just a few years of incarceration when caught? Or should we, albeit reluctantly, take lessons from such countries as Singapore or China? Perhaps on this issue one ought to send out our national jury for a decision.

Another of these random thoughts come when I occasionally wish I had a daughter. If I had, and if I had any say in the man she might marry, what would my choice be? Unhesitatingly I would choose a kind, honest, but unsophisticated man instead of a clever and ambitious one. The latter might give her a wealthier life style but when has money in itself brought happiness? The former man would not only offer her comfort and understanding but in addition his ambience and behaviour would spread around them like a healing balm and bring them friends everywhere.

Then there is the thought of our becoming an integral part of Europe. I know that in England we have many doubters, and I understand their concern. But I must ask how many of these have lived through the hell of a European war. At least a unified Europe should prevent such a catastrophe again. Then there is the new structure of the world to consider. Today nations that were once little more than land masses packed with impoverished peasants are now becoming huge industrial nations with millions of skilled workers. How will we fare, a small island with a relatively small population, against giants like China, India, and Brazil? Only a closely knit Europe with its combined population will be able to sit at the world's table with them. For precisely the same reason, those among us who cry for an independent Wales or Scotland should face the fact that the future world will consist of huge blocks of nations, and minute countries would have as much chance of survival as minnows in a tank full of hungry trout.

Ironically, perhaps when wine has flowed too freely, there are the moments when one's doppelganger mocks at all such speculations. What a load of piffle about nothing, it jeers. For when all is said and done, what are we in this boundless universe but microbes playing our silly games on a speck of dust? So why waste one's time on what microbes should do or not do? It will only take one adjacent red star to explode into a super nova and our speck of dust will be gone forever.

The antidote to this nanotechnological thought is usually to finish the bottle of wine or, even better, to open a second one. After that it will matter even less whether we are microbes or men!

But not all these random thoughts are so negative. Some, born of experience, are very positive. One is that few of the ordeals one has to face in the future are as stressful as the anxiety that precedes them. Imagination colours, distorts, and exaggerates one's misgivings until reality becomes almost an anti climax.

On that note I had better conclude my memoirs. I hope my criticisms, although often harsh, do not give the impression that I believe we humans are beyond redemption? On the contrary I most definitely do not. With the necessary desire, we can very swiftly change ourselves. And we have one great asset. Our ability to love. Love in its many manifestations: tolerance, kindness, forgiveness, charity, is the one human characteristic that has no dark side. Here I can call upon the Christian Holy Bible for support. To paraphrase the words of St. Paul to the Corinthians: "Although I speak with the tongues of angels and possess their other virtues, I am still nothing unless I have charity".

It is so true. Charity, the biblical word for love, conquers all. Our ability to love, with all its manifestations, offers credence to the assertion of many religions that man is made in the image of God. Love in material terms means not only aiding our loved ones and friends, but in the wider world means adopting policies that, instead of impoverishing its needy, provides support and sustenance for them. In such practical terms love can work wonders in any sphere of life and turn the bitterest of enemies into friends.

Not that anyone who gives it must expect to profit materially. Those who give love totally and unselfishly often gain hostages to fate. They also might find occasionally that those they help find forgiveness too difficult to accept. This means a man needs perseverance and courage with his love. Courage that does not allow him to falter until the day when he reaches that bright welcoming star that is his own. But what a rich reward that day brings him.

There is no doubt whatever in my mind that the man who puts the love of his fellow men before his ambitions, or the man who is beaten and bloodied by his enemy and yet can still find the charity to hold out a forgiving hand, is a million miles nearer to divinity than the churchgoer who lights candles, sings hymns, and then drives off in his expensive limousine to commit another shady business deal. Sadly, as my instinct is to fight back when robbed or attacked, I cannot claim a place in the Pantheon of such people.

But perhaps it is never too late to change. Perhaps this is the moment to put my money where my mouth is and say I forgive all the publishers and others who have given me such a hard time in the past. After all, if I believe that challenges and disappointments are good for the soul, I should be grateful to them. They have braced me, they have never allowed me to grow rich and fat, and they have forced me to write more and more books when, if they had been kinder to me, I might have sat back on my profits. They have taught me that life is never seen in perspective when disaster strikes. It is only later that one realizes it takes rain as well as sunshine to ripen the corn. Perhaps in that moment of realization one becomes a man. I can only hope so.

END

Other titles by Frederick E. Smith curently available

A YOUTHFUL ABSURDITY
An autobiography: Volume 1
Pb. £10.50 inc.p&p   Hb. £16.50 inc.p&p (was £25)

In the author's own words:
"... Because this book covers my earlier years and because my age fated me to serve throughout the second world war, some of these events took place during that conflict.

"But ... it covers in the main the painful, the bizarre, and the often downright absurd events that plagued me from birth up to my twenty-sixth year...."

....

AN AUTHOR'S ABSURDITIES
An autobiography: Volume 2
Pb. £9.50 inc.p.&p.

The final volume in this riveting autobiography of the writer's life continues to enthral. A fighter who believes in peace, a peacemaker who confronts bullies, a man of quiet courage with a steely determination to retain his independence and integrity as a full-time writer, whatever the frowns of fortune, and who never loses his sense of humour or fighting spirit.

....

THE MYSTERIOUS AFFAIR
Frederick E. Smith £8.95 each (inc.p&p)

THE MYSTERIOUS AFFAIR is a gripping story about the strange liaison between RAF Flight Lieutenant Sean Hammond, DFC, a fighter-pilot and confirmed atheist who volunteers in 1939 because his hatred of bullies outweighs his distrust of patriotism, and Linda Martin, a devoted and married Christian with a deep, patriotic love of her country.

Inexplicably drawn to one another by forces beyond their control, they are totally unaware of the massive difference their chance meeting is to make on both themselves and the world around them.

ORDER FORM
Other Titles by FREDERICK E. SMITH
(All prices include post and packing in the UK)

QTY.	TITLE	PRICE	TOTAL
....	The Mysterious Affair	£8.95	....
....	A Youthful Absurdity (Vol 1: pb)	£10.50	....
....	A Youthful Absurdity (Vol 1: hb)	£16.50	....
....	An Author's Absurdities (Vol 2: pb)	£9.50	....
....	The Final Absurdities (Vol 3: pb)	£9.50	....

TOTAL £

Please send your order with cheque/postal order made payable to:
Emissary Publishing at PO Box 33, Bicester, OX26 2BU, UK.
(Add £3.00 per book for Overseas Postage; ensure cheque is for sterling and drawn on an English Clearing Bank).

Alternatively, please visit our website at: *www.emissary-publishing.com*

Name..

Address...

....

....

Post Code .... Date....................................

Tel :(in case of query)..

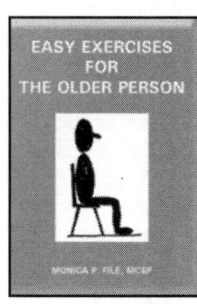

EASY EXERCISES FOR THE OLDER PERSON
by
Monica P. File, MCSP
Cover design and illustrations:
William T. File
(£5.50 inc. p.&p.)

This book is intended for older people and carers.

It is easy to read and understand, giving beneficial exercises and general tips designed to help older or disabled people to maintain their health and independence.

The author is a chartered physiotherapist with forty years experience.

ON A CLEAR DAY YOU CAN SEE GOD
by
Daphne Ayles
(£8.50 inc. p.&p.)

With a light touch, a honed mind and unerring accuracy, Ms Ayles goes 'Shopping for God' as she probes the perennial questions asked by Man. Who is God? What makes Him tick? Where can you find Him?

The refreshing thing about *On A Clear Day . . .* is that it has a rhythm all its own, like nature on a spring morning, fresh, impulsive and irresistible. With simplicity and clarity, she plumbs the deepest waters, (still or stormy), climbs the highest mountain, (Snowdon for a start: it can only be seen on a clear day), travels the furthest reaches of the mind, (from Heaven to Hell), and comes up smiling, laughing, and, yes, loving, too.

This is one of those compelling books which provoke a re-evaluation of one's own life style and place in the scheme of things, making it very personal, very caring, and very well worth reading.

It is also the kind of book you'll want to share, especially its simple, honest recipe for day to day living and loving that puts us on the right road — the clear road — to see God.

Award-winning novelist and author of over forty novels, Frederick E. Smith is no genre writer. Titles as diverse as **633 SQUADRON,** made into a film which broke box office records; the hugely successful novel, **LYDIA TRENDENNIS**, written from a woman's viewpoint; **LAWS BE THEIR ENEMY,** an attack on apartheid which was banned in South Africa and brought him death threats from fanatics; **DEVIL DOLL,** a film made from one of his short stories, winning the award at the *2002 Manchester Fantasy Film Festival*; **A KILLING FOR THE HAWKS** which won him the *American Mark Twain Literary Award,* to name but a few, are testament to his independence and integrity as a writer.

The third and final volume of his autobiography, **THE FINAL ABSURDITIES**, highlights the pitfalls and traumas, the graft, the grind and the glory of becoming a full-time author.

THE FINAL ABSURDITIES

This concluding volume focuses on the latter half of the author's life.

It covers the exhilarating and enormously liberating times. The struggle to retain integrity, vision and independence in the face of adversity. How the happiness and wellbeing of his family were threatened by his refusal to sacrifice integrity and how his selfless wife was his bedrock and inspiration.

It touches on the ruthless exploitation by some publishers and agents and his Jekyll and Hyde character which occasionally got out of control. And it reflects upon the cruel tricks that life has played upon him.

But mostly, in his later years, he feels enriched by his life experience, justified in his self belief that he was born to be a writer. And because he has remained true to himself, and never lost his sense of humour, despite the vagaries of life, he can now sit back with a satisfied smile, knowing he would not have wanted to play the game of life any other way.

EMISSARY PUBLISHING
Price: £8.50 in U.K.
ISBN: 978-1-874490-82-1